YOU AIN'T SEEN

nothing

YET.

(75% healthy, 25% butter)

· · · · · · · · · · · · · · ·

WHOLESOME DAILY EATS &
DELECTABLE OCCASIONAL TREATS

The Bite Me Balance COOKBOOK

JULIE ALBERT & LISA GNAT

appetite
by RANDOM HOUSE

Appetite by Random House® and colophon are registered trademarks of Penguin Random House LLC.

Library and Archives Canada Cataloguing in Publication is available upon request.
ISBN: 978-0-525-61054-0
eBook ISBN: 978-0-525-61055-7

Photography by Maya Visnyei
Book and jacket design by Raquel Waldman Buchbinder
Printed and bound in China

Published in Canada by Appetite by Random House®,
a division of Penguin Random House Canada Limited.

www.penguinrandomhouse.ca

10 9 8 7 6 5 4 3 2 1

BUT WAIT, THERE'S

more.

   @bitememore
bitememore.com

We dedicate this book
to those who endure
our twisted sisterhood:

our families.

··········

To Kenny, Jamie, Perry, Benjy & Billie

To Jordan, Emmy, Alex, Lauren & Sophie

table of contents

breakfast & brunch

lunch

weeknight dinners

gatherings

introduction

How do you sum up a lifetime of belly laughs, of conversations spoken only with your eyes, of shared delicious, joy-filled meals, and family you've fiercely loved? It's not easy, but this natural give and take my sister Lisa and I have is what's always kept us balanced. We're sisters who know when to step in and prop the other up, and when to stand back and let the other shine. We cheer each other on, and we always have each other's backs (rolls and all). We cross our arms over our chests in unison not because we're closed off, but because it's comfy. We still get sent away from our parents' dinner table for being naughty, we're always on the same page (even when we're not—it happens, sometimes), we share a deep love for dogs, we talk endlessly about nothing, and together, we've built a business that caters to each other's strengths. My (being Julie's) deep love for the written word and design partners perfectly with the bionic palate that has helped guide Lisa in developing over a thousand unbelievably tasty and doable recipes in three best-selling cookbooks and on our Bite Me More website. She'd never boast about that, but I can.

> "WE ALWAYS HAVE EACH OTHER'S BACKS (ROLLS & ALL)."

WHY THE BALANCE?

Since we both always try to tell it like it is, here's the skinny on our waistlines: we've sweated to the oldies, we've tried and failed to build buns of steel, and we ate fat-free for way too long. We fervently bought into (and boy, do we wish we could have our money back) the idea of the quick fix, the sure thing, and the next fad that would surely make us the masters of our thighs. But, eventually, too hungry and too tired, we waved the white flag, and shockingly, the moment we gave up on all-or-nothing extremism, everything fell into place. We had no idea how starving we were to be free of dodgy diet claims and constant fork-in-hand self-flagellation until we discovered that all that time wasted on calorie counting (btw, I'm superbad at math), obsessing over forbidden fruit (and, no, it wasn't apples), and holding our breath as we stepped on the scale would be way better spent *listening* to *what* our *bodies* were telling us about what we needed to be nourished, energized, and, of course, satisfied.

"MODERATION IS THE GRANNY PANTIES OF THE DIET WORLD."

Here's the boring truth of our hard-won know-how: there's no magic bullet when it comes to health and wellness for either of us, and there's nothing sexy about our approach—moderation is the granny panties of the diet world—which comes down to a lifelong commitment to eating smarter and moving more. Yuppers, you read that right: eat smarter and move more. And while we haven't included our calisthenics routine in this book (though Lisa does dish on dips and I serve up some epic burpees), we can most definitely help you with the eating part.

Finding the right balance between healthy and indulgent eating means different things to different people, but we're hoping to arm you with the tools (aka everyday amazing, easy, delicious, well-tested, healthy-ish recipes) that will allow you, and us, to bake that cake and eat it too.

STRIKING THE BALANCE

While it didn't happen overnight, we've broken the cycle of obsession-deprivation-binge-guilt, a loop that's harmful to both body and brain. Food is no longer our enemy, but our bestie, there to nourish us, and at times, even comfort us. We have become mindful eaters and feeders by following these easy-to-keep habits:

- We fuel our bodies daily with whole foods, and fill our plates with quality ingredients that are high in fiber, good fats such as avocado, eggs, and nuts, and protein-packed powerhouses like fish, beans, and lean meats.

- We try to be good to ourselves, and serve up healthy options at every meal—be it a grab-and-go breakfast, lazy weekend brunch, working lunch, busy weekday dinner, or gathering of friends and family—so that making the smart choice is easy.

- We listen to our body's signals, eating when hungry and stopping when full (sounds simplistic but very effective), signals that can be best heard not standing at the counter shoveling food with our fingers, but when we slow down, sit down, and pay attention.

- And, finally, since no food is off the table when eating in a balanced and intuitive way, we occasionally indulge in deliciously decadent dessert, because, simply put, life without dessert is just sad. So instead of trying to satisfy our sweet cravings with a whole sleeve of processed cookies, we know through experience that we're way better off and satisfied savoring every bite of one ultimate cookie, one made with real, quality ingredients.

THE BALANCE IN A NUTSHELL

Lisa's giving me the "wrap it up" signal so I better keep this brief (too late, am I right?), but know one thing for certain—you're in great hands. Lisa's skills are the real deal and under her tutelage, even I can rock mealtime. As for the both of us, our hope is that The Bite Me Balance means to you what it does to our sister act: the freedom found when fad diets are replaced with self-acceptance and mindful eating, the pleasure that comes with loving every bite, and the confidence in knowing you can bring friends and family to the table for joy-filled, delicious, and wholesome meals.

"LIFE
WITHOUT
DESSERT
IS JUST
SAD."

what's inside

THE BALANCE?

We have very few dos and don'ts when it comes to mastering your culinary and diet domains. With this book, we're giving you the recipe roadmap, but you're still the one in the driver's seat. Here are a few pointers to get the most out of *The Bite Me Balance*.

THE CHAPTERS

This book of 138 original recipes is broken down into four sections: Breakfast and Brunch, Lunch, Weeknight Dinners, and Gatherings. Each chapter serves up approachable recipes, along with prep and cook times for each. While we've categorized the recipes as such, feel free to mix and match, with breakfast for dinner and lunch for brunch.

THE LESSONS FROM LISA

She speaks. And boy, when I let her have the floor, she dishes up some gold nuggets. Yup, I'm finally letting Lisa serve up some of her brilliant food for thought, with her invaluable tips and tricks sure to make your life easier and tastier in the kitchen. You're welcome.

THE ICONS

If cooking were a tennis match (and, well, isn't it kinda, with Lisa acing every meal, while I grunt and serve?), these icons would be your game, set, and match. They will not only help you navigate mealtime when you're at your breaking point (with meals for the time-pressed and dishes that are freezer-friendly), but also have you smashing dietary challenges with vegetarian and gluten-free recipes galore. Yes, champ, these six icons will help you call the shots and bring home some major grand slam winners.

 FAST (40 MINS OR LESS)

 FREEZES WELL

 MAKE IT GLUTEN-FREE

 VEGETARIAN

 GLUTEN-FREE

 OCCASIONAL TREAT

THE GLUTEN-FREE RECIPES

The Bite Me Balance has 96 recipes that are marked gluten-free or can easily be adapted to be gluten-free. Here are a few notes, thanks to my and your gluten-free goddess, RonniLyn Pustil, founder of Gluten Free Garage.

While many of the recipes include items that are naturally gluten-free, it's always important to read the labels, or better yet, buy brands that are labeled gluten-free. Some of the gluten-free ingredients to watch for include:

- Seeds and nuts (peanuts, almonds, cashews, pistachios, walnuts, pine nuts, sunflower seeds, pumpkin seeds, hemp seeds)

- Baking ingredients (vanilla extract, cocoa powder, old-fashioned oats, steel-cut oats)

- Condiments (Dijon mustard, ketchup, mango chutney, maple syrup, horseradish)

- Broth (chicken, vegetable)

- Spreads (peanut butter, almond butter)

- Asian ingredients (mirin, sake, wasabi, white miso paste, fish sauce)

- Roasted deli chicken

oh baby,

WE'VE GOT 96 GLUTEN-FREE RECIPES.

kitchen

You don't need to stock your shelves with useless gizmos (read: banana cutter), but there are five essential tools we recommend having on hand to up your healthy-eating game.

BLENDERS

A high-powered blender is key for whipping up smoothies and dressings, while the can't-live-without-it handheld immersion blender expertly purees soups right in the pot, giving them a creamy texture sans cream or mess.

MEASURING CUPS & SPOONS

Sounds obvious (we heard you think, "duh"), but don't dismiss how essential these tools are for staying trim. While we've all thought, "I'll just eyeball it" at one time or another, we're all bad at getting that teaspoon or serving size accurate without these cups and spoons on hand.

KITCHEN SHEARS

While Lisa won't let me cut her hair with the kitchen shears (the party pooper does need a trim, just saying), she lets me go wild snipping fresh herbs and veggies with this terrific tool.

KNIFE & BOARD

If you're going to be in the kitchen, you need a great chef's knife and wooden cutting board. This versatile knife will have you chopping, slicing, and dicing like a pro, while giving your sturdy (not to mention more sanitary than plastic) board a workout.

MINI FOOD PROCESSOR

While you'll have the big boy on hand for big-batch jobs, this small-but-mighty appliance (we love the 3.5-cup size) is indispensable—it's a space saver, cleans up easily, chops onions, garlic, and herbs in a snap, and makes for endless sauce, dip, and vinaigrette possibilities.

BONUS: A SOUS CHEF

OK, so not an actual living, breathing person, but there are tools that keep us working smarter, not harder. For expert help in the kitchen, we recommend a silicone baking mat, a handheld citrus juicer, a variety of Microplane graters/zesters, a mandoline, and a pair of 'Ove' Gloves.

CHOP, CHOP,

let's get to it.

THE
healthy highs

We know that one menu doesn't always fit all, depending on how you personally like to eat, so here we're highlighting five recipes in each of the categories below to help you hit both the highs and lows of healthy eating.

breakfast & brunch

I f you were disappointed upon discovering that *The Breakfast Club* had nothing to do with your favorite morning meal, we share your frustration. Such food deserves the spotlight, food that can be enjoyed day and night (hello naysayers, it's why there's all-day breakfast and why brinner, aka breakfast for dinner, is a thing), whether you're dining on the run or hunkering down for an eatathon with friends and family. Whatever your needs, we've got the tastiest, most nutritious ways to power you through the weekday rush, and the most scrumptious eats to satisfy your Sunday slow down. So, press pause on your VCR because that '80s classic film has little to do with food (save for a power-hungry principal and an "Eat my shorts" bad boy), and get cooking because these blockbuster recipes are guaranteed to get you top breakfast and brunch billing.

breakfast quinoa

WITH BLUEBERRIES & ALMONDS

Does your pillow lure you over to the dark side? Are you sick of hitting snooze? Well, if you're more a middle-of-the-day-than-morning person, we've got something that's going to change your whole outlook on the sun rising: quinoa for breakfast. Sure to shake your cobwebs, this bowl has all the nutrition your body needs to get started—protein- and fiber-rich quinoa, almond milk, and almonds are joined by the super-spice cinnamon and topped with roasted blueberries full of antioxidants. So it's time to stop letting morning kick your butt; get ready, thanks to this epically energizing, wholesome, and hearty breakfast, to start kicking butt yourself.

SERVES: 3–4   PREP TIME: 10 MINS   COOK TIME: 25 MINS

Blueberry Topping

3 cups fresh blueberries, divided

2 tsp honey

Pinch kosher salt

Quinoa

1 cup uncooked quinoa

2 cups unsweetened almond milk

½ tsp vanilla extract

¼ tsp ground cinnamon

¼ tsp kosher salt

Garnish

⅓ cup toasted sliced almonds

⅓ cup toasted unsweetened coconut flakes

Honey (optional)

1. For the blueberry topping, preheat the oven to 425°F and line a baking sheet with parchment paper. In a medium bowl, toss 2 cups of blueberries with the honey and a pinch of salt. Place on prepared baking sheet and roast for 6–7 minutes, until the blueberries start to burst and release their juices. Remove from the oven and carefully transfer the berries and liquid to a bowl. Stir in the remaining 1 cup blueberries. Set aside.

2. For the quinoa, place quinoa in a strainer, rinsing and draining well before cooking. In a medium saucepan, bring the quinoa, almond milk, vanilla, cinnamon, and salt to a boil. Reduce the heat, cover, and simmer for 15 minutes. Remove from the heat and let sit covered for 5 minutes.

3. Scoop the quinoa into serving bowls and top with blueberry mixture, almonds, and coconut. Drizzle with honey.

lessons *from* lisa

★ *Toast sliced almonds by spreading them in a single layer on a baking sheet and baking at 350°F for 3–5 minutes, until fragrant and lightly browned, shaking the pan occasionally.*

> 66 *Morning is wonderful. Its only drawback is that it comes at such an inconvenient time of day.* —GLEN COOK

tropical mango smoothie bowl

Forget the conch shell. When you hold this bountiful smoothie bowl close, you'll hear waves hitting the shore, sand crunching underfoot, and squawking seagulls. Yup, grab your shades and SPF because this dreamy breakfast will transport you to the tropics with the sweet taste of mango, pineapple, and banana, blended with zesty lime and topped with a homemade coconut hemp granola. Baked up in only 10 minutes, super-speedy golden granola adds a satisfying crunch to each fruity, healthy spoonful. With paradisiacal fresh flavors, this ice cream–like bowl will tide you over until your next meal, a mouthwatering reminder that yes, life *is* a beach.

SERVES: 4   PREP TIME: 10 MINS   COOK TIME: 10 MINS

Coconut Granola

½ cup old-fashioned oats

3 tbsp unsweetened coconut flakes

2 tbsp hemp seeds

⅛ tsp kosher salt

1 tbsp olive oil

1 tbsp honey

Smoothie Bowl

2 cups frozen cubed mango

1½ cups frozen pineapple chunks

2 ripe bananas, frozen

2 tbsp fresh lime juice

1 tbsp honey

½ tsp lime zest

½ tsp vanilla extract

1½ cups unsweetened almond milk

1 mango, peeled and chopped

1 kiwi, peeled and chopped

1. Preheat the oven to 325°F. Line a baking sheet with parchment paper.

2. For the granola, in a medium mixing bowl, combine the oats, coconut flakes, hemp seeds, and salt. Add the olive oil and honey, tossing well to coat. Spread onto the prepared baking sheet and bake for 5 minutes. Stir and continue to bake for 5 minutes more. Let the granola cool without stirring to create some clumpy pieces as it cools. Set aside.

3. For the smoothie bowl, in a blender, combine the mango, pineapple, bananas, lime juice, honey, lime zest, vanilla, and almond milk. Blend until smooth but still thick. Pour into bowls and top with granola, mango, and kiwi. Serve immediately.

lessons *from* lisa

★ *Frozen fruit helps thicken your smoothie bowl. If your fruit isn't frozen, you'll need to add a large handful of ice cubes before blending.*

banana date oatmeal bowl

D o you sit at breakfast, staring down the box of bland and boring cereal, wondering where the days of sowing your wild oats went? People, we're here for you with a bowl that makes getting out of bed worthwhile, delivering all the excitement of your youth without a trip to the free clinic. While it may taste naughty, this bowl is anything but—full of wholesome goodness, steel-cut oats are one of the healthiest grains you can eat. Retaining their chewy texture, the fiber-rich oats get a touch of natural sweetness and loads of vitamins and minerals from banana and dates, to say nothing of the creaminess from the almond milk. Get ready, because you're going to feel hot to trot after a steaming bowl of this incredibly satisfying breakfast-with-benefits.

SERVES: 4   PREP TIME: 10 MINS   COOK TIME: 20 MINS

Oatmeal Bowl

3 cups water

1 cup unsweetened almond milk

1 cup steel-cut oats

1 large ripe banana, mashed

4 large dates, pitted and chopped

1 tsp vanilla extract

¼ tsp ground cinnamon

¼ tsp ground ginger

¼ tsp kosher salt

Toppings

1 banana, sliced

½ cup chopped toasted walnuts

¼ cup dark chocolate chips

Maple syrup, for drizzling (optional)

1. In a large saucepan, bring the water and almond milk to a boil. Stir in the oats, banana, dates, vanilla, cinnamon, ginger, and salt. Mix well. Lower the heat and let the oatmeal mixture simmer for 20 minutes, stirring occasionally. Let rest for 5 minutes before serving.

2. To serve, scoop into bowls and top with banana slices, chopped walnuts, chocolate chips, and a drizzle of maple syrup.

> *Most of us spend the first six days of each week sowing wild oats; then we go to church on Sunday and pray for a crop failure.* —FRED ALLEN

maple ginger granola

Oh, granola. You've had a charmed existence, protected by a health halo and the endorsement of hikers and outdoorsy types alike. Well, sorry, we're pulling back the flannel curtain and exposing you for what you are—a cereal with enough sugar and fat to put a chocolate cake to shame. Lisa may not know what to do with a carabiner, but she blazes a trail, with her creative compass pointing straight to the N in nutrition. Her granola has thrown butter over the cliff and replaced it with heart-healthy olive oil, high-fiber chia seeds and oats, and protein-packed cashews and pecans. Add a hint of ginger, toasted coconut and pumpkin seeds, and a dash of maple syrup, and you've got an energy booster with a satisfying crunch that you (and your waistline) will love.

MAKES: 8 CUPS   PREP TIME: 10 MINS   COOK TIME: 40 MINS

3 cups old-fashioned oats

½ cup chopped raw pecans

½ cup chopped raw cashews

½ cup unsweetened coconut flakes

½ cup raw pumpkin seeds

¼ cup chia seeds

¼ cup chopped crystallized ginger

1 tsp ground cinnamon

1 tsp kosher salt

¼ tsp ground ginger

⅓ cup olive oil

¼ cup pure maple syrup

3 tbsp honey

1. Preheat the oven to 300°F and line a rimmed baking sheet with parchment paper.

2. In a large bowl, combine the oats, pecans, cashews, coconut flakes, pumpkin seeds, chia seeds, crystallized ginger, cinnamon, salt, and ground ginger.

3. In a small bowl, whisk together the olive oil, maple syrup, and honey. Pour over oat mixture and toss to combine. Spread the granola evenly over the prepared baking sheet. Bake for 18–20 minutes and stir carefully. Continue baking for another 18–20 minutes, until golden. Remove from the oven and let cool completely on the baking sheet. Once cool, break the granola apart and store at room temperature in an airtight container for up to 1 week.

G et blending because these scrumptious and satisfying smoothies are the perfect vitamin-packed breakfast, nutritious snack, or afternoon pick-me-up, guaranteed to do your brain and body good.

MANGO GREEN SMOOTHIE

3 cups packed fresh baby spinach leaves

2 cups frozen mango chunks

1 large frozen ripe banana

2 cups coconut water

Fresh mango, chopped, for garnish

Black chia seeds, for garnish

SERVES: 2

1. Using a blender, combine the spinach, mango, banana, and coconut water. Blend on high until smooth and pour into serving glasses. Garnish with the fresh mango and chia seeds, if desired.

STRAWBERRY, RASPBERRY & ALMOND SMOOTHIE

2 cups frozen strawberries

¾ cup frozen raspberries

1 ripe banana

2¼ cups almond milk

2 tbsp almond butter

1 tbsp honey

1 tsp vanilla extract

Fresh raspberries, for garnish

Chopped toasted almonds, for garnish

SERVES: 2–3

1. Using a blender, combine the strawberries, raspberries, banana, almond milk, almond butter, honey, and vanilla. Blend on high until smooth and pour into serving glasses. Garnish with fresh raspberries and chopped almonds, if desired.

BANANA, PEANUT BUTTER & DATE SMOOTHIE

2 frozen ripe bananas

6 pitted dates, chopped

3 tbsp smooth peanut butter

½ cup old-fashioned oats

2 cups almond milk

½ tsp vanilla extract

Pinch ground cinnamon

Pinch kosher salt

8 ice cubes

Crushed roasted peanuts, for garnish

SERVES: 2

1. Using a blender, combine the bananas, dates, peanut butter, oats, almond milk, vanilla, cinnamon, salt, and ice cubes. Blend on high until smooth and pour into serving glasses. Garnish with crushed roasted peanuts, if desired.

banana breakfast cookies

I told Lisa she couldn't reveal the secret ingredient in these healthy breakfast cookies. Hello, Sister, people would pay zillions for the Colonel's closely guarded formula, and still she's opening the vault and giving away what makes these breakfast cookies the ultimate busy-morning bite: tahini. You read that right, tahini, the Middle Eastern sesame paste, subs in for butter and lends a nutty and nutritious bent to these breakfast beauties. Add ground flaxseed (in place of eggs), bananas, dates, and dark chocolate, and you've got a superfast, wholesome, and moist power breakfast that delivers quite the tasty bang for your buck. Thanks, blabbermouth.

MAKES: 8 LARGE BREAKFAST COOKIES   **PREP TIME: 10 MINS**   **COOK TIME: 15 MINS**

1½ cups old-fashioned oats

½ cup oat bran

¼ cup ground flaxseed

1 tsp ground cinnamon

½ tsp baking soda

½ tsp kosher salt

½ cup tahini

⅓ cup mashed ripe banana
 (about 1 large banana)

¼ cup maple syrup

1 tsp vanilla extract

½ cup chopped pitted dates

½ cup chopped dark chocolate

1. Preheat the oven to 350°F. Line a baking sheet with parchment paper and set aside.

2. In a large bowl, combine the oats, oat bran, flaxseed, cinnamon, baking soda, and salt.

3. In a medium bowl, whisk together the tahini, mashed banana, maple syrup, and vanilla. Pour into the oat mixture and stir in dates and chocolate. Mix until the ingredients are well combined.

4. Drop ¼ cup of dough per cookie onto the prepared baking sheet. Bake for 14 minutes, until the edges are golden.

✛ **Make it gluten-free:** Use gluten-free oat bran

lessons *from* lisa

★ *These breakfast cookies can be refrigerated (and enjoyed) for up to a week.*

read us like a *book*

Here's a bit of a deep (yet shallow) dive on us sisters: what makes us tick, click, and have schtick.

SMALL THINGS THAT MAKE MY DAY

Julie: Bubble wrap
Lisa: A superhot cup of coffee

SMALL THINGS THAT DAMPEN MY DAY

Julie: Reply All
Lisa: Having to shake hands

FAVE QUOTE

Julie: "The 'Duh' is silent."
— Rachel Maddow
Lisa: "A dog is the only thing on earth that loves you more than you love yourself."
— Josh Billings

A WORD I LOVE

Julie: Sugoi
Lisa: Truffle

A WORD YOU'LL NEVER HEAR ME SAY

Julie: Irregardless
Lisa: Touché

THINGS I THOUGHT I'D GROW OUT OF

Julie: Getting sent to my room
Lisa: Drinking from a straw

I FEEL OLD WHEN

Julie: I scroll to my birth year
Lisa: I realize I'm 10 years older than Diet Coke

#1 PLAYED SONG

Julie: "Mack the Knife," Bobby Darin
Lisa: "Banana Pancakes," Jack Johnson

MY DOG-EARED BOOK

Julie: Roget's Thesaurus
Lisa: The Way to Cook, Julia Child

MOVIE TITLE THAT DESCRIBES MY LIFE

Julie: Raging Bull
Lisa: Spice World

OLDEST THING IN MY FRIDGE

Julie: Blue cheese
Lisa: Miso paste

SOMETHING THAT SHOULD BE ON MY RÉSUMÉ

Julie: I'm immune to brain freeze
Lisa: I've never burped

MUSIC TO MY EARS

Julie: "Would you like to see the dessert menu?"
Lisa: An egg frying

IF ONLY I COULD WEAR THIS SMELL AS PERFUME

Julie: My dog's popcorn paws
Lisa: Chocolate

A TV CATCHPHRASE I OVERUSE

Julie: "Marcia, Marcia, Marcia."
Lisa: "Make it work."

WORTH SPENDING MORE ON TO GET THE BEST

Julie: Everything
Lisa: Olive oil

SOMETHING I'LL NEVER EXPERIENCE

Julie: Naked yoga
Lisa: Jumping out of an airplane

SOMETHING I'M DYING TO EXPERIENCE

Julie: A police ride-along
Lisa: Stomping grapes (with socks on, of course)

THE ONE THING I COULD EAT FOR THE REST OF MY LIFE

Julie: Chili dogs
Lisa: Pizza

WHAT I HOPE MY LAST WORDS WILL BE

Julie: Tag. You're it.
Lisa: Don't overmix

> 66 *When I was a kid I got no respect. I played hide-and-seek. They wouldn't even look for me.* —RODNEY DANGERFIELD

zucchini lime muffins

When it comes to hide-and-seek, we've got game. While I'm masterful at hiding my muffin top (thanks, high-waisted jeans), Lisa's stealth at hiding vegetables in plain sight. Ready or not, Lisa, in her quest to make fat-laden muffins lighter, has enlisted the help of zucchini, a champ at adding nutrients and moisture to baked goods. Close your eyes and take a big bite because this subtly flavored vegetable, along with zesty lime and a golden crumble topping, makes these speedy (pantry-to-oven before I can count to 900) snacks surefire game winners. One . . . two . . . three . . .

MAKES: 12 MUFFINS   PREP TIME: 15 MINS   COOK TIME: 20 MINS

Crumble Topping

¼ cup flour

¼ cup sugar

2 tbsp butter, softened

¼ tsp lime zest

Zucchini Lime Muffins

1½ cups flour

2 tsp lime zest

1 tsp baking powder

½ tsp baking soda

½ tsp kosher salt

¼ cup canola oil

¼ cup melted butter

¾ cup sugar

1 egg

1 tbsp fresh lime juice

2 tsp vanilla extract

1½ cups shredded zucchini
  (do not squeeze liquid out)

1. For the crumble topping, in a small bowl, combine the flour and sugar. Add the butter and lime zest and mix with a fork until crumbly. Set aside.

2. Preheat the oven to 350°F. Coat a 12-cup muffin tin with nonstick cooking spray and line with muffin cups.

3. For the muffins, in a large bowl, combine the flour, lime zest, baking powder, baking soda, and salt. Mix well.

4. In a medium bowl, whisk together the canola oil, melted butter, sugar, egg, lime juice, and vanilla. Pour over the flour mixture along with the shredded zucchini. Stir just until blended, being careful not to overmix.

5. Spoon the batter evenly into the prepared muffin tin. Sprinkle the crumble topping over the muffins and bake for 20 minutes, or until the muffins are golden and spring back when gently pressed. Remove from the oven and let cool slightly before removing from the pan.

banana chocolate chip muffins

Since muffins get a bad rap (think: monstrous coffee shop versions), I tried to convince Lisa to make these into flourless vegan muffins loaded with wheat germ and flax. She passed. As she explained, there's a time for mega-nutrition in our balanced diets, and then there's a time for homemade, lightened-up muffins that contain all the essentials and on top of that, deliver delicious comfort: oatmeal, bananas, and chocolate. Packed with the goodness of rolled oats and loaded with banana flavor, you can have these moist and tender beauties hot and fresh from the oven in 30 minutes, like scrumptious grab-and-go bowls of warm oatmeal.

MAKES: 12 MUFFINS   PREP TIME: 10 MINS   COOK TIME: 20 MINS

1½ cups flour

1 cup old-fashioned oats

1½ tsp baking powder

½ tsp baking soda

½ tsp kosher salt

½ tsp ground cinnamon

1½ cups mashed very ripe bananas

½ cup sugar

¼ cup brown sugar

⅓ cup vegetable oil

⅓ cup buttermilk

1 egg

1 tsp vanilla extract

1 cup semisweet or dark chocolate chips

1. Preheat the oven to 400°F. Line 12 muffin cups with paper liners and lightly coat with nonstick cooking spray. Set aside.

2. In a large bowl, combine the flour, oats, baking powder, baking soda, salt, and cinnamon. In a second bowl, whisk together the mashed bananas, sugar, brown sugar, vegetable oil, buttermilk, egg, and vanilla. Fold the banana mixture into the flour mixture along with the chocolate chips, mixing just until the flour disappears.

3. Divide the batter between the prepared muffin cups, filling the cups to the top. Bake for 16–18 minutes, until the muffins spring back when gently touched. Remove from the tins and cool.

It's always nice to have a stud muffin at the table. —JANET EVANOVICH

GLAZED blueberry lemon loaf

I f ever there were a recipe to epitomize my sister, this would be it. First, her wish is to set everyone up for success, and this simple, foolproof loaf makes instant bakers out of all of us. Second is her consideration for the time-strapped—this is a quick bread with emphasis on the "quick," meaning you can get this delicious delight from pantry to oven in 15 minutes. Third, in keeping with her motto, "Silence is golden," she's gone mixer-free on this one, leaving us free to bake in peace (unless of course you have me clamoring in the kitchen), and whenever inspiration strikes. Finally, and most importantly, is her attention to flavor, striking the perfect balance between sweet and sour in this moist lemon-infused loaf studded with fresh, juicy blueberries and topped with a zesty, glorious glaze. This loaf is so Lisa: easygoing, speedy, quiet, sweet, and a tad tart.

MAKES: 10–12 SLICES   PREP TIME: 15 MINS   COOK TIME: 55 MINS

Blueberry Lemon Loaf

½ cup melted butter

1 cup sugar

2 eggs

1 tsp vanilla extract

1 heaping tbsp lemon zest
  (from 2 large lemons)

1½ cups flour

1 tsp baking powder

¾ tsp kosher salt

½ cup whole milk

1 cup fresh blueberries tossed
  with 1 tbsp flour, divided

Lemon Glaze

½ cup icing sugar

1 tbsp fresh lemon juice

Pinch kosher salt

Lemon zest, for garnish

1. Preheat the oven to 350°F. Line a 9-by-5-inch loaf pan with parchment paper.

2. For the loaf, in a large bowl, whisk the butter, sugar, and eggs until the sugar is dissolved and well combined. Add the vanilla and lemon zest.

3. In a small bowl, combine the flour, baking powder, and salt. Stir half the flour mixture into the wet ingredients, alternating with adding the milk, just until combined.

4. Fold in half the blueberries and pour into the prepared loaf pan. Place the remaining blueberries evenly on the batter and gently push them in—this will help make sure all blueberries don't end up at the bottom of the loaf. Bake for 50–55 minutes, until a toothpick inserted into the center comes out clean. Cool the bread for 15 minutes before removing it from the pan.

5. For the glaze, in a small bowl, whisk together the icing sugar, lemon juice, and salt.

6. Once the loaf is completely cool, spread the glaze over top and garnish with the extra lemon zest.

CRANBERRY, orange & ginger scones

W hile my accent is wanting and stiff upper lip nonexistent, I adore everything across the pond, including lawyers in wigs, fish and chips, footie (go, Liverpool!), and of course, afternoon tea. I always fancy a brew, but have to say, I have trouble choking down those scones that can be as dry as British wit. So, instead of learning the Heimlich maneuver, Lisa has created a bloody delicious scone dominated by the trio of cranberry, orange, and ginger, that is crisp on the outside and tender and soft on the inside. Every bite bursts with bright flavors and sweet citrus, with the warm spice of crystallized ginger balancing out the tartness of the cranberries. Flaky, ultra-moist, and 28 minutes from start to finish, these stellar scones are everyone's cup of tea.

MAKES: 8 SCONES   **PREP TIME: 10 MINS**   **COOK TIME: 20 MINS**

Scones

2 cups flour

¼ cup sugar

1 tbsp baking powder

2 tsp orange zest

½ tsp ground cinnamon

½ tsp kosher salt

¼ tsp ground ginger

3 tbsp chopped crystallized ginger

6 tbsp cold butter, cut in small pieces

½ cup half and half cream

1 egg

1 tsp vanilla extract

1 cup coarsely chopped frozen cranberries

Orange Glaze

½ cup icing sugar

1 tbsp orange juice

Orange zest, for garnish

1. Preheat the oven to 400°F and line a baking sheet with parchment paper.

2. To make the scones, in a large bowl, combine the flour, sugar, baking powder, orange zest, cinnamon, salt, ground ginger, and crystallized ginger. Cut in the butter until it is in pea-sized crumbs.

3. In a small bowl, whisk together the cream, egg, and vanilla. Add to flour mixture, along with the frozen cranberries. Using a wooden spoon, stir until the dough holds together.

4. On a lightly floured surface, knead the dough by folding it over itself 4 or 5 times. Form into an 8-inch circle and cut into 8 wedges. Place on the prepared baking sheet and bake for 18 minutes until golden. Remove from the oven and allow to cool completely before glazing.

5. For the glaze, in a small bowl, whisk together the icing sugar and orange juice. Drizzle over the cooled scones and garnish with the orange zest.

lessons *from* lisa

★ *Cold ingredients are the secret to flaky, tender scones. Cut the butter in small pieces and put them back in the fridge while you are doing the other prep, and chop the cranberries and throw them in the freezer until you are ready to mix them in.*

NIBBLE

NIBBLE

Ditch those preservative-laden energy bars, because you're going to be a ball of healthy energy with these protein-packed bites that are full of deliciously wholesome ingredients.

NO-BAKE
energy bites

ALMOND COCONUT BITES

1 cup pitted dates

3 tbsp almond flour

2 tbsp almond butter

3 tbsp unsweetened shredded coconut

1 tbsp water

½ tsp vanilla extract

¼ tsp ground cinnamon

¼ tsp kosher salt

Heaping tablespoon of unsweetened shredded coconut, to roll balls in

MAKES: 20 BITES

1. In the bowl of a food processor or blender, add the dates, almond flour, and almond butter. Pulse on and off until the mixture is well chopped and combined.

2. Place in a large mixing bowl and stir in the coconut, water, vanilla, cinnamon, and salt. Mix until the ingredients are well incorporated. Refrigerate the mixture for 10 minutes.

3. Form each ball out of 2 teaspoons of dough. Roll the balls in shredded coconut and refrigerate in a covered container until ready to serve.

PEANUT BUTTER OAT BITES

1 cup pitted dates

1 cup old-fashioned oats

½ cup smooth peanut butter

2 tbsp honey

½ tsp vanilla extract

¼ tsp kosher salt

Melted dark chocolate, for drizzling (about 1 tbsp)

Sea salt, for sprinkling

MAKES: 20 BITES

1. In the bowl of a food processor or blender, add the dates, oats, peanut butter, honey, vanilla, and salt. Pulse until ingredients are finely chopped.

2. Refrigerate for 10 minutes and then roll into balls, using 1 tablespoon of dough for each ball.

3. Drizzle the finished balls with melted dark chocolate and sprinkle sea salt over them. Refrigerate in a covered container until ready to serve.

CHOCOLATE RAISIN PECAN BITES

½ cup almond butter

¼ cup honey

¼ cup cocoa powder

1 cup old-fashioned oats

½ cup unsweetened shredded coconut

½ cup finely chopped pecans

½ cup semisweet chocolate chips

½ cup chopped raisins

¼ tsp kosher salt

MAKES: 30 BITES

1. In a large bowl, mix together the almond butter, honey, and cocoa powder. Stir in the oats, coconut, pecans, chocolate, raisins, and salt, mixing until well combined.

2. Roll the dough into balls, using 1 tablespoon for each ball. Refrigerate in a covered container until ready to serve.

sensational shakshuka

What do Liberace and shakshuka have in common? Pizazz, that's what. Much like the rhinestone capes and diamond-encrusted pianos, shakshuka is bold, with dazzling flavors that hit all the high notes: salty, sweet, sour, and spicy. Never to be outshone by other brunch (or lunch or dinner) dishes, eggs are poached in a smoky, spice-packed, chunky tomato sauce and sprinkled with tangy feta in this fast (less than 30 minutes) and easy meal that's all the rage at Middle Eastern tables. The richness of slightly runny yolks mingling with tasty tomato sauce begs to be mopped up with crusty bread, so don't delay; be like Mr. Showmanship—with the snap of your fingers, awe your gastronomic groupies with your spectacular one-skillet shakshuka.

SERVES: 4–6   PREP TIME: 5 MINS   COOK TIME: 20 MINS

2 tbsp olive oil

1 medium yellow onion, chopped

1 red bell pepper, chopped

2 garlic cloves, minced

1 tsp smoked paprika

1 tsp ground cumin

1 tsp kosher salt

½ tsp freshly ground black pepper

½ tsp ground coriander

½ tsp fennel seeds (crushed or whole)

1 (28 oz) can San Marzano tomatoes

½ tsp sugar

6 eggs

½ cup crumbled feta cheese

¼ cup chopped fresh flat-leaf parsley

1. In a 12-inch heavy-bottomed or cast-iron skillet, heat the olive oil over medium heat. Add the onions and red peppers and cook until softened, 6–8 minutes.

2. Add the garlic, smoked paprika, cumin, salt, pepper, coriander, and fennel seeds. Continuously stir for 1 minute. Add the San Marzano tomatoes, breaking them up with a wooden spoon to create smaller chunks. Stir in the sugar and bring to a boil. Reduce the heat and simmer the sauce for 8–10 minutes.

3. Make 6 indentations in the sauce and crack an egg into each indentation. Cover and cook over low heat for 3 minutes, until the eggs are just set.

4. Remove from the heat and top with feta and parsley. Serve with toasted sourdough or pita bread.

> *Why don't I just step out and slip into something more spectacular?* —LIBERACE

smoked salmon breakfast salad

WITH PUMPERNICKEL CROUTONS

"Wake up and smell the salad." "Would you like coffee with your arugula?" "Breakfast salad is the most important meal of the day." I'm trying out all these phrases because while I don't have a crystal ball, I can predict with certainty that this breakfast salad is going to become your rise-and-shine ritual. Taking a cue from Middle Eastern morning meals, Lisa's swapped out the cereal bowl for the salad one, full of freshness (baby spinach, arugula, cucumber), protein (smoked salmon, eggs), and fruit (blueberries, avocado), tossed with a zesty Greek yogurt dill dressing, and finished with salty capers and crunchy pumpernickel croutons. Even the breakfast traditionalist will agree that this bright, crisp, and savory salad is worth getting out of bed for.

SERVES: 4   PREP TIME: 15 MINS   COOK TIME: 15 MINS

Creamy Lemon Dressing

½ cup 2% plain Greek yogurt

3 tbsp olive oil

1 tbsp fresh lemon juice

2 tsp chopped fresh dill

1 tsp honey

½ tsp Dijon mustard

½ tsp lemon zest

¼ tsp garlic powder

¼ tsp kosher salt

¼ tsp freshly ground black pepper

Pumpernickel Croutons

2 cups cubed pumpernickel bread

2 tsp olive oil

⅛ tsp kosher salt

⅛ tsp freshly ground black pepper

continued on next page

1. For the dressing, whisk together the yogurt, olive oil, lemon juice, dill, honey, mustard, lemon zest, garlic powder, salt, and pepper. Cover and refrigerate until ready to serve.

2. For the croutons, preheat the oven to 350°F. Toss the cubed bread with the olive oil, salt, and pepper and spread in a single layer on a parchment-lined baking sheet. Bake for 12–15 minutes, stirring once halfway through, until the croutons are golden and crunchy. Remove from the oven and allow to cool. Set aside.

3. For the salad, in a large bowl, toss the baby spinach, arugula, blueberries, cucumber, avocado, and croutons with a few spoons of dressing. Divide among 4 plates, top with the smoked salmon and hard-boiled eggs, and sprinkle each plate with capers. Top with more dressing if desired. Serve immediately.

+ Make it gluten-free: Use gluten-free bread

lessons *from* lisa

★ *For perfect hard-boiled eggs, place the eggs in a saucepan with just enough cold water to cover the eggs. Bring the water to a boil, cover the pot, and then let the eggs sit off the heat for about 10 minutes. Run under cold water and peel.*

ingredients continued

Salad

3 cups baby spinach

3 cups arugula

1 cup fresh blueberries

1 cup cubed English cucumber

1 large ripe avocado, cubed

8 oz smoked salmon, sliced

4 hard-boiled eggs, quartered

1 tbsp capers, rinsed and drained

smoked salmon & goat cheese FRITTATA

Hakuna Frittata. Not sure if you've heard this phrase, but it loosely translates to, "No brunch worries for the rest of your days." Our very own Lioness Lisa has created a healthy, flavor-packed one-dish delight that ain't no passing craze. The salty goodness of smoked salmon and sun-dried tomatoes is mixed with the creaminess of goat cheese, the freshness of dill and parsley, and the tanginess of kale and Greek yogurt. Packed with protein and simple to whip together, you're going to go whole hog on this rustic, loaded Italian omelet (think: Pumbaa).

SERVES: 6   PREP TIME: 10 MINS   COOK TIME: 25 MINS

2 tbsp olive oil

1 large leek, washed well, white and light green parts chopped

1 large shallot, chopped

1 garlic clove, minced

3 cups chopped kale

10 eggs

½ cup plain Greek yogurt

¼ cup milk

6 oz (about ½ cup) coarsely chopped smoked salmon

3 tbsp coarsely chopped oil-packed sun-dried tomatoes

¼ cup chopped fresh flat-leaf parsley

2 tbsp chopped fresh dill

½ tsp kosher salt

½ tsp freshly ground black pepper

½ cup crumbled goat cheese

1. Preheat the oven to 425°F.

2. Heat the olive oil over medium heat in a 10-inch ovenproof skillet. Add the leeks, shallots, and garlic and cook, stirring constantly, for 3 minutes. Add the kale and cook for 1 minute. Remove the skillet from the heat.

3. In a large bowl, whisk together the eggs, yogurt, and milk. Stir in the salmon, sun-dried tomatoes, parsley, dill, salt, and pepper. Pour the egg mixture evenly over the kale mixture in the skillet. Drop the crumbled goat cheese over top of the frittata.

4. Transfer to the oven and bake for 20–25 minutes, until puffed and set in the middle. Let cool for a few minutes, cut in wedges, and serve.

There has never been a sadness that can't be cured by breakfast food.

—RON SWANSON, *PARKS & RECREATION*

VEGETABLE hash with poached eggs

There's a hashtag for everything. Search #inappropriatefuneralsongs and you're bound to find "Rolling in the Deep" and "Another One Bites the Dust." So, I've come up with a hashtag for this healthy vegetable and protein-packed meal: #thishashisdope. Forget the greasy-spoon fare you once knew—our meatless hash is a powerhouse, loaded with chopped potatoes, onions, zucchini, red peppers, spinach, and fresh herbs. Made in one skillet and topped with poached eggs, this addictive blend is hearty, simple, and savory, sure to satisfy all your taste buds. #putthatinyourskilletandmakeit

SERVES: 4   PREP TIME: 20 MINS   COOK TIME: 30 MINS

Vegetable Hash

2 tbsp olive oil

1 large (about 1 lb) Yukon gold potato, scrubbed and cubed

1 large (about 1 lb) sweet potato, scrubbed and cubed

1 medium yellow onion, chopped

1 red bell pepper, chopped

1 medium zucchini, chopped

3 garlic cloves, minced

2 tsp chopped fresh thyme

1 tsp chopped fresh rosemary

1 tsp kosher salt

½ tsp freshly ground black pepper

⅛–¼ tsp crushed red pepper flakes

3 cups coarsely chopped baby spinach

Poached Eggs

1 tbsp white vinegar

6–8 eggs

Kosher salt and freshly ground black pepper, to season

1. For the hash, heat the olive oil in a large skillet over medium heat. Add the Yukon gold potatoes and sweet potatoes, mixing well to coat the potatoes with the oil. Cover the skillet and cook for 8 minutes, stirring occasionally. Add the onions, peppers, and zucchini. Continue cooking, uncovered, for 6–8 minutes, or until the potatoes are tender. Add the garlic, thyme, rosemary, salt, pepper, and red pepper flakes. Cook, stirring, for 1–2 minutes. Stir in the spinach and cook until wilted, about 1 minute. Remove from the heat.

2. For the poached eggs, over high heat, bring a medium saucepan of cold water to a boil. Reduce the heat to medium and add the vinegar. Crack each egg into its own small bowl. Give the water a quick whisk right before adding the eggs. Slide 2 eggs into the water and poach for 3 minutes. Remove with a slotted spoon and drain on a paper towel. Repeat with the remaining eggs, poaching 2 at a time.

3. To serve, place 1–2 poached eggs over each serving of hash, seasoning the eggs with salt and freshly ground black pepper. Serve immediately.

lessons *from* lisa

★ *Try to cut your veggies the same size so their cooking time is the same.*

savory kale & mushroom STRATA

Lisa runs her kitchen with military precision. Here, the Kitchen Colonel provides us with a brunch blueprint, a game plan for the most foolproof, flavorful, crowd-pleasing, and strategic strata. This well-thought-out, savory strata (aka bread pudding) is perfect for holiday brunch—so simple, it's prepped in advance and assures satisfyingly glorious grub for all. Keeping it easy yet elegant, earthy mushrooms are sautéed with red onion, garlic, and thyme, combined with fresh kale, and folded into a mixture of crusty bread, sharp Gruyère, white cheddar, and Parmesan. Baked until warm and golden, this scrumptious strata is a fuss-free winner, chow that makes it super simple to earn your stripes. Bravo Zulu, Lisa.

SERVES: 6–8   PREP TIME: 15 MINS (+ resting)   COOK TIME: 60 MINS

8 cups cubed rustic or French bread

1 tbsp olive oil

1 tbsp butter

1 medium red onion, chopped

12 oz sliced cremini mushrooms

2 garlic cloves, minced

2 tsp chopped fresh thyme

1 tsp kosher salt, divided

½ tsp freshly ground black pepper

6 cups coarsely chopped fresh kale

6 eggs

2 cups whole milk

1 tbsp Dijon mustard

1½ cups grated Gruyère cheese

1½ cups grated white cheddar cheese, divided

1 cup freshly grated Parmesan cheese, divided

1. Preheat the oven to 350°F and coat a 13-by-9-inch baking dish with nonstick cooking spray.

2. Place the cubed bread in a large mixing bowl and set it aside. In a large skillet over medium heat, add the olive oil and butter. Stir in the red onions and cook for 4 minutes. Increase the heat to medium-high and add the mushrooms. Cook for 5 minutes, stirring occasionally. Add the garlic, thyme, ¾ tsp of the salt, and the pepper and stir for 1 minute. Lower the heat to medium, add the kale, and cook for 1 minute, until the kale has wilted. Remove from the heat and toss with the bread cubes. Let cool for a few minutes.

3. In a separate bowl, whisk together the eggs, milk, mustard, and the remaining ¼ tsp salt. Set aside.

4. Add the Gruyère, 1 cup of the grated white cheddar, and ½ cup of the Parmesan to the bread mixture and stir. Pour the bread mixture into the prepared baking dish. Pour the egg mixture over the bread and press the ingredients lightly. Top with the remaining ½ cup of white cheddar and ½ cup of Parmesan. Either cover and refrigerate overnight before baking, or let the mixture stand covered at room temperature for 30 minutes before baking.

5. Bake uncovered in a preheated 350°F oven for 45–50 minutes, until the top is golden and the middle is set. Let stand for a few minutes before serving.

+ **Make it gluten-free: Use gluten-free bread**

gingerbread waffles

What does this Jewess want for Christmas? Everything. From tinsel and trees to carols and candy canes, I want it all. And though I'm often a bit more naughty than nice, Lisa's still busy in her workshop, whisking up everything on my list, including these warm and wondrous Gingerbread Waffles with Apple Cinnamon Syrup. An epic combination of ginger, molasses, and buttermilk, these festively flavored waffles have a fluffy texture with a crisp exterior. Smothered in sweet-yet-tart apple cinnamon syrup, these are the stuff that brunch miracles are made of. Wait until I get that saintly sister of mine under the mistletoe.

MAKES: 8 LARGE WAFFLES   PREP TIME: 15 MINS   COOK TIME: 10 MINS

Gingerbread Waffles

2 cups flour

¼ cup brown sugar

1 tbsp baking powder

2 tsp ground ginger

1½ tsp ground cinnamon

½ tsp kosher salt

¼ tsp ground nutmeg

2 egg yolks

1½ cups buttermilk, room temperature

⅓ cup melted butter

⅓ cup molasses

1 tsp vanilla extract

4 egg whites

2 tbsp sugar

continued on next page

1. Preheat the waffle iron.

2. For the waffles, in a large mixing bowl, combine the flour, brown sugar, baking powder, ginger, cinnamon, salt, and nutmeg.

3. In another bowl, whisk the egg yolks, buttermilk, melted butter, molasses, and vanilla extract until well combined. Add the egg mixture to the flour mixture and stir just until combined. Do not overmix; a few small lumps are all right.

4. Using an electric mixer, whip the egg whites on high speed until foamy. Add the sugar and continue to beat until soft peaks form. Very gently fold the egg whites into the batter just until incorporated.

5. Coat the heated waffle iron with nonstick cooking spray and spoon batter into the waffle iron. Close the lid and let cook for 4 minutes, until the waffles are golden brown. Repeat with remaining batter.

Apple Cinnamon Syrup

2 tbsp butter

¼ cup brown sugar

¼ cup maple syrup

⅛ tsp ground cinnamon

2 Granny Smith apples, peeled and diced

6. While the waffles are cooking, make the apple cinnamon syrup. In a medium saucepan, melt the butter over medium heat. Stir in the brown sugar, maple syrup, and cinnamon. Cook for 2 minutes, until the sugar is dissolved. Add the apples and continue to cook just until apples are slightly tender, 2–3 minutes. Remove from the heat and serve with the waffles.

lessons *from* lisa

★ You can make your own buttermilk: combine 1 tablespoon lemon juice or white vinegar with 1 cup milk, let sit 5 minutes, then whisk.

★ For easy removal, let the waffles sit for 30 seconds after you open the waffle iron.

★ If you aren't serving the waffles right away, crisp them up by putting them directly on the oven rack for 5 minutes at 250°F.

I LIKE HASHTAGS BECAUSE THEY LOOK LIKE

waffles #

OUR

top 10 pet peeves

Since we sisters don't sweat the small stuff, here's a list of the big stuff that really steams us up . . .

01. **Watching someone eat yogurt**

02. **Zealous finger licking**

03. **Major mastication**

04. **Toast crumbs in the butter**

05. **Not clearing the microwave timer**

06. **People who talk about dieting while we're chowing down**

07. **Peanut butter knuckles**

08. **Honey on the honey jar**

09. **Ketchup water**

10. **Paper straws**

apple pie

FRENCH TOAST BAKE

I like to coin expressions, and after devouring this Apple Pie French Toast Bake, "Go big and stay home" immediately sprung to mind. Why, after Lisa has pulled out all the scrumptious stops, would I ever go out to eat brunch again? This is last meal material, folks, we're talking the no regrets kind of eats where every extravagant bite is fulfilling to the extreme. Apples are sautéed in brown sugar and cinnamon, layered between cubes of sweet brioche, and topped with a pie-like crumble that gets crunchy and golden when baked. Prepped in advance, this is the definition of "easy as pie," and most definitely a weekend wonder—to coin a new phrase, you're going to want to "Put all your eggs in this bake." Take that, Cervantes.

SERVES: 8–10   PREP TIME: 30 MINS (+ refrigeration)   COOK TIME: 50 MINS

Apple Mixture

⅓ cup brown sugar

¼ cup butter

1 tsp ground cinnamon

6 Granny Smith apples, peeled and cut into chunks

Crumble Topping

1¼ cups flour

½ cup brown sugar

1 tsp ground cinnamon

¼ tsp kosher salt

½ cup butter, cut into pieces

French Toast

2 cups whole milk

1 cup heavy cream

½ cup brown sugar

¼ cup sugar

6 eggs

1 tbsp vanilla extract

14 cups cubed brioche or challah bread

1. For the apple mixture, in a large skillet, melt the brown sugar and butter over medium heat. Stir constantly until the sugar is dissolved. Stir in the cinnamon and apples and cook over low heat for 5 minutes, stirring occasionally. Remove from the heat and allow to cool slightly.

2. For the crumble topping, in a medium bowl, combine the flour, brown sugar, cinnamon, and salt. Add the butter and combine with your fingers or a fork until the mixture is crumbly. Set aside.

3. For the French toast, coat a 9-by-13-inch baking dish with nonstick cooking spray. In a large bowl, whisk the milk, heavy cream, brown sugar, sugar, eggs, and vanilla extract until well combined.

4. To assemble, place half the cubed bread in the bottom of the prepared baking dish. Top with half the apple mixture. Top with the remaining cubed bread and scatter the remaining apples and any accumulated liquid from the apples over top. Pour the milk mixture evenly over the bread. Sprinkle the crumble evenly over top. Cover and refrigerate for several hours or overnight.

5. When ready to bake, remove from refrigerator and preheat the oven to 350°F. Bake for 40–45 minutes, or until set and golden brown. Serve with maple syrup, if desired.

buttermilk pancakes

WITH FRESH BERRY SAUCE

Have you ever attempted to wake a teenage boy? It's not pretty. My son has endured the ice water treatment, sonic-boom alarm blare, and tickling of his man-sized feet. Nothing mobilized the sleeping beaut until I called on my secret weapon and scent specialist sister Lisa, the genius behind these buttermilk beauties. Blanketing the house in a pancake perfume, the aroma of freshly baked cake with notes of rich buttermilk, sweet butter, and warm vanilla travels up stairs and under bedroom doors, awakening sleeping minds in a flippin' fantastic fashion. Drool-worthy for sure, these fluffy flapjacks are served up with a scrumptious triple berry sauce that bursts with fresh flavor. Now if only this sanity-saving, sky-high stack could get him to make his bed.

MAKES: 15 PANCAKES   PREP TIME: 10 MINS   COOK TIME: 20 MINS

Fresh Berry Sauce

1 cup fresh raspberries, divided

1 cup fresh blueberries, divided

1 cup hulled and sliced fresh
  strawberries, divided

⅓ cup sugar

2 tsp fresh lemon juice

Buttermilk Pancakes

1½ cups flour

2 tbsp sugar

1 tsp baking powder

½ tsp baking soda

¼ tsp kosher salt

1¼ cups buttermilk, room
  temperature

3 tbsp melted butter

1 egg

1 tsp vanilla extract

Butter, for greasing the skillet
  or griddle

1. For the berry sauce, in a medium saucepan, combine ¾ cup of the raspberries, ¾ cup of the blueberries, ¾ cup of the strawberries, and the sugar and lemon juice. Bring to a simmer over medium heat. Cook for 10 minutes, stirring occasionally. Remove from the heat and stir in the remaining raspberries, blueberries, and strawberries. Set aside.

2. For the pancakes, in a large mixing bowl, combine the flour, sugar, baking powder, baking soda, and salt. In a medium bowl, whisk together the buttermilk, melted butter, egg, and vanilla. Stir the buttermilk mixture into the dry ingredients. Do not overmix.

3. Heat a skillet or griddle over medium heat. Lightly grease it with butter. Drop 2 tablespoons of batter into the skillet and cook until bubbles form, then flip the pancake over and cook on the other side until golden. Serve the pancakes with the berry sauce.

lessons *from* lisa

★ Be careful not to overmix your batter or you'll end up with dense, flat pancakes.

coffee cake

We have a friendship philosophy. If you like *Seinfeld*, we like you. It's that simple. This epic show that began in the '80s provides us with daily points of reference, from "man hands," "close talkers," and "puffy shirts" to "serenity now," "you gotta see the baby," and "shmoopie." This crumble-topped cake is our edible homage to Jerry, to the episode where he tried to bribe Newman with a Drake's Coffee Cake. Elaine devoured the entire cake, but really, how could anyone resist a classic New York coffee cake that's moist, buttery, and loaded with a super-cinnamony crumble? Quick and easy, you're going to want to giddy-up and get baking this irresistible coffee cake—we guarantee it's gold, people, gold.

SERVES: 12–14   PREP TIME: 15 MINS   COOK TIME: 50 MINS

Crumble Topping

1¼ cups flour

½ cup sugar

½ cup brown sugar

1 tbsp ground cinnamon

¼ tsp kosher salt

½ cup melted butter

Cinnamon Filling

½ cup sugar

1 tbsp ground cinnamon

Coffee Cake

2 cups flour

1 tsp baking powder

½ tsp baking soda

½ tsp kosher salt

½ cup melted butter

½ cup sugar

½ cup brown sugar

2 eggs

2 tsp vanilla extract

1 cup sour cream

⅓ cup milk

1. Preheat the oven to 350°F. Coat a 9-inch square baking pan with nonstick cooking spray and line with parchment paper.

2. For the crumble topping, in a bowl, combine the flour, sugar, brown sugar, cinnamon, and salt. Add the melted butter and stir with a fork until the mixture is combined and crumbly. Set aside.

3. For the cinnamon filling, combine the sugar and cinnamon in a small bowl and set aside.

4. For the coffee cake, in a large bowl, stir together the flour, baking powder, baking soda, and salt.

5. In a separate bowl, whisk the melted butter, sugar, brown sugar, eggs, vanilla, sour cream, and milk until well combined. Add the wet ingredients to the dry ingredients and stir just until combined.

6. Pour half the cake batter into the prepared baking pan. Sprinkle the cinnamon filling evenly over the batter. Pour in the remaining cake batter and spread it across the pan. Sprinkle the crumble topping evenly over top. Bake in the preheated oven for 48–50 minutes, until the crumble top is golden and the cake is baked through.

lunch

> *Lunch? Aw, you gotta be kidding. Lunch is for wimps.*
>
> —GORDON GEKKO, *WALL STREET*, 1987

• • • • • • •

If lunch is for wimps, then we're the biggest sissy sisters of all time. Whether dining al desko, taking the opportunity to lunch with the ladies, or simply looking for a nutritious nooner, we've got amazing recipes that'll power you through straight until supper. From warming soups and mealtime salads to light bites and simple sandwiches, never before has "Let's do lunch" sounded so deliciously easy.

green minestrone
WITH KALE PESTO

As kids, Lisa and I fought twice. Once, I scratched her (banished to my room for that), and another time, I twisted her arm. She's waited 40 years to take her revenge, has dropped the gloves and walloped my devotion to the classic tomato minestrone. Being the purist I am, I threatened an atomic wedgie, but one spoonful of this aromatic, ingenious green minestrone and my outrage was extinguished. This healthy soup is packed with crunchy green vegetables, fresh herbs, and creamy white beans, and it's finished with a pesto that packs a sharp, lemony punch. Once again, Lisa has had the last laugh, with me twisted around her little finger, begging for another bowl of this vibrant, scrumptious soup.

SERVES: 8–10   PREP TIME: 20 MINS   COOK TIME: 20 MINS

Green Minestrone

1 tbsp olive oil

1 large leek, white part only, cut in half lengthwise and chopped (about 1½ cups), rinsed well

2 large shallots, chopped

2 celery stalks, chopped

2 garlic cloves, finely minced

1 tsp dried Italian spices

1 tsp kosher salt

½ tsp freshly ground black pepper

½ tsp red pepper flakes

¼ cup dry white wine

10 cups vegetable broth

2 small zucchini, chopped (about 1½ cups)

1 cup fresh or thawed frozen green peas

25 green beans, ends trimmed and beans cut in half

1¼ cups canned cannellini (white kidney) beans, rinsed and drained

continued on next page

1. For the minestrone, in a large soup pot, heat the olive oil over medium heat. Add the leek, shallots, and celery and cook for 6 minutes, until the vegetables soften. Stir in the garlic, Italian spices, salt, pepper, and red pepper flakes. Cook for 1 minute, stirring constantly. Add the white wine and let evaporate, about 1 minute. Add the vegetable broth and bring to a boil. Reduce the heat to medium and stir in the zucchini, peas, green beans, cannellini beans, and pasta. Cook for 10 minutes, stirring occasionally.

2. For the kale pesto, place the kale, basil, almond flour, garlic, salt, and pepper in a food processor. Process for 10 seconds to chop. Scrape down the sides of the bowl. With the machine running, slowly pour in the olive oil in a steady stream until the mixture is smooth, about 10 seconds. Add the Parmesan and lemon juice and pulse a few times until incorporated.

3. Once the soup is finished cooking, stir in the kale, basil, parsley, and Parmesan and cook for 2 minutes. Serve immediately, topping each serving with a dollop of kale pesto.

+ Make it gluten-free: Use gluten-free pasta

lessons *from* lisa

★ *If you don't have dried Italian spices, use a mixture of equal parts dried oregano and thyme.*

ingredients continued

¾ cup uncooked tiny bow-shaped pasta (or any small shape)

4 cups chopped baby kale

¼ cup chopped fresh basil

¼ cup chopped fresh flat-leaf parsley

¼ cup freshly grated Parmesan cheese

Kale Pesto

1 cup chopped baby kale

½ cup chopped fresh basil

¼ cup almond flour (finely ground almonds)

1 small garlic clove

Scant ½ tsp kosher salt

¼ tsp freshly ground black pepper

⅓ cup olive oil

¼ cup freshly grated Parmesan cheese

1 tbsp fresh lemon juice

TOMAYTO ·········· ·········· TOMAHTO

tomato basil soup

WITH CRUNCHY GARLIC CROUTONS

Lisa thinks outside the can. Just when I figure she can't possibly reinvent tomato soup (she's created countless stellar versions), she serves up a bowl of this steamy, healthy tomato basil soup. While my descriptions of her past masterpieces—"creamy yet creamless," "a comfort food classic," "velvety goodness"—all apply, this smooth and spectacular iteration is something unto its own. The genius additions of red peppers and carrots add sweetness, a touch of cayenne brings a bit of spice, basil offers up a fresh pop, and crunchy garlic croutons give a tasty bite to this bursting-with-flavor soup. Once again, we all reap the benefits of Lisa's can-do attitude and pro palate.

SERVES: 4   PREP TIME: 10 MINS   COOK TIME: 30 MINS

Tomato Basil Soup

2 tbsp olive oil

1 medium red onion, chopped

2 carrots, peeled and chopped

1 red bell pepper, chopped

2 garlic cloves, minced

2 tbsp tomato paste

2 tsp sugar

1 tsp kosher salt

½ tsp freshly ground black pepper

Pinch cayenne pepper

3 cups chicken broth

1 (28 oz) can San Marzano tomatoes, crushed with hands

2 tsp red wine vinegar

¼ cup chopped fresh basil

Garlic Croutons

3 cups cubed rustic bread

2 tbsp olive oil

1 garlic clove, finely minced

1 tbsp chopped fresh flat-leaf parsley

¼ tsp kosher salt

1. For the soup, in a large soup pot, heat the olive oil over medium heat. Add the red onions and carrots, cooking for 6 minutes. Stir in the red peppers and garlic, continuing to cook for 4 minutes. Add the tomato paste, sugar, salt, black pepper, and cayenne pepper, stirring constantly for 1 minute. Add the chicken broth and tomatoes. Bring to a boil, reduce the heat to low, and allow the soup to simmer for 20 minutes, stirring occasionally.

2. Meanwhile, for the croutons, preheat the oven to 375°F and line a baking sheet with parchment paper. In a medium bowl, toss the cubed bread with the olive oil, garlic, parsley, and salt. Place the cubes in a single layer on the prepared baking sheet. Bake 14–16 minutes, stirring once halfway through baking, until the bread is lightly golden. Remove from the oven and allow to cool.

3. Remove the soup from heat and puree in 2 batches using a countertop blender, or in the pot using a handheld immersion blender. Stir in red wine vinegar and basil. Ladle into serving bowls and top with garlic bread croutons.

+ Make it gluten-free: Use gluten-free bread

EASY thai chicken noodle soup

While Elsa sang, "Let It Go," in *Frozen*, it's hard to let those chicks leave the nest and spread their wings. What can ease the pain? How about this creative combo of two classic cuisines, a soul-soothing crossover of Phuket and Poland, the merger of popular Thai street food with the steamy star of Jewish cooking? Easy, warm, and filling, our Easy Thai Chicken Noodle Soup is the gold standard in solace—in no time at all, you can have a comforting meal-in-a-bowl broth boosted by spicy red curry, smooth peanut butter, and savory lime and finished with creamy coconut milk. Chicken and rice noodles add hearty goodness to this mega-flavorful, fragrant, and filling masterpiece, each spoonful guaranteed to comfort you until the chickens come home to roost.

SERVES: 4   PREP TIME: 10 MINS   COOK TIME: 20 MINS

1 tbsp olive oil

1 red bell pepper, chopped

2 large shallots, halved and thinly sliced

2 garlic cloves, minced

⅓ cup smooth peanut butter

2 tbsp red curry paste

2 tsp grated fresh ginger

5 cups chicken broth

4 oz rice vermicelli noodles, uncooked

2 cups shredded roasted deli chicken breast

1 cup canned coconut milk

2 tbsp soy sauce

2 tbsp fresh lime juice

2 tbsp chopped cilantro

1 tsp lime zest

Lime, sliced for garnish (optional)

Thai chili pepper, sliced for garnish (optional, very spicy)

1. In a soup pot, heat the olive oil over medium-high heat. Add the red pepper, shallots, and garlic and cook, stirring frequently, for 5 minutes until softened. Stir in the peanut butter, red curry paste, and ginger and cook for 1 minute. Add the chicken broth and bring to a boil. Reduce the heat and simmer the soup for 10 minutes.

2. While the soup simmers, bring a medium pot of water to a boil. Cook the vermicelli noodles until tender, drain, and divide between 4 serving bowls.

3. To finish the soup, over low heat, stir in the shredded chicken, coconut milk, soy sauce, lime juice, cilantro, and lime zest. Heat through for 2 minutes, and then ladle the soup over the noodles and garnish with the lime slices and sliced Thai chili pepper, if desired.

+ Make it gluten-free: Replace soy sauce with gluten-free tamari or gluten-free soy sauce

The empty nest is underrated. —NORA EPHRON

SPICY tuna & cucumber sashimi bites

Want to be a sushi chef? It can take up to five years of apprenticeship before you're even allowed to make rice. Fear not: these riceless sashimi bites cut your training down by 1,825 days, by piling crisp cucumber slices high with creamy avocado, tender tuna, spicy wasabi sauce, and crunchy peas. The ideal light lunch or easy app, these fuss-free bites are impressive looking, superb tasting, and, in our crash course to becoming a lunchtime legend or entertaining expert, will take you only 20 minutes to master.

SERVES: 6   PREP TIME: 20 MINS   COOK TIME: 0 MINS

Marinade

2 tbsp soy sauce

2 tsp mirin

1 tsp rice vinegar

½ tsp sesame oil

¼ tsp wasabi paste

¼ tsp grated fresh ginger

Wasabi Sauce

¼ cup mayonnaise

¼ tsp wasabi paste

Sashimi Bites

½ lb sushi grade tuna, cut into small cubes

1 English cucumber, sliced on the diagonal

1 firm ripe avocado, thinly sliced

½ cup coarsely chopped wasabi peas, for garnish

Black sesame seeds, for garnish

1. To make the marinade, in a medium bowl, whisk together the soy sauce, mirin, rice vinegar, sesame oil, wasabi paste, and ginger. Add the cubed tuna and toss well to coat. Set aside to marinate for 10 minutes.

2. For the wasabi sauce, in a small bowl, whisk together the mayonnaise and wasabi paste.

3. To assemble the sashimi bites, place the sliced cucumber on a serving platter and top each slice with a thin slice of avocado. Place a dollop of wasabi sauce on top. Drain the marinade and spoon the tuna over the sauce. Finish with a sprinkling of chopped wasabi peas and sesame seeds.

+ **Make it gluten-free:** Use gluten-free tamari or gluten-free soy sauce, and wasabi peas coated in cornstarch or omit from recipe

A good rule to remember for life is that when it comes to plastic surgery and sushi, never be attracted by a bargain.

—GRAHAM NORTON

fresh salad rolls

WITH PEANUT SAUCE

While I was slightly miffed that I got an LOL text from some fella ("Lots of love?" I hardly know you), I was super excited to get ROFL from my sister, knowing this could only mean one thing: "Rolling out the freshest lunch." My enthusiasm multiplied as I thought about these healthy Asian-style rolls, a vibrant rainbow of fresh vegetables and herbs, all tucked together in tender rice paper and dunked in a delectable peanut sauce. So versatile (change up the veggies, add lean protein) and easy to master (trust us, you'll be on a roll in no time), these deliciously refreshing bites are full of OMG. Yes, that's short for "overpowering mega-greatness."

MAKES: 12 RICE PAPER ROLLS   PREP TIME: 35 MINS   COOK TIME: <5 MINS

Peanut Dipping Sauce

6 tbsp smooth peanut butter

2 tbsp rice vinegar

2 tbsp water

1 tbsp soy sauce

1 tbsp honey

1 tsp sesame oil

1 tsp Sriracha hot sauce

¼ cup finely chopped roasted peanuts

Salad Rolls

4 oz rice vermicelli noodles, uncooked

12 (9-inch) rice paper wrappers

1 red bell pepper, sliced into long strips

1½ cups English cucumber, sliced into long strips

1¼ cups peeled and shredded carrots

1 cup shredded purple cabbage

24 fresh basil leaves

2 tbsp black sesame seeds

1. For the peanut sauce, in a small bowl, whisk the peanut butter, rice vinegar, water, soy sauce, honey, sesame oil, and Sriracha until smooth. Stir in the chopped peanuts. Cover and set aside.

2. To make the salad rolls, bring a small saucepan of water to a boil. Add the vermicelli and cook 3–4 minutes, until tender. Drain, rinse under cold water, and drain well again.

3. Fill a shallow dish with warm water. Dip a rice paper wrapper into the water, allowing it to soften, about 15 seconds. Transfer it to a flat surface like a cutting board. Place a small handful of cooked vermicelli noodles in the center of the wrap. Top with red pepper, cucumber, carrots, cabbage, and 2 basil leaves, and top with a sprinkle of sesame seeds. Assemble like a burrito, folding in the sides, and then rolling away from you, tucking the filling in as you roll. Repeat with the remaining ingredients. To serve, cut the rolls in half and serve with the peanut dipping sauce.

+ Make it gluten-free: Use gluten-free tamari or gluten-free soy sauce, and gluten-free chili hot sauce

lessons *from* lisa

★ To make ahead, place the finished rice paper wrappers on a platter, cover with a damp paper towel, and wrap the platter in plastic wrap. Another option is to wrap each roll individually in plastic wrap and place it in an airtight container in the refrigerator.

★ These rolls go by many names: summer rolls, spring rolls, Vietnamese rice paper rolls, Thai fresh rolls, cold rolls, and Gỏi cuốn.

BERRY, baby kale & fennel salad

I n the world of extreme sports, BASE jumping and bull riding are walks in the park compared to current-day foodie photography. We're noshing in an age of highly competitive eat-your-heart-out Instagrammers, where only the ultra-fast, mega-tasty, and most photo-worthy dishes win. Our courageous culinarian Lisa has fearlessly tossed her toque (aka chef's hat) in the ring and whipped up this speedy, nutritious, and stunning salad: baby kale combined with crunchy fennel, juicy 'n' tart fresh and dried berries, along with maple shallot dressing and sweet 'n' spicy pecans. Sit back and relax because these over-the-top forkfuls of delicious tastes and textures are guaranteed to push your green grub game first over the finish.

SERVES: 4–6   PREP TIME: 15 MINS   COOK TIME: 15 MINS

Toasted Pecans

1½ cups pecan halves

1 tbsp honey

1 tbsp sugar

½ tsp kosher salt

Pinch cayenne pepper

Maple Shallot Vinaigrette

6 tbsp olive oil

2 tbsp champagne vinegar

1 tbsp maple syrup

1 tsp Dijon mustard

1 tsp finely chopped shallots

½ tsp chopped fresh thyme

¼ tsp kosher salt

Salad

10 cups packed baby kale

½ bulb fennel, thinly sliced

1 cup fresh blueberries

1 cup fresh sliced strawberries

¼ cup dried blueberries

¼ cup dried cherries

1. For the pecans, preheat the oven to 325°F. Line a baking sheet with parchment paper.

2. In a bowl, toss the pecans, honey, sugar, salt, and cayenne pepper. Place the pecans on the baking sheet and bake in the preheated oven for 5 minutes. Stir and bake for 10 minutes more, until toasted. Set aside and allow to cool.

3. For the dressing, in a medium bowl, whisk together the olive oil, champagne vinegar, maple syrup, mustard, shallots, thyme, and salt.

4. To assemble the salad, in a large serving bowl, place the kale, fennel, blueberries, strawberries, dried blueberries, dried cherries, and half the toasted pecans. Add a few tablespoons of the maple dressing and toss to combine. Drizzle with remaining dressing and sprinkle with pecans. Serve immediately.

Champions keep playing until they get it right.

—BILLIE JEAN KING

These tasty twists on the classic chickpea dip are super simple to make, will punch up your protein, and will satisfy all your snack cravings.

JALAPEÑO HUMMUS

1 large jalapeño pepper, chopped, pith and seeds removed

1 cup canned chickpeas, rinsed and drained

½ cup chopped fresh cilantro

3 tbsp tahini

3 tbsp olive oil

2 tbsp fresh lime juice

1 garlic clove, minced

½ tsp ground cumin

½ tsp kosher salt

2 tbsp water

Olive oil, for garnish

Jalapeño peppers, sliced, for garnish

MAKES: 1½ CUPS

1. Place the chopped jalapeño in a food processor or blender. Add the chickpeas, cilantro, tahini, olive oil, lime juice, garlic, cumin, and salt. Blend the ingredients thoroughly. Gradually add water while the blender is running until the hummus is smooth. Place in a serving bowl and garnish with a drizzle of olive oil and the sliced jalapeño peppers.

ROASTED CARROT HUMMUS

4 large (about 1 lb) carrots, peeled and cut into ½-inch pieces

¼ cup + 1 tsp olive oil, divided

Pinch kosher salt and freshly ground black pepper

1 cup canned chickpeas, rinsed and drained

3 tbsp tahini

2 tbsp fresh lemon juice

1 garlic clove, minced

½ tsp kosher salt

¼ tsp ground cumin

Pinch crushed red pepper flakes

2 tbsp water

Olive oil, for garnish

Za'atar, for garnish

continued on next page

MAKES: 2 CUPS

1. Preheat the oven to 425°F. Line a baking sheet with parchment paper.

2. Toss together the carrots, 1 teaspoon of the olive oil, and a pinch of salt and pepper. Spread evenly over the baking sheet. Roast for 20 minutes, stirring twice, until the carrots are tender. Remove from the oven and allow to cool slightly.

3. Place the carrots in a food processor or blender with the chickpeas, tahini, remaining ¼ cup of olive oil, lemon juice, garlic, salt, cumin, and crushed red pepper flakes. Blend the ingredients thoroughly. Gradually add water while the blender is running until the hummus is smooth. Place in a serving bowl and garnish with a drizzle of olive oil and a generous pinch of za'atar.

+ **Make it gluten-free: Use gluten-free za'atar**

SUN-DRIED TOMATO HUMMUS

⅓ cup chopped oil-packed
  sun-dried tomatoes

1 cup canned chickpeas, rinsed
  and drained

3 tbsp tahini

¼ cup olive oil

2 tbsp fresh lemon juice

1 garlic clove, minced

2 tbsp water

2 tbsp chopped fresh basil

Olive oil, for garnish

Chopped oil-packed sun-dried
  tomatoes, for garnish

Fresh basil, for garnish

1. Place the sun-dried tomatoes, chickpeas, tahini, olive oil, lemon juice, and garlic in a food processor or blender. Blend the ingredients thoroughly. Gradually add water while the blender is running until the hummus is smooth. Add the basil and pulse until chopped. Place in a serving bowl and garnish with a drizzle of olive oil, the chopped sun-dried tomatoes, and the basil.

WE'RE ALL

hummusapiens.

top 10 meals

IN-A-BOWL

Bowls aren't just for soup and cereal—fill 'em to the brim with these nutrient-packed, fresh and fantastic one-bowl meals.

fattoush salad

WITH JAMMY EGGS

There's no doubt words feed our minds, especially those considered most beautiful-sounding such as *serendipity* and *epiphany*. Now, finally, comes a word as amazing to say as it is to devour: *fattoush*. Fattoush (pronounced "fuh-toosh") is a Lebanese chopped salad that's healthy and has terrific tastes and textures—fresh cucumbers, tomatoes, and mint mingle with a zesty sumac dressing, crunchy spice-baked pita chips, and jammy soft-boiled eggs. Here's some music to your ears—even the most salad-averse will eat their words when it comes to this fast, filling, and fantastic fattoush.

SERVES: 4–6   PREP TIME: 25 MINS   COOK TIME: 20 MINS

Crunchy Pita Chips

2 (9-inch) pita bread rounds

2 tbsp olive oil

1 tsp ground sumac

¼ tsp kosher salt

Lemon Sumac Dressing

6 tbsp olive oil

2 tbsp fresh lemon juice

1 tsp ground sumac

1 small garlic clove, finely minced

1 tsp apple cider vinegar

1 tsp honey

½ tsp kosher salt

Salad

4–6 eggs

6 cups shredded romaine lettuce

3 cups coarsely chopped arugula

½ cup chopped fresh flat-leaf parsley

¼ cup chopped fresh mint

2 cups chopped English cucumber

3 large tomatoes, cored and cut in chunks

6–8 radishes, thinly sliced

1. For the pita chips, preheat the oven to 375°F. Line a baking sheet with parchment paper. Split the pitas open horizontally. Brush the rough side with the olive oil and sprinkle with the sumac and salt. Cut each pita into 2-inch pieces and spread out on the baking sheet. Bake for 10 minutes, stirring halfway through. Remove from the oven and allow to cool.

2. For the dressing, whisk the olive oil, lemon juice, sumac, garlic, apple cider vinegar, honey, and salt until well combined. Set aside.

3. For the jammy soft-boiled eggs, bring a large saucepan of water to a boil. Lower the heat and gently add the eggs to the pot. Raise the heat back to medium to maintain a gentle boil and cook the eggs for 6½ minutes. Immediately place the eggs in an ice bath to stop the cooking. Once they are cool, gently peel the eggs and cut in half.

4. To assemble the salad, in a large bowl, combine the romaine lettuce, arugula, parsley, mint, cucumbers, tomatoes, and radishes. Toss with a few tablespoons of dressing at a time to coat the salad. Divide salad between serving plates and top with the pita chips and eggs.

+ Make it gluten-free: Use gluten-free pita chips

lessons *from* lisa

* Sumac is a spice known for its anti-inflammatory properties and ability to add a lemony pop of flavor to any dish.

vegetable power bowl

WITH MISO DRESSING

Your Powerball numbers just hit. The odds may have been 1 in 292 million, but it's no wonder because you've got Lucky Lisa on your side, creating this mega-winning power bowl, guaranteed to change your life. Almost too good to be true, it's got it all: your greens (kale), your grains (brown rice), your veggies (butternut squash, Brussels sprouts, cauliflower, beets), and your protein (hemp seeds, miso). A truly satisfying prize, complete with a drinkable dressing and popcorn-like toasted hemp seeds, you can finally claim your winnings and be full and healthy. Playing the numbers really pays off.

SERVES: 4   PREP TIME: 25 MINS   COOK TIME: 45 MINS

Miso Dressing

2 tbsp white miso paste

2 tbsp olive oil

2 tbsp rice vinegar

1½ tbsp maple syrup

1 tbsp warm water

2 tsp tahini

1 tsp sesame oil

1 tsp grated fresh ginger

Rice Bowl

1 cup uncooked brown basmati rice

1¾ cups water

3 cups cubed butternut squash

3 cups halved Brussels sprouts

3 cups cauliflower florets

3 tbsp olive oil, divided

Kosher salt and freshly ground black pepper, to taste

1 bunch beets (4–5 small beets), peeled and cut into ½-inch wedges

continued on next page

1. For the miso dressing, whisk the miso paste, olive oil, rice vinegar, maple syrup, warm water, tahini, sesame oil, and ginger until well combined. Cover and refrigerate to allow flavors to develop.

2. For the rice bowl, in a saucepan, combine rice with the water and bring to a boil over high heat. Cover and reduce the heat to low. Simmer for 40 minutes and then remove from the heat and leave covered for 5 minutes.

3. While the rice is cooking, preheat the oven to 400°F. Line 2 baking sheets with parchment paper. In a large bowl, toss the butternut squash, Brussels sprouts, and cauliflower with 2 tablespoons of the olive oil and season with salt and pepper. Spread evenly on 1 baking sheet. Roast for 15 minutes, then stir and continue for 10 minutes more until tender and golden.

4. Toss the beets with the remaining tablespoon of olive oil and season with salt and pepper. Place the beets on the second baking sheet. Roast the beets for 20 minutes, then stir and continue roasting for 10–15 minutes more, until tender.

5. Prepare the hemp seed crunch. In a small bowl, toss the hemp seeds, parsley, olive oil, lemon zest, and salt together. Spread the mixture out on a parchment-lined baking sheet and bake at 400°F for 6 minutes, until lightly toasted.

6. To assemble the bowls, divide the cooked rice between 4 serving bowls. Top with the roasted vegetables and chopped kale. Drizzle miso dressing over each bowl and sprinkle with toasted hemp seeds.

ingredients continued

Hemp Seed Crunch

½ cup hemp seeds

2 tsp chopped fresh flat-leaf
  parsley

1 tsp olive oil

¼ tsp lemon zest

¼ tsp kosher salt

3 cups chopped kale

quinoa niçoise
SALAD

Lisa's a tastemaker. She invented avocado toast, was a turducken trailblazer, and led the ramen pizza revolution, so it shouldn't come as a surprise that she's taken a French classic and made it her own. Say bonjour to Le Quinoise™, a healthy, simple, and protein-packed collision of quinoa and Niçoise, a salad that puts the heart in hearty. I feel like the picture of health just listing what's in this meal-in-a-bowl: tuna and eggs are artfully combined with quinoa, avocado, green beans, tomatoes, and arugula, finished with olives and crispy capers (these surprising salty crunches are *everything*), and dressed in a lemon shallot vinaigrette. One forkful is proof positive that Lisa's taste buds are tops.

SERVES: 4   PREP TIME: 25 MINS   COOK TIME: 20 MINS

Lemon Shallot Vinaigrette

¼ cup olive oil

2 tbsp fresh lemon juice

1 tbsp sherry vinegar

1 tsp minced shallot

1 tsp Dijon mustard

1 tsp honey

½ tsp dried thyme

½ tsp kosher salt

½ tsp freshly ground black pepper

Crunchy Capers

¼ cup capers, rinsed and drained

2 tbsp cornmeal

1 tbsp olive oil

Salad

⅔ cup quinoa, rinsed

1⅓ cups water

¼ tsp kosher salt

4 eggs

½ lb green beans, ends trimmed and cut in half

3 cups lightly packed baby arugula

1. For the vinaigrette, whisk together the olive oil, lemon juice, sherry vinegar, shallot, mustard, honey, thyme, salt, and pepper. Cover and set aside.

2. For the capers, toss with cornmeal and shake off any excess. Heat the olive oil in a small skillet over medium heat. Add the capers and cook for 3–4 minutes, until golden, stirring gently and shaking the pan occasionally to move them around. Remove from the heat and drain on paper towel. Set aside.

3. To cook the quinoa, combine the quinoa, water, and salt in a saucepan. Bring to a boil over high heat. Reduce the heat to a simmer, cover, and cook for 12–14 minutes until tender. Remove from the heat and let sit covered for 5 minutes. Drain any remaining water. Set aside to cool.

4. While the quinoa cooks, prepare the eggs. Place the eggs in a medium saucepan and cover with cold water. Bring to a boil over medium-high heat. Once the water has boiled, cover the pan, remove from the heat, and let sit for 12 minutes. Drain and place the eggs in ice water to cool quickly. After 5 minutes, peel and halve the eggs.

5. For the green beans, bring a medium saucepan of water to a boil. Lower to a simmer and then add the green beans and cook for 2 minutes. Transfer the beans to a bowl of ice water to stop the cooking and keep them bright green. Drain well and set aside.

continued on next page

1 cup halved cherry tomatoes

2 cans (6 oz each) water-packed tuna, drained and broken into chunks

¾ cup Kalamata olives, pitted

2 firm, ripe avocados, pitted and cubed

6. To assemble, place the quinoa, avocados, green beans, tomatoes, tuna, arugula, eggs, and olives in a large serving bowl. Drizzle with a few spoonfuls of dressing. Top with the capers. Drizzle with the remaining dressing.

lessons *from* lisa

★ For easy peeling, boil eggs that are at least a week old.

★ Quinoa, a staple of the ancient Incas, is high in protein and has all of the essential amino acids.

I haven't trusted polls since I read that 62% of women had affairs during their lunch hour. I've never met a woman in my life who would give up lunch for sex.

—ERMA BOMBECK

top 10 food duos

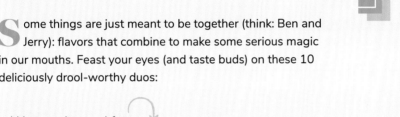

S ome things are just meant to be together (think: Ben and Jerry): flavors that combine to make some serious magic in our mouths. Feast your eyes (and taste buds) on these 10 deliciously drool-worthy duos:

mason jar salad

Say goodbye to sad desk salad. Thanks to Lisa-the-Lunchtime-Liberator, we're shaking up your midday meal, taking it from monotonous to marvelous with this healthy, quick, and easy-to-assemble chopped Italian salad in a jar. Get ready to feast on forkfuls of fresh and fantastic ingredients—at the base is a light and savory Italian dressing, followed by layers of creamy chickpeas, crunchy carrots and cucumbers, sharp white cheddar, juicy tomatoes, peppers, lettuce, and parsley. Portable and packed with protein, you're not going to keep a lid on this genius lunch, guaranteed to break you free of your salad slump.

SERVES: 4   PREP TIME: 20 MINS   COOK TIME: 0 MINS

Italian Dressing

3 tbsp olive oil

3 tbsp vegetable oil

2 tbsp white wine vinegar

½ tsp dried oregano

½ tsp dried basil

½ tsp kosher salt

¼ tsp freshly ground black pepper

¼ tsp garlic powder

Pinch sugar

Pinch red pepper flakes

3 tbsp freshly grated Parmesan cheese

Mason Jar Salad

1½ cups canned chickpeas, rinsed and drained

2 cups peeled and finely sliced carrots

2 cups chopped, unpeeled English cucumber

1 cup cubed sharp white cheddar cheese

2 cups halved cherry tomatoes

1 large green bell pepper, chopped

6 cups chopped romaine lettuce

¼ cup chopped fresh flat-leaf parsley

1. For the dressing, in a medium bowl, whisk together the olive oil, vegetable oil, white wine vinegar, oregano, basil, salt, pepper, garlic powder, sugar, and red pepper flakes. Stir in the Parmesan cheese. Refrigerate until ready to use.

2. To prepare the mason jar salads, divide the salad dressing between 4 mason jars (32 ounces each). Top with the chickpeas and carrots, followed by cucumbers, cheddar, tomatoes, green peppers, romaine lettuce, and chopped parsley. Put the lid on each jar and refrigerate until ready to eat.

My favorite exercise is a cross between a lunge and a crunch . . . I call it lunch. —ANONYMOUS

mediterranean farro
& BEAN SALAD

Farro was found in the tombs of Egyptian kings, nestled among amulets, jewels, and chariots. Makes perfect sense because in addition to *farro* and *pharaoh* being cool homophones, this ancient whole grain is gold—top of the nutritional pyramid, rich in protein, fiber, and vitamins. While nutty-flavored and chewy-textured farro first cropped up in the Middle East, the ever-versatile grain has become a staple in Mediterranean dishes and works beautifully in this hieroglyphic-free—it's super easy to decipher, and you won't have to slave away to enjoy zesty bites of beans, tomatoes, peppers, and fresh herbs. Trust us, everyone is going to dig this superfood salad.

SERVES: 6–8   PREP TIME: 15 MINS   COOK TIME: 30 MINS

Red Wine Vinaigrette

¼ cup olive oil

2 tbsp red wine vinegar

2 tsp fresh lemon juice

1 small garlic clove, minced

1 tsp sugar

1 tsp dried oregano

½ tsp Dijon mustard

½ tsp lemon zest

½ tsp kosher salt

¼ tsp dried basil

¼ tsp freshly ground black pepper

Farro & Bean Salad

1½ cups uncooked farro

4 cups water

Pinch kosher salt

½ lb green beans, ends trimmed, cut in half

1¼ cups canned cannellini (white kidney) beans, rinsed and drained

1¼ cups canned chickpeas, rinsed and drained

1½ cups halved cherry tomatoes

1 red bell pepper, diced

1 yellow bell pepper, diced

¼ cup chopped oil-packed sun-dried tomatoes, rinsed and dried

¼ cup chopped fresh flat-leaf parsley

¼ cup chopped fresh basil

1. For the vinaigrette, whisk together the olive oil, red wine vinegar, lemon juice, garlic, sugar, oregano, mustard, lemon zest, salt, basil, and pepper. Set aside.

2. For the farro and bean salad, rinse the farro well and drain it. Place the farro, water, and salt in a saucepan. Bring to a boil. Reduce the heat to low, cover, and simmer for 25 minutes, until tender but still chewy. Drain any remaining liquid and place the farro in a large serving bowl.

3. To cook the green beans, bring a medium pot of salted water to a boil. Add the green beans and cook on low heat until tender-crisp, about 2–3 minutes. Drain and rinse under cold water to stop them cooking. Add the beans to the farro, along with the cannellini beans, chickpeas, tomatoes, red and yellow peppers, sun-dried tomatoes, parsley, and basil. Toss to coat well with dressing.

lessons *from* lisa

★ *Rinse canned beans to cut almost 40 percent of the sodium.*

chopped salad

If you are what you eat, then I'm the walking picture of wellness after chowing down on this superb salad, my body and brain boosted from iron- and protein-packed lentils, chicken, and chickpeas, from fiber-rich dates, and from omega-loaded pumpkin seeds. Tossed in a massively flavorful coconut mango dressing, this satisfying salad serves up major Dr. Feelgood forkfuls.

SERVES: 4–6   PREP TIME: 15 MINS   COOK TIME: 20 MINS

Coconut Mango Dressing

½ cup canned coconut milk

3 tbsp smooth peanut butter

2 tbsp fresh lime juice

2 tbsp mango chutney

1 tsp curry powder

½ tsp kosher salt

Roasted Pumpkin Seeds

1 cup raw pumpkin seeds (pepitas)

1 tsp olive oil

¼ tsp kosher salt

Salad

½ cup dried green lentils, rinsed well

3 cups water

8 cups chopped romaine lettuce

2 cups cubed roasted deli chicken breast meat

2 mangoes, peeled and chopped

½ cup chopped dates

½ cup canned chickpeas, rinsed and drained

¼ cup chopped fresh flat-leaf parsley

1 cup unsweetened coconut flakes, toasted, for garnish

1. For the dressing, using a small blender, combine the coconut milk, peanut butter, lime juice, mango chutney, curry powder, and salt until well blended and smooth. Refrigerate until ready to serve.

2. For the pumpkin seeds, preheat the oven to 300°F and line a baking sheet with parchment paper. Toss the pumpkin seeds with the olive oil and salt, and spread them on the baking sheet. Roast the seeds for 18–20 minutes, stirring once halfway through. Remove from the oven and allow to cool slightly.

3. Meanwhile, cook the lentils. In a small saucepan, bring the lentils and water to a boil. Reduce the heat to a simmer and cook, uncovered, until just tender with a little bite to them, 16–18 minutes. Drain well and set aside to cool while you prepare the rest of the salad.

4. In a large serving bowl, combine the cooked lentils, lettuce, chicken, mangoes, dates, chickpeas, parsley, and roasted pumpkin seeds. Toss the salad with the coconut mango dressing and garnish with the coconut flakes.

lessons *from* lisa

★ To toast coconut flakes, place the coconut on a baking sheet and toast in a 325°F oven for 4–5 minutes until golden, watching carefully because coconut burns easily.

chicken & rice salad

WITH GINGER DRESSING

Nice to know I'm not alone. Like 70 percent of folks, I regularly dine al desko (read: pretend to eat outdoors while inside working) and am super aware of the desk don'ts, like smelly and sloppy food. With that in mind, Lisa's created a moveable feast that covers all the dos of desk dining: a delish, healthy, and refreshing meal of chicken, fresh veggies, and rice that won't kill my keyboard or choke my coworkers.

SERVES: 6   PREP TIME: 20 MINS   COOK TIME: 15 MINS (+ cooling)

1¼ cups uncooked jasmine rice, rinsed and drained

1¾ cups water

½ tsp kosher salt

Ginger Dressing

½ cup creamy peanut butter

¼ cup rice vinegar

2 tbsp honey

2 tbsp soy sauce

1 tbsp vegetable oil

1 tbsp sesame oil

1 tbsp grated fresh ginger

1 garlic clove, finely minced

Salad

2 cups chopped roasted deli chicken breast meat

2 cups shredded purple cabbage

1 cup peeled and shredded carrots

1 cup unpeeled chopped English cucumber

1 red bell pepper, chopped

½ cup chopped fresh flat-leaf parsley

¼ cup chopped green onions

1 cup chopped roasted peanuts, for garnish

1. For the rice, in a medium saucepan, combine the rice, water, and salt and bring to a boil. Cover with a tight-fitting lid, reduce the heat to low, and simmer for 15 minutes. Remove from the heat and leave covered for 10 minutes. Place the rice in a large bowl to cool further.

2. For the dressing, in a medium bowl, whisk together the peanut butter, rice vinegar, honey, soy sauce, vegetable oil, sesame oil, ginger, and garlic until well combined. Set aside.

3. For the salad, add the chopped chicken, cabbage, carrots, cucumbers, red pepper, parsley, and green onions to the rice bowl. Toss the salad with the dressing and garnish with the roasted peanuts.

+ **Make it gluten-free: Use gluten-free tamari or gluten-free soy sauce**

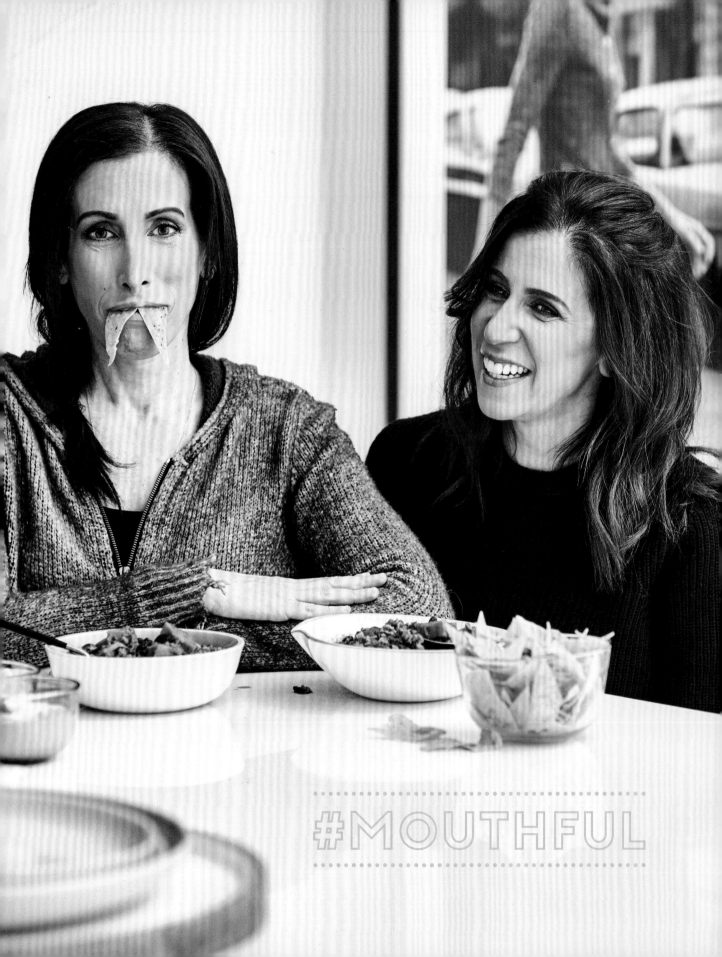

#MOUTHFUL

vegetarian chili

Entering a chili cook-off is high on our (okay, my) bucket list. Step one is to come up with a kickin' slogan for our saucy sister duo—Lisa nixed both Chili Chili Bang Bang and Cooking with Gas, so we settled on Cumin Get It. Step two is to create the most mouthwatering championship chili, and my red-hot sis has done it with this smoky, sweet, and winning combination of tender chunks of vegetables, perfectly balanced spices (cumin and smoked paprika lend earthiness and a little kick in the pants), fiber-rich beans, and farro, the protein-packed whole grain that serves up a "meaty" bite. There's no stopping us now—armed with steaming bowls of this hearty-yet-healthy comfort food, we're certain our chili sans carne is just what the judges have been waiting for.

SERVES: 6–8   PREP TIME: 15 MINS   COOK TIME: 40 MINS

1 cup uncooked farro

3 cups water

Pinch kosher salt

1 tbsp olive oil

4 cups peeled and cubed butternut squash

1 medium yellow onion, chopped

2 large carrots, peeled and chopped

1 red bell pepper, chopped

2 tbsp tomato paste

2 garlic cloves, minced

1 jalapeño, seeds and ribs removed, finely minced

2 tbsp chili powder

1 tsp ground cumin

1 tsp smoked paprika

1 tsp dried oregano

1 tsp kosher salt

4 cups vegetable broth

1 (28 oz) can diced tomatoes

1¼ cups canned black beans, rinsed and drained

1¼ cups canned kidney beans, rinsed and drained

1 tbsp fresh lime juice

Garnishes

Sour cream

Chopped fresh flat-leaf parsley

Shredded cheddar cheese

Tortilla chips

1. Rinse the farro well and drain. In a saucepan, combine the farro, water, and salt. Bring to a boil, reduce the heat to low, cover, and simmer for 22–24 minutes, until tender but still chewy. Drain any remaining water and set the farro aside.

2. While the farro is cooking, heat the olive oil in a large soup pot over medium heat. Add the butternut squash, onion, carrots, and red pepper. Cook, stirring occasionally, for 5 minutes. Stir in the tomato paste, garlic, jalapeño, chili powder, cumin, smoked paprika, oregano, and salt. Stir continuously for 2 minutes. Add the vegetable broth, diced tomatoes, black beans, and kidney beans. Bring to a boil. Reduce heat and let simmer uncovered for 15 minutes. Stir in the cooked farro and continue to simmer for 15 minutes more. Remove from the heat and stir in the lime juice. Serve garnished with sour cream, parsley, cheddar, and a side of tortilla chips.

peanut noodles with tofu

I think Lisa developed this fast and fantastic recipe because she was sick of me calling her cell (FYI 416-970-4926) and placing a takeout order. That's fine, because I was most unimpressed by her delivery time. Now, in no time at all, I can whip up this vegan dish, a scrumptious combination of peanut and sesame noodles (this silky sauce is to die for) with tender vegetables and crisp golden tofu. In fact, this marvelous midweek meal is so easy, it will not only save you time, but also the 20 percent gratuity Lisa tacks on.

Peanut Sesame Sauce

½ cup smooth peanut butter

2 tbsp soy sauce

2 tbsp toasted sesame seeds

2 tbsp rice vinegar

2 tbsp dry sherry

1 tbsp honey

1 garlic clove, chopped

1 tsp grated fresh ginger

1 tsp sesame oil

1 tsp Sriracha hot sauce

4 tbsp hot water

Noodles

1 (12 oz) package Chinese egg noodles, soba noodles, or thin spaghetti noodles

2 tsp sesame oil

1 (12 oz) package extra-firm tofu, pressed between paper towels for 10 minutes, then cut into 1-inch cubes

1 tbsp cornstarch

¼ tsp kosher salt

⅛ tsp freshly ground black pepper

2 tbsp vegetable oil, divided

1 red bell pepper, sliced into strips

1 yellow bell pepper, sliced into strips

1 carrot, peeled, thinly sliced on the diagonal

¼ cup chopped fresh basil

¼ cup chopped roasted peanuts, for garnish

1 tsp toasted sesame seeds, for garnish

1. For the peanut sesame sauce, in a blender, combine the peanut butter, soy sauce, sesame seeds, rice vinegar, sherry, honey, garlic, ginger, sesame oil, and Sriracha. Blend until smooth. Add the hot water and continue to blend until the sauce is a pourable consistency.

2. Bring a large pot of salted water to a boil. Cook the noodles according to the package directions. Drain, rinse with cold water, and toss with the sesame oil.

3. To prepare the tofu, toss the tofu cubes with the cornstarch, salt, and pepper. Heat 1 tablespoon of the vegetable oil in a large skillet over medium-high heat. Add the tofu and let cook 1 minute before stirring. Continue to cook for 4 minutes, flipping as needed, until all sides are golden. Transfer to a plate. Reduce the heat to medium and add the remaining 1 tablespoon of oil. Stir in the red pepper, yellow pepper, and carrots and cook for 3 minutes, until the vegetables are tender. Turn the heat to low and add the basil, noodles, tofu, and peanut sesame sauce. Stir until heated through. Remove from the heat and garnish each serving with peanuts and sesame seeds. Best served immediately.

lessons *from* lisa

....

⭐ Remove the thin peel on the ginger by scraping it with a small spoon—it's easier than using a knife around the bumpy parts.

thai chicken wraps

WITH PINEAPPLE SALSA

I'm going to blow your mind. There's like no degree of separation between Lisa and Diane von Furstenberg, creator of the iconic wrap dress. You see, LCG and DVF both created empires from scratch (albeit from butter, sugar, and flour in Lisa's case), they've both created wraps so revolutionary they've changed lives (and lunchtimes), and finally, they both get us—they know how to do easy, tasteful, and totally awesome. While DVF's flattering frock is a must, you're going to devour Lisa's Thai wrap like it's going out of style. Chicken coated in a delectable peanut sauce is rolled up with a vibrant pineapple salsa, fresh romaine, and crunchy roasted peanuts. An innovative combo of savory, sweet, and spicy bites, this priceless power lunch is kind of like the power dress, but cheaper. See? These legendary ladies are cut from the same cloth.

SERVES: 4   PREP TIME: 15 MINS   COOK TIME: 10 MINS

Pineapple Salsa

1 cup diced English cucumber

¾ cup diced fresh pineapple

3 tbsp diced red onion

2 tbsp chopped fresh flat-leaf parsley

2 tsp fresh lime juice

1 tsp sugar

¼ tsp kosher salt

Peanut Sauce

½ cup creamy peanut butter

3 tbsp soy sauce

2 tbsp honey

1 tbsp fresh lime juice

2 tsp Sriracha hot sauce
 (1 tsp if you don't want spice)

1 garlic clove, finely minced

1 tsp grated fresh ginger

continued above

Wraps

2 tbsp olive oil

3 boneless, skinless chicken breasts, cut into long, thin strips

Pinch kosher salt

Pinch freshly ground black pepper

4 (10-inch) flour tortillas, warmed if desired

1 cup shredded romaine lettuce

¼ cup chopped roasted peanuts

1. For the salsa, in a medium bowl, combine the cucumber, pineapple, red onion, parsley, lime juice, sugar, and salt. Toss well, cover, and refrigerate until you are ready to assemble the wraps.

2. For the peanut sauce, in a small bowl, whisk together the peanut butter, soy sauce, honey, lime juice, Sriracha, garlic, and ginger. Set aside.

3. To cook the chicken, heat the olive oil in a large skillet over medium-high heat. Season the chicken strips with salt and pepper. Add the chicken to the skillet, cooking 4 minutes per side, until golden brown and cooked through. Turn the heat to low and stir in ¼ cup of the peanut sauce. Toss to coat and remove from the heat.

4. To assemble, spread a spoonful of the remaining peanut sauce on the base of each tortilla. Top with the chicken, pineapple salsa, shredded romaine, and chopped peanuts. Roll up the tortillas, slice in half and serve.

+ **Make it gluten-free: Use gluten-free tamari or gluten-free soy sauce, and gluten-free tortillas**

hoisin beef

LETTUCE CUPS

What do we sisters have in common with famed rapper Drake? We attended the same high school (Go, Falcons!), our moms are Jewish (more brisket, Aubrey?) and we too like to sing (albeit, nasally and pitchy) about our cups running over. Literally, when considering this amazing handheld appetizer of lettuce cups mounded high with hoisin beef and red peppers, crunchy carrots, and cucumbers. Topped with a smooth peanut sauce, there's an abundance of flavor and crunch in each sweet and spicy bite. Simple to whip up (as Drizzy advises, start from the bottom), this recipe can be transformed into a main course by swapping out the lettuce for rice, resulting in a hit-making meal.

SERVES: 6   PREP TIME: 15 MINS   COOK TIME: 15 MINS

Spicy Peanut Sauce

¼ cup smooth peanut butter

1 tbsp soy sauce

1 tsp Sriracha hot sauce

1 tsp honey

½ tsp freshly grated ginger

¼ cup water

Hoisin Beef

¼ cup hoisin sauce

2 tbsp rice vinegar

1 tsp soy sauce

1 tsp honey

1 tsp sesame oil

2 tsp vegetable oil

1 small red onion, diced

1 lb lean ground beef

1 red bell pepper, diced·

2 garlic cloves, minced

1 tsp freshly grated ginger

¼ tsp freshly ground black pepper

1 head butter or Bibb lettuce

2 carrots, peeled and cut into matchsticks

1 large English cucumber, cut into matchsticks

¼ cup chopped green onions, for garnish

1. For the peanut sauce, in a small bowl, whisk together the peanut butter, soy sauce, Sriracha, honey, ginger, and water until well combined. Set aside.

2. For the hoisin beef, in another small bowl, whisk together the hoisin sauce, rice vinegar, soy sauce, honey, and sesame oil.

3. In a large skillet, heat the vegetable oil over medium-high heat. Add the onion and cook, stirring, for 2 minutes. Add the beef and continue to cook for 4 minutes, stirring frequently. Transfer mixture to a strainer, draining off any fat. Return the beef and onion mixture to the skillet and add the red pepper, garlic, ginger, and pepper. Cook for 1 minute, stirring continuously. Add the hoisin mixture and continue cooking over low heat for 5 minutes.

4. To assemble, arrange the lettuce leaves on a serving platter. Spoon the peanut sauce on the base of each lettuce leaf. Top with a generous spoonful of hoisin meat, carrots, and cucumbers. Garnish with the green onions.

+ **Make it gluten-free: Use gluten-free tamari or gluten-free soy sauce, and gluten-free hoisin**

steak tartine
WITH CARAMELIZED ONION JAM

hings sound so much lovelier when said in French; an umbrella is a *parapluie*, and *tartine* is a fancy way of saying "open-face sandwich." Literally translated to "a slice of bread," this is that and so much more, its *incroyable* toppings including a spicy horseradish spread, pan-seared steak, caramelized onion jam, peppery arugula, and creamy goat cheese. With all these luscious layers, it's clear Lisa's fluent in tasty tartine terminology.

SERVES: 4–6   PREP TIME: 20 MINS   COOK TIME: 40 MINS (+ resting)

Caramelized Onion Jam

2 tbsp olive oil

2 lb yellow onions, halved and thinly sliced

⅓ cup sugar

½ cup balsamic vinegar

¼ cup sherry vinegar

2 fresh thyme sprigs

¾ tsp kosher salt

½ tsp freshly ground black pepper

Horseradish Spread

½ cup light mayonnaise

1 tbsp jarred horseradish

1 tbsp sherry vinegar

1 tsp Dijon mustard

¼ tsp kosher salt

¼ tsp freshly ground black pepper

Rib Eye Steaks

1 tsp kosher salt

½ tsp paprika

½ tsp garlic powder

¼ tsp dried oregano

¼ tsp freshly ground black pepper

1½ lb boneless rib eye steaks, room temperature

1 tbsp vegetable oil

Rustic white or sourdough loaf, sliced lengthwise and toasted (6–8 slices)

1 cup baby arugula

¾ cup crumbled goat cheese

1. For the onion jam, in a large skillet, heat the olive oil over medium heat. Add the onions and cook for 10 minutes, stirring occasionally, until softened and golden. Sprinkle evenly with the sugar and cook for 1 minute without stirring. Add the balsamic vinegar, sherry vinegar, thyme, salt, and pepper and bring to a boil. Reduce the heat to low and cook for 20 minutes, until all of the liquid is evaporated and onions have a jammy consistency. Remove from the heat, discard thyme sprigs, and set aside.

2. For the horseradish spread, in a small bowl, whisk together the mayonnaise, horseradish, sherry vinegar, mustard, salt, and freshly ground black pepper. Cover and refrigerate until ready to assemble.

3. For the steak, in a small bowl, combine the salt, paprika, garlic powder, oregano, and pepper. Sprinkle both sides of the steak with the mixture. Place a cast-iron skillet over medium-high heat and add the vegetable oil. Once hot, add the steaks and cook for 3–4 minutes, then flip and continue cooking for 4–6 minutes more, until the internal temperature is between 135°F and 140°F. Remove from the heat and let rest for 10 minutes before slicing thinly.

4. To assemble, place the toasted bread on a serving platter. Spread the horseradish spread on each slice, and layer with sliced steak, onion jam, and arugula, finishing with crumbled goat cheese.

+ **Make it gluten-free: Use gluten-free bread**

lessons *from* lisa

⋆ *Don't use expensive balsamic vinegar because it cooks right down until all that's left is syrupy goodness.*

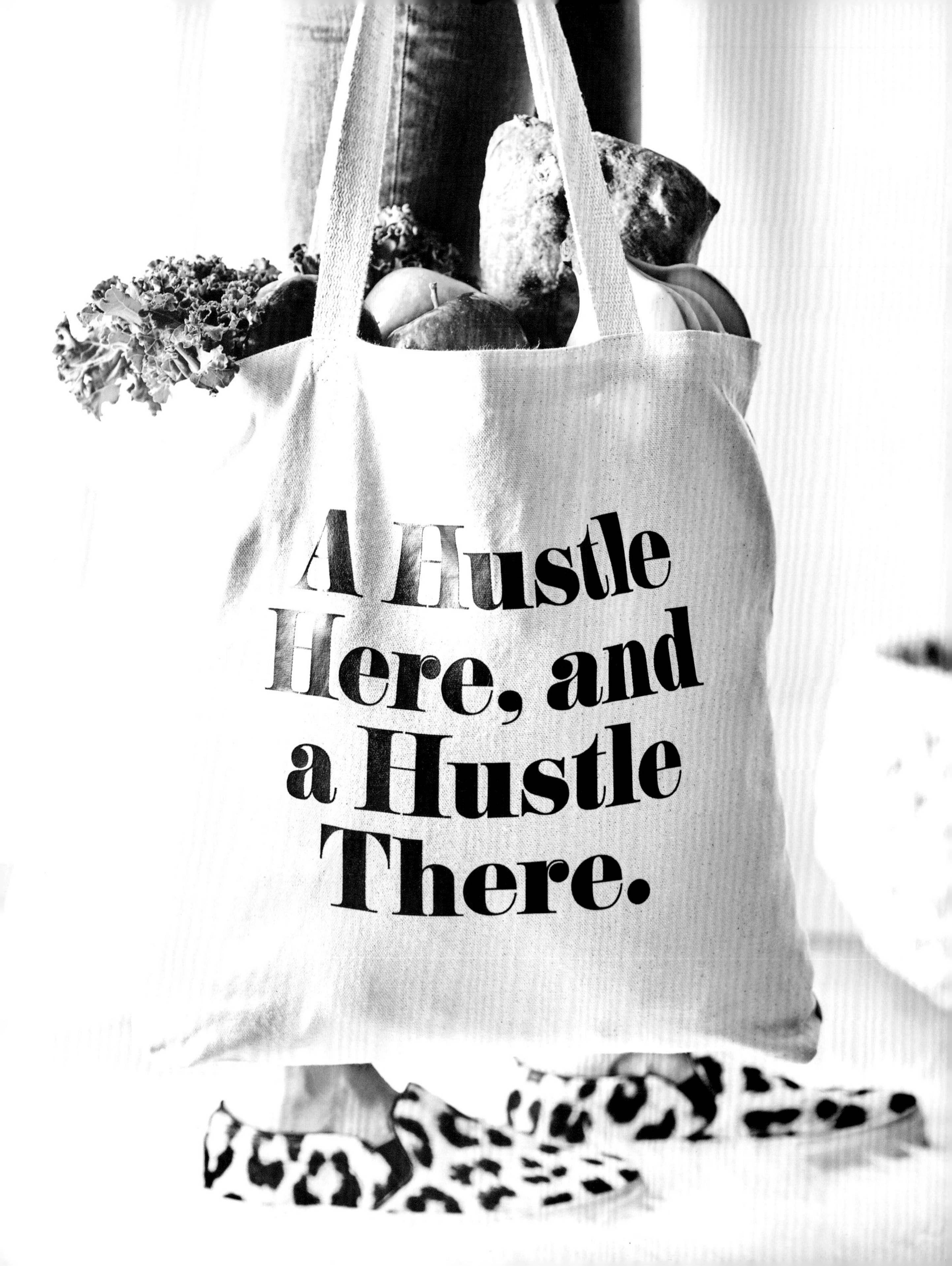
A Hustle
Here, and
a Hustle
There.

weeknight dinners

The reality is, weeknight meals can take on the feel of *The Hunger Games*, where the fight to get food into hangry mouths is an epic challenge, let alone sitting down together as a family. Well, your hunt for fresh, quick, nutritious, and satisfying staples is done like dinner—we're here to help you bite off exactly what you can chew: food for the busy, the tired, and the starving. These family-friendly meals are low on cleanup and high on compliments, and they're sure to get everyone to the table in a timely fashion.

vegetable soup

When the temperature dips below zero, it's time for my season-long snooze, staying curled up in my den until the bitter cold ends. But how do I lazily hole up and hibernate without packing on the winter weight? The answer is deliciously simple—steaming bowls of this healthy, hearty, flavorful soup, a magical mix of earthy root vegetables, fresh herbs, and white wine finished with creamy, tangy goat cheese. Quick and easy to pull together (prep time is 10 minutes), this robust cold-weather soup means more time spent by the fire, where the forecast is always warm and toasty.

SERVES: 4–6   PREP TIME: 10 MINS   COOK TIME: 25 MINS

2 tbsp olive oil

1 medium yellow onion, chopped

½ cup chopped leeks, white and light green part only

2 large carrots, peeled and cut into ½-inch cubes

1½ cups ½-inch-cubed peeled parsnips

2 garlic cloves, minced

1 tsp chopped fresh thyme

½ tsp kosher salt

½ tsp freshly ground black pepper

⅛ tsp cayenne pepper

½ cup dry white wine

2 cups ½-inch-cubed peeled Yukon gold potatoes

2 cups ½-inch-cubed peeled sweet potatoes

6 cups chicken broth

1 tbsp fresh lemon juice

Crumbled goat cheese, for garnish

Fresh thyme sprigs, for garnish

1. In a large soup pot, heat the olive oil over medium heat. Add the onion, leeks, carrots, and parsnips. Cook for 8 minutes, until softened. Add the garlic, thyme, salt, pepper, and cayenne pepper. Cook, stirring, for 1 minute. Add the white wine and let evaporate over high heat for 2 minutes. Stir in the potatoes, sweet potatoes, and chicken broth. Bring the soup to a boil, reduce the heat to low, and simmer until the potatoes are softened, about 15 minutes.

2. When the soup is finished cooking, remove 3 cups of soup and place in a blender. Puree and then stir back into the soup pot with the lemon juice. Garnish each serving with crumbled goat cheese and a sprig of thyme.

Winter is nature's way of saying, 'Up yours.'

—ROBERT BYRNE

sweet potato & carrot soup WITH KALE CHIPS

Lisa told me to shut my eyes and open my mouth. I did as requested (read: demanded) and was fed the most velvety smooth and richly flavored soup. How dare she? She knows I loathe cream soups. I told her so much, and she rolled her eyes, telling me that there's no dairy in this delight. I was gobsmacked by my soup-savvy sis. In her bag (or in this case, bowl) of tricks, she uses nutrient-rich sweet potatoes to add creaminess, and combines them with carrots to create steamy spoonfuls with hints of thyme, ginger, and garlic. Topped with crunchy baked kale chips, this bright-orange soup is hearty and healthy, proving once again that Lisa really is the cream of the crop.

SERVES: 6   PREP TIME: 20 MINS   COOK TIME: 40 MINS

Kale Chips

½ lb kale

1 tbsp olive oil

½ tsp kosher salt

Sweet Potato & Carrot Soup

2 tbsp olive oil

1 medium red onion, chopped

2 carrots, peeled and chopped

3 garlic cloves, minced

2 tsp grated fresh ginger

2 tsp chopped fresh thyme

1 tsp kosher salt

¼ tsp freshly ground black pepper

⅛ tsp red pepper flakes

2 lb (2 large or 3 medium) sweet potatoes, peeled and cubed

1 tbsp honey

6 cups chicken broth

1 tbsp fresh lemon juice

1. For the kale chips, preheat the oven to 350°F. Line 2 baking sheets with parchment paper and set aside.

2. To prepare the kale, remove the center stem and tear the kale into large pieces. Wash well and dry completely. In a large bowl, toss the kale leaves with the olive oil and sprinkle with the salt. Place the kale in a single layer on the baking sheets and bake for 10 minutes. Remove any pieces that are crispy and golden. Continue to bake another 3–4 minutes, until all the pieces are crispy. Remove from the oven and allow to cool.

3. For the soup, in a large soup pot, heat the olive oil over medium heat. Add the onion and carrots, cooking 4–5 minutes until softened. Stir in the garlic, ginger, thyme, salt, pepper, and red pepper flakes and cook for 1 minute, stirring constantly. Stir in the sweet potatoes and honey until well combined. Add the chicken broth and bring to a boil. Reduce the heat and simmer uncovered for 20 minutes, until the potatoes are tender.

4. Remove from the heat and puree the soup in 2 batches using a countertop blender, or in the pot using a handheld immersion blender. Stir in the lemon juice and garnish each serving with kale chips.

lessons *from* lisa

★ Dry the kale completely, or it won't get crispy.

HEAL THYSELF chicken noodle soup

Our mom isn't the stereotypical Jewish mother—she doesn't nag, guilt, or pressure us. In fact, she didn't even insist we marry doctors. She was sure we'd have the chops to stand on our own and do our best to help repair the world, and we're doing our best, one bowl at a time, with this amped-up cold-busting version of Jewish penicillin, complete with the healing powers of immunity-boosting turmeric and fresh ginger. Easy to pull together, this superb soup is perfect for a speedy recovery, is always on call, and, without fail, has a great tableside manner. Just what the doc (and Mom) ordered.

SERVES: 6   PREP TIME: 15 MINS   COOK TIME: 35 MINS

1 tbsp olive oil

2 large carrots, peeled and chopped

2 celery stalks, chopped

1 medium yellow onion, chopped

3 garlic cloves, minced

1 tbsp grated fresh ginger

2 tsp ground turmeric powder

½ tsp ground coriander

½ tsp kosher salt

½ tsp freshly ground black pepper

8 cups chicken broth

½ lb (8 oz package) egg noodles, uncooked

2 roasted deli chicken breasts, cubed

1 cup fresh or thawed frozen green peas

1 cup chopped zucchini

1 tbsp fresh lemon juice

1. In a large soup pot, heat the olive oil over medium heat. Stir in the carrots, celery, and onion and cook until tender, about 6 minutes. Add the garlic, ginger, turmeric, coriander, salt, and pepper. Continue to cook, stirring, for 1 minute. Add the chicken broth and bring to a boil. Reduce the heat and simmer covered for 20 minutes.

2. While the soup simmers, prepare the noodles. Bring a large pot of salted water to a boil. Add the noodles and cook 6–8 minutes, or until tender. Drain and divide between individual serving bowls.

3. Once the soup finishes cooking, add the cubed chicken, peas, and zucchini. Simmer uncovered for 5 minutes more and then stir in the lemon juice and add to the serving bowls with the noodles.

+ **Make it gluten-free: Use gluten-free pasta**

> **Isn't it a bit unnerving that doctors call what they do practice?**
>
> —GEORGE CARLIN

couscous salad

We're calling out spring here, but really, this is a 365 salad—super speedy to make, it's a green-lover's dream. Perfect for picnics, backyard barbecues, or a frosty February day (yes, it's a light-yet-comforting combo of flavors and textures), this salad has couscous coated in a fragrant basil dressing, and is loaded with fresh asparagus and peas, salty feta, and crunchy roasted almonds. Refreshing and easy to whip together, this scrumptious salad is sure to put a spring in your step.

SERVES: 6   PREP TIME: 10 MINS   COOK TIME: <10 MINS

Fresh Basil Dressing

¾ cup packed fresh basil leaves

¼ cup olive oil

2 tbsp champagne vinegar

1 tbsp fresh lemon juice

1 small garlic clove, minced

1 tsp minced shallots

1 tsp honey

½ tsp kosher salt

Salad

1½ cups couscous

1 tbsp olive oil

1½ cups boiling water

1½ cups fresh or frozen green peas

1 small bunch asparagus, ends trimmed and cut into thirds

¼ cup chopped fresh flat-leaf parsley

½ cup crumbled feta cheese

½ cup chopped roasted almonds

1. For the basil dressing, in a blender, combine the basil, olive oil, champagne vinegar, lemon juice, garlic, shallots, honey, and salt. Blend until well combined and set aside.

2. For the couscous, in a large bowl, combine the couscous, olive oil, and boiling water. Cover and let stand for 5 minutes. Fluff with a fork.

3. Bring a large pot of salted water to boil. Reduce the heat to low and add peas and asparagus. Cook for 2 minutes.

4. Drain and plunge the vegetables into a bowl of ice water (this will keep your vegetables bright green and crunchy). Then drain again and add to couscous. Add the parsley and toss with the dressing. Place in a large serving bowl and top with the feta cheese and almonds.

+ Make it gluten-free: Replace couscous with quinoa

lessons *from* lisa

★ Five ounces of asparagus provides 60 percent of your daily folic acid requirements.

★ Choose firm asparagus stalks that are smooth and brightly colored, with tightly closed tips.

★ Make it a meal by adding some sliced grilled chicken.

kale salad

I'm going to say one of the most divisive words in the culinary world: cilantro. Now, before you start picketing, cool your jets because we've got you covered—if these zesty leaves are a meal-breaker, swap 'em out for fresh flat-leaf parsley and get tossing this superfood salad. Chock-full of kale, beans, corn, and avocado, and lightly coated in a Southwestern-inspired jalapeño yogurt dressing, this crunchy, creamy, and bountiful bowl has the power to unite everyone and bring mega-nutrients to your Taco Tuesday or Fajita Friday.

SERVES: 4–6   PREP TIME: 15 MINS   COOK TIME: 0 MINS

Jalapeño Yogurt Dressing

½ cup plain Greek yogurt

¼ cup olive oil

¼ cup chopped fresh cilantro

2 tbsp fresh lime juice

2 tbsp light mayonnaise

1 tbsp chopped jalapeño pepper, seeds removed

1 garlic clove, minced

½ tsp kosher salt

¼ tsp freshly ground black pepper

Salad

6 cups chopped kale, stalks removed

1 cup canned black beans, rinsed and drained

1 cup fresh or thawed frozen corn

1 green bell pepper, chopped

1 red bell pepper, chopped

1 large ripe avocado, chopped

2 large tomatoes, seeded and chopped

½ cup chopped fresh cilantro

1 cup roasted salted pumpkin seeds

Jalapeño peppers, sliced, for garnish

---

1. For the dressing, in a blender, combine the yogurt, olive oil, cilantro, lime juice, mayonnaise, jalapeño pepper, garlic, salt, and pepper. Blend until smooth and set aside.

2. For the salad, in a large serving bowl, toss the chopped kale with the black beans, corn, green peppers, red peppers, avocado, tomatoes, and cilantro. Mix with a few tablespoons of dressing until well coated. Add the roasted pumpkin seeds and serve with sliced jalapeño peppers to garnish.

I would pick it out if I saw it and throw it on the floor.

—JULIA CHILD, ON CILANTRO

*THROWING SALAD IS NOT RECOMMENDED.

PROTEIN-PACKED asian chopped salad

Lisa's the CEO of our chop shop, and you best stand back because she's a-choppin', wiping out all the hidden fats (read: crispy fried noodles, heavy peanut dressing) often found in Asian salads. Amping up the fresh and healthy parts, protein is aplenty with the addition of tender edamame, spiced nuts, and creamy avocado. Toasted sesame seeds, almonds, and cashews lend golden nutty richness and superb crunch, light vinaigrette contrasts perfectly with sweet chunks of mango, and cabbage, snow peas, and parsley serve up some stellar green power. With this satisfying, nutritious, and delicious marriage of textures and flavors, Lisa's truly a master mechanic at maintaining our midriffs.

SERVES: 6–8   PREP TIME: 30 MINS   COOK TIME: 10 MINS

Sesame Soy Vinaigrette

3 tbsp vegetable oil

1 tbsp sesame oil

2 tbsp rice vinegar

1 tbsp soy sauce

1 tbsp toasted sesame seeds

2 tsp fresh lime juice

2 tsp honey

1 small garlic clove, finely minced

Roasted Spiced Nuts

1 cup coarsely chopped raw almonds

1 cup coarsely chopped raw cashews

1 tbsp olive oil

1 tsp toasted sesame seeds

1 tsp sugar

½ tsp kosher salt

¼ tsp ground ginger

Pinch cayenne pepper

¼ tsp lime zest

Chopped Salad

8 cups thinly sliced napa cabbage

2 cups thinly sliced purple cabbage

1 cup shelled and cooked edamame

2 mangoes, peeled and chopped

1 ripe avocado, chopped

1 cup snow peas, sliced in half on the diagonal

½ cup chopped fresh flat-leaf parsley

1. For the vinaigrette, in a small bowl, whisk together the vegetable oil, sesame oil, rice vinegar, soy sauce, sesame seeds, lime juice, honey, and garlic until combined. Set aside.

2. For the spiced nuts, preheat the oven to 375°F. In a medium bowl, combine the almonds, cashews, olive oil, sesame seeds, sugar, salt, ginger, and cayenne pepper. Toss well to combine and spread out on a parchment-lined baking sheet. Bake for 8–10 minutes, until lightly toasted. Remove from the oven and toss with lime zest. Set aside to cool.

3. For the salad, in a large serving bowl, combine the napa cabbage, purple cabbage, edamame, mangoes, avocado, snow peas, parsley, and half the nuts. Toss the salad with dressing just before serving and top with the remaining nuts.

╋ **Make it gluten-free:** Use gluten-free tamari or gluten-free soy sauce

charred corn & zucchini
ORZO SALAD

If this salad had a theme song, it'd be The Beatles' hit tune "I'll Follow the Sun." It wouldn't be a stretch to say that the sun rises and sets on this salad, blazing with the brilliance of vivid veggies, each light and refreshing bite bursting with the dazzling combination of corn, zucchini, and Southwestern flavors. Made in minutes (30, to be exact), fresh corn and zucchini get a barbecue-like boost when charred on the stove and are mixed with salty queso fresco, a little kickin' chili powder, and a tangy lime dressing. Using small, tender orzo allows each forkful to shine, carrying the perfect balance of creamy, tangy, and smoky flavors, sure to bring brightness to every mouthful. Blue skies ahead, baby.

SERVES: 4–6   PREP TIME: 10 MINS   COOK TIME: 20 MINS

Chili Lime Dressing

¼ cup olive oil

2 tbsp fresh lime juice

2 tsp apple cider vinegar

1 tsp minced shallots

1 tsp honey

½ tsp chili powder

½ tsp kosher salt

¼ tsp freshly ground black pepper

Salad

3 ears corn, shucked

2 medium zucchini, ends trimmed, cut in half lengthwise

1 tbsp olive oil

Pinch kosher salt

Pinch freshly ground black pepper

½ lb uncooked orzo pasta

¾ cup crumbled queso fresco cheese

¼ cup chopped fresh cilantro

1. For the dressing, in a small bowl, whisk together the olive oil, lime juice, apple cider vinegar, shallots, honey, chili powder, salt, and pepper. Set aside.

2. For the salad, first char the corn and zucchini. Heat a grill pan over medium-high heat. Brush the corn and zucchini with olive oil and sprinkle with a pinch of salt and pepper. Add the zucchini and corn until charred on all sides. The corn will take about 8 minutes of spinning to make sure all sides are charred, and the zucchini will take 6–8 minutes, flipping halfway through.

3. Cut the kernels off the cobs and chop the zucchini. Place in a large mixing bowl.

4. While the vegetables are grilling, bring a large pot of salted cold water to a boil. Cook the orzo until al dente. Drain, rinse under cold water, and drain well. Add the orzo to the corn and zucchini, along with the crumbled queso fresco and chopped cilantro. Toss with the chili lime dressing until well coated.

+ **Make it gluten-free: Use gluten-free pasta**

lessons *from* lisa

★ *Queso fresco is a Mexican cheese with a salty-sour flavor that is great crumbled on everything from grilled vegetables to egg dishes.*

★ *This salad keeps well in the refrigerator, only getting more flavorful as it sits.*

tuscan pasta salad
WITH SHERRY VINAIGRETTE

Drawing inspiration from Tuscany, our Mona Lisa has used her noodle and transformed the traditionally bland and oily pasta salad into an ambrosial work of art. Rustic yet elegant, her masterpiece is characterized by authentic flavors, simplicity, and heartiness. Roasted red peppers add a sweet smokiness, nutty sherry vinegar combines with Dijon mustard and garlic to create a next-level dressing, and nutrient-rich cherry and sun-dried tomatoes, spinach, and chickpeas combine to bring juiciness and creaminess to every bite. Much like Leonardo and his love of symmetry, Lisa da Vinci has created perfectly balanced bites and restored Last Supper–level glory to the pasta salad.

SERVES: 6–8   PREP TIME: 15 MINS   COOK TIME: 20 MINS

Sherry Vinaigrette

6 tbsp olive oil

2 tbsp sherry vinegar

1 garlic clove, finely minced

1 tsp Dijon mustard

1 tsp honey

½ tsp kosher salt

¼ tsp freshly ground black pepper

Pasta Salad

1 lb uncooked rigatoni pasta

2 red bell peppers

3 cups packed baby spinach leaves, coarsely chopped

1½ cups halved cherry tomatoes

1 cup canned chickpeas, rinsed and drained

½ cup chopped fresh basil

½ cup freshly grated Parmesan cheese

¼ cup finely chopped oil-packed sun-dried tomatoes, rinsed and dried

1. For the sherry vinaigrette, in a medium glass jar, combine the olive oil, sherry vinegar, garlic, mustard, honey, salt, and pepper. Shake well and refrigerate until ready to use.

2. For the pasta salad, in a large pot of boiling salted water, cook the pasta according to package directions until just tender. Drain and rinse with cold water. Place in a large serving bowl.

3. Place the red peppers directly on the burner of a gas stove and turn to high heat. When 1 side is charred, rotate the pepper until all sides are charred.

4. Place the peppers in a bowl, cover, and let them steam. After 5–10 minutes, slip off the charred skin and remove the core and seeds of the peppers. Chop the peppers and add to the cooked pasta. Add the spinach, cherry tomatoes, chickpeas, basil, Parmesan, and sun-dried tomatoes. Pour the dressing over the pasta salad and toss to coat.

+ **Make it gluten-free:** Use gluten-free pasta

lessons *from* lisa

★ *If you don't have a gas stove, char the pepper skins under the broiler in your oven and continue with the steaming step.*

★ *Sun-dried tomatoes are concentrated sources of vitamins C and K, iron, and lycopene.*

steak salad

WITH RANCH DRESSING

I'm taking my cue from Elmer Wheeler, who in the 1920s coined the sales phrase, "Don't sell the steak—sell the sizzle!" So I'm not going to tell you that this pan-seared rib eye is incredibly tender, flavorful, and juicy. I'm also not going to try to persuade you with this light, creamy, and tangy Greek yogurt ranch dressing. And, I'm most certainly not going to lure you with the perfectly healthy balance that's created when you combine a cooked-to-a-T steak with a whole host of crunchy, superbly refreshing vegetables. Easy and impressive, great for last-minute company or a weeknight family meal, this speedy, satisfying, and scrumptious steak salad sells itself every time.

SERVES: 4   PREP TIME: 15 MINS   COOK TIME: 10 MINS

Greek Yogurt Ranch Dressing

1 cup plain Greek yogurt

¼ cup 1% milk

1 tbsp freshly grated Parmesan cheese

1 tbsp chopped fresh flat-leaf parsley

2 tsp chopped fresh chives

2 tsp apple cider vinegar

½ tsp garlic powder

½ tsp kosher salt

¼ tsp freshly ground black pepper

Steak Salad

1½ lb rib eye steak

¾ tsp kosher salt

½ tsp freshly ground black pepper

1 tbsp vegetable oil

8 cups chopped romaine lettuce

1½ cups chopped celery

1½ cups chopped English cucumber

1 cup halved cherry tomatoes

1 cup sliced hearts of palm

½ cup thinly sliced radishes

1. For the dressing, in a medium bowl, whisk together the yogurt, milk, Parmesan cheese, parsley, chives, apple cider vinegar, garlic powder, salt, and black pepper. Cover and refrigerate while preparing the salad.

2. For the steak salad, preheat the oven to 400°F. Season the steak on both sides with salt and pepper. Using a cast-iron pan or a heavy ovenproof skillet, heat the vegetable oil over medium-high heat. Sear the steak for 4 minutes, flip and sear for 4 minutes more. For medium doneness, finish in the oven for 3 minutes. Let the steak rest before slicing. Slice thinly across the grain and set aside.

3. To assemble the salad, place the lettuce on a serving platter and drizzle with a few spoonfuls of dressing. Add the sliced steak to the platter and place the celery, cucumber, tomatoes, hearts of palm, and radishes around the steak and over the lettuce. Serve with the remaining dressing.

> *Steak and sex, my favorite pair. I get them both very rare.*
>
> —RODNEY DANGERFIELD

10 things you can do on a sunday (TO MAKE MONDAY LESS LIKE, WELL, MONDAY)

I used to start the week with the best, healthiest intentions, but somewhere around Wednesday, when life had turned me into a whirling dervish (Lisa's description, not mine), I'd start thumbing through food delivery apps or fall victim to my bad habit, otherwise known as I'll-just-eat-toast-for-dinner. Well, thanks to Lisa's brilliant foresight and organizational skills, a little prep goes a long way, and now I have nutritious options at my frantic fingertips all week long. You can too. Here's how.

BREAKFAST

Get ahead of weekday mornings by pre-making recipes that can be kept in the refrigerator and enjoyed for days afterwards

Pre-measure smoothie ingredients into packs to store in your freezer, leaving you with just a dump-and-blend morning

Be sure to prep portable healthy breakfast options for when you're in a rush

LUNCH

Prep your weekday salads ahead of time by washing and chopping vegetables, cooking protein, and making dressing, then all you need to do on the day is toss

Try making a soup that eats like a meal

Opt for dinner recipes that work well as leftovers for lunch

SNACKS

Pre-stock your fridge with healthy snacks and light bites, perfect options for when the afternoon munchies hit

DINNER

Make the after-work rush more manageable by prepping the whole grain and lean protein that's the base of a dish ahead of time

Make spice mixes that can be kept in airtight containers for weeks at a time

Get a head start on a recipe by making sauces, dips, and spreads that can be kept in the refrigerator for the week

CHOPPED buffalo chicken salad

R *ah! Rah! Sis boom bah.* This is how I cheer Lisa on, especially when she pulls out a huge win, successfully punting fattening fan-favorite buffalo chicken wings into the healthy zone. Sure to become the MVP of game-day eats, lean chicken breasts are marinated and cooked in a spicy sauce, tossed in a hot honey glaze, and teamed up with crunchy lettuce, carrots, celery, cucumbers, and avocado. Dressed in a tangy blue cheese that gives a cool and creamy balance to the mix, it's clear that my sis is the culinary champ, the creator of epic forkfuls that give us something to cheer about from the table. *Gimme an L. Gimme an I. Gimme an S. Gimme an A. What does that spell? Tasty touchdown.*

SERVES: 4   PREP TIME: 15 MINS (+ marinating)   COOK TIME: 15 MINS (+ resting)

3 boneless, skinless chicken breasts

Marinade and Glaze

¼ cup Frank's Original Red Hot Sauce

3 tbsp olive oil

1 tbsp fresh lime juice

½ tsp paprika

½ tsp kosher salt

¼ tsp garlic powder

¼ tsp freshly ground black pepper

1 tbsp honey

Blue Cheese Dressing

⅓ cup light sour cream

¼ cup light mayonnaise

2 tbsp milk

1 tbsp finely chopped shallots

1 tbsp white wine vinegar

continued on next page

1. Place chicken breasts in a medium bowl.

2. To make the marinade, in a separate bowl, whisk together the hot sauce, olive oil, lime juice, paprika, salt, garlic powder, and pepper. Toss the chicken breasts with 3 tablespoons of sauce and let marinate 30 minutes at room temperature while preparing the rest of the salad. To make the glaze with the remaining marinade, whisk in the honey and set aside until the chicken is cooked and chopped.

3. For the dressing, whisk together the sour cream, mayonnaise, milk, shallots, white wine vinegar, sugar, salt, and pepper until well combined. Fold in the blue cheese and cover and refrigerate until ready to serve.

4. Preheat a lightly oiled grill to medium-high heat. Place the chicken on the grill and cook for 5–7 minutes per side, until cooked through. Remove from the grill and let the chicken rest for 5 minutes before chopping. Alternatively, prepare the chicken as above and bake at 425°F for 15 minutes. Allow the chicken to rest for 5 minutes before cutting.

5. When cool enough to handle, chop the chicken into 1-inch chunks and toss with remaining glaze until all the pieces are well coated.

6. To make the salad, in a large bowl, toss the lettuce, celery, carrots, cucumber, and avocado with enough dressing to coat the salad. Divide the salad between 4 serving plates and top with the chicken, blue cheese, and green onions.

ingredients continued

½ tsp sugar

½ tsp kosher salt

¼ tsp freshly ground black
pepper

½ cup crumbled blue cheese
(or feta, if desired)

Salad

10 cups chopped romaine lettuce

3 celery stalks, chopped

2 carrots, peeled and chopped

1½ cups chopped English
cucumber

1 large ripe avocado, chopped

¼ cup crumbled blue cheese
(or feta), for garnish

2 tbsp chopped green onions, for
garnish

CRISPY baked carrot fries

Would I like fries with that? Is rain wet? Of course I'd like fries with everything, and in the case of these carrot fries, supersize it, please. In a brilliant move for our taste buds and waistlines alike, Lisa has swapped out potatoes for carrots and the deep fryer for the oven to make these baked beauties. Hand cut and coated in a golden panko Parmesan mixture, carrots are baked to a fry-like crisp and served with a refreshing, zesty lime and basil dip, sure to satisfy crunch cravings and French-fry fanatics everywhere.

SERVES: 4   PREP TIME: 20 MINS   COOK TIME: 20 MINS

Zesty Lime Dip

½ cup light sour cream

¼ cup light mayonnaise

2 tsp fresh lime juice

½ tsp lime zest

½ tsp kosher salt

¼ tsp freshly ground black pepper

¼ tsp garlic powder

2 tbsp chopped fresh basil

Carrot Fries

½ cup panko (Japanese breadcrumbs)

⅓ cup freshly grated Parmesan cheese

½ tsp dried oregano

¼ tsp garlic powder

¼ tsp kosher salt

Pinch cayenne pepper

1 egg, lightly whisked

4 large carrots, peeled and cut into long pieces, to resemble French fries

2 tsp olive oil

1. For the dip, in a medium bowl, whisk together the sour cream, mayonnaise, lime juice, lime zest, salt, pepper, and garlic powder. Stir in the chopped basil and cover and refrigerate until ready to serve.

2. Preheat the oven to 400°F and line a baking sheet with parchment paper.

3. For the carrot fries, in a medium bowl, combine the panko, Parmesan, oregano, garlic powder, salt, and cayenne.

4. In a second bowl, whisk the egg. Dip each carrot stick into the egg, allow excess to drip off, and then dredge in the panko mixture, patting gently to help the crumbs stick. Place on the prepared baking sheet in a single layer and repeat until all the carrots have been used. Drizzle the coated carrots with the olive oil and bake for 16–18 minutes, flipping halfway through, until the carrots are tender, slightly crispy, and golden. Serve with the dip.

— **Make it gluten-free:** Use gluten-free panko

fried "rice"

When Lisa and I clash, it can get out of hand. She'll put her palm out to quiet me and I'll pepper her with air quotes, effectively covering off the two most irritating and theatrical gestures. Imagine the scrap that ensued over this recipe with her talk-to-the-handing me and my quote-blasting her that cauliflower isn't "rice." Well, I'm so "glad" I didn't bite the hand that feeds me because while cauliflower might not be "rice," it's the perfect way to make this Chinese takeout classic healthy. Easy and superfast to whip up, riced cauliflower is stir-fried with vegetables and eggs, cutting carbs and calories in this Asian fare. Two thumbs up, Lisa. See? I can be "nice."

SERVES: 4   PREP TIME: 15 MINS   COOK TIME: <10 MINS

1 large cauliflower

1 tbsp sesame oil

1 small yellow onion, chopped

2 garlic cloves, minced

¾ cup peeled, chopped carrots

¾ cup fresh or thawed frozen green peas

½ tsp kosher salt

2 eggs, lightly whisked

2 tbsp soy sauce

Chopped green onions, for garnish

Roasted peanuts, for garnish

1. To rice the cauliflower, cut cauliflower into florets. Working in 2–3 batches, put the florets in a food processor and pulse on and off until they become small rice-sized pieces, totaling approximately 4 cups. Set aside.

2. In a wok or large skillet, heat the sesame oil over medium heat. Add the onion, cooking for 2 minutes. Stir in the garlic, carrots, peas, and salt and continue to cook for 2 minutes more. Push the vegetables to the side of your pan, pour the eggs in, and scramble for 1 minute. Mix the eggs in with the vegetables. Add the cauliflower and stir well to coat. Stir in the soy sauce and cook for 2 minutes, until the cauliflower is tender. Garnish with the scallions and roasted peanuts. Serve immediately.

lessons *from* lisa

★ When buying cauliflower, look for clean, white compact curds and a head that is surrounded by a lot of thick green leaves—it will be better protected.

★ Riced cauliflower can be refrigerated in a reusable plastic bag for 4 days.

> *I 'believe' you, too. See the quotations I'm making with my claw hands? It means I DON'T believe you!*
>
> —BAD COP, *THE LEGO MOVIE*

EASY mexican street corn

I didn't eat corn for two years after seeing *Children of the Corn*. But, fictional murderous minors aside, there's nothing that should stop you from enjoying fresh corn, comfort-on-a-cob, one of life's simplest and greatest pleasures. Forget the false claim that this veggie will make you husky—sweet juicy niblets are chock-full of fiber, vitamins, and antioxidants, each cob having less sugar than a beet, banana, or apple. So, armed with dental floss, let's all go hog wild for Lisa's version of Mexican elotes (aka street corn): lightly charred cobs slathered in a salty (cotija), spicy (chipotle chili powder), and savory (lime zest and cilantro) sauce. Delivering a delicious kick to your taste buds, this smoky, spicy, sweet, and tangy cream-of-the-crop side dish will have everyone grinning from ear to ear.

MAKES: 6 EARS OF CORN   PREP TIME: 10 MINS   COOK TIME: 15 MINS

Cotija Topping

⅓ cup light sour cream

¼ cup light mayonnaise

⅓ cup chopped fresh cilantro, divided

1 tsp lime zest

½ tsp chipotle chili powder

¼ tsp kosher salt

¾ cup crumbled cotija cheese, divided

Corn

6 ears corn, husks and corn silk removed

1 tbsp olive oil

Pinch chipotle chili powder, for garnish (optional)

1 lime, cut into 6 wedges

1. For the cotija topping, in a small bowl, whisk together the sour cream, mayonnaise, ¼ cup of the cilantro, lime zest, chipotle chili powder, and salt. Stir in ½ cup of the cotija cheese. Set aside.

2. For the corn, heat a cast-iron grill pan or if using an outdoor grill, preheat to medium-high heat. Rub the ears of corn with the olive oil and place in the grill pan or on the grill. Cook for 10–12 minutes in the grill pan or about 8 minutes on the grill, turning the cobs occasionally until the kernels are lightly charred and the corn is just tender.

3. Remove from the grill and brush cotija mixture over each ear of corn. Sprinkle with the remaining cotija cheese, remaining cilantro, and a pinch of chipotle chili powder. Serve with a wedge of lime.

lessons *from* lisa

★ *Cotija, a salty and crumbly Mexican hard cheese, is sold at most large grocery stores; however, if you have trouble finding it, you can use feta in its place.*

CRISPY ROASTED

smashed potatoes

I may have been a potato sack star (reigning champ '84–'87), but my sister has it in the bag when it comes to turning the humble spud into a showstopper. Here, she has created a smashing success of a side dish: mini potatoes are boiled until fork tender, and then gently "smashed," seasoned with olive oil and garlic, and baked until crisp on the outside and creamy on the inside. The perfect marriage of golden French fries and fluffy baked potatoes, these superb spuds are finished with a little Parmesan and topped with sour cream and chives. Impressive (much like my race ribbons) and super simple, these tasty tubers are Lisa's very own triumphant hop to glory.

SERVES: 6   PREP TIME: 10 MINS   COOK TIME: 40 MINS

22 mini red or mini Yukon gold potatoes (about 2 lb), scrubbed clean

3 tbsp olive oil

1 garlic clove, finely minced

½ tsp kosher salt

¼ tsp freshly ground black pepper, divided

¼ tsp dried thyme, divided

¼ cup freshly grated Parmesan cheese

½ cup sour cream, for garnish

2 tbsp chopped fresh chives, for garnish

1. Preheat the oven to 450°F. Line a baking sheet with parchment paper.

2. In a medium pot, cover the potatoes with cold water and add a generous sprinkle of salt. Bring to a boil over medium heat and cook for 14–16 minutes, until fork tender. Drain and set aside until cool enough to handle.

3. Place the potatoes on a flat surface and use a potato masher or the bottom of a glass or jar to lightly press each potato to a ¾-inch thickness. The potatoes don't have to be completely flat; you want to keep them in one piece. Transfer each smashed potato onto the prepared baking sheet.

4. In a small bowl, combine the olive oil and garlic. Brush the top of each potato with half the mixture.

5. In a separate small bowl, mix the salt, pepper, and thyme. Sprinkle half the mixture over the potatoes and roast for 10 minutes. Flip the potatoes and brush with the remaining olive oil mixture and sprinkle with the remaining salt mixture. Return to the oven and bake for 10 minutes more. Remove from the oven and sprinkle Parmesan over the potatoes. Return to the oven to melt for 1 minute.

6. To serve, top each smashed potato with a dollop of sour cream and some chopped chives.

> *My sister was with two men in one night. She could hardly walk after that. Can you imagine? Two dinners!* —SARAH SILVERMAN

twice-baked potatoes

When I'm deliriously hungry and looking to eat that something special, I pretend to log onto Gninder (yuppers, that's Chef Gnat + Tinder). I imagine myself scrolling through countless drool-worthy dishes, until I feast my eyes on this double-the-pleasure potato. This union of two steakhouse staples—the twice-baked stuffed potato and creamed spinach—is a match made in heaven. These ingredients have some real chemistry—onions and garlic are sautéed, spinach and dairy are added, and then the lightened-up mixture is mashed with tender potato filling, topped with sharp Swiss, and again baked until golden. Transformed from tiresome tuber to sensational spud, this is no one-night stand. I'm so swiping right.

SERVES: 6–8   PREP TIME: 15 MINS   COOK TIME: 75 MINS

6 large baking potatoes, washed

2 tbsp butter

1 small yellow onion, chopped

2 garlic cloves, minced

1½ tsp kosher salt

½ tsp freshly ground black pepper

1 (10 oz) package frozen chopped spinach, thawed and squeezed out

4 oz light cream cheese

¼ cup 2% milk

¾ cup light sour cream

1¼ cups shredded Swiss cheese, divided

1. Preheat the oven to 425°F. Pierce each potato with a fork several times and place on a baking sheet. Bake for 50–60 minutes, until tender.

2. While the potatoes bake, melt the butter in a large skillet over medium heat. Add the onion and cook for 3 minutes, until softened. Add the garlic, salt, and pepper and cook for 1 minute. Reduce the heat to low and stir in the spinach, cream cheese, and milk. Cook, stirring, until the cream cheese has melted and the mixture is well combined, about 2 minutes. Remove from the heat and set aside.

3. Lower the oven temperature to 400°F. Once the potatoes are cool enough to handle, cut lengthwise and scoop out the potato flesh, leaving a thin layer to keep the potato shell's shape.

4. Place the potato flesh in a large mixing bowl and mash together with the spinach mixture, sour cream, and ¾ cup of the Swiss cheese.

5. Scoop and mound the potato mixture into 8 of the shell halves (you can use the 4 empty shells for potato skins) and sprinkle the remaining ½ cup of Swiss cheese over the potatoes. Bake at 400°F for 10 minutes, until heated through and cheese is melted.

ginger tofu stir-fry
WITH COCONUT RICE

I can't read a balance sheet to save my life, but as this book's keeper, I can assure you that with this stir-fry there is accounting for taste. The building block, protein-rich tofu, gets crisped (but not fried) until golden, and along with a veritable vegetable garden, is smothered in a savory and spicy stir-fry sauce. With the value-add of aromatic, fluffy coconut rice, this majorly marketable meal is a weeknight whiz that's quick, easy, and healthy. All assets, no liabilities—you're going to get a huge return on your investment when you heat up your wok and get cooking the book(s). See? It all adds up.

Coconut Rice

1½ cups jasmine rice, rinsed and drained

1¾ cups canned coconut milk

1 cup water

½ tsp kosher salt

Stir-Fry Sauce

¼ cup soy sauce

¼ cup + 1 tbsp water, divided

2 tbsp honey

1 tbsp fresh lime juice

1 tbsp oyster sauce

½ tsp chili paste (such as sambal oelek)

2 tbsp cornstarch

Tofu

1 (12 oz) package extra-firm tofu

⅛ tsp kosher salt

⅛ tsp freshly ground black pepper

1 tbsp cornstarch

1 tbsp vegetable oil

Stir-Fry

1 small yellow onion, thinly sliced

1½ cups sugar snap peas

1 red bell pepper, sliced into strips

1 carrot, peeled and sliced on the diagonal

2 garlic cloves, minced

2 tsp grated fresh ginger

3 tbsp chopped fresh basil

1. For the coconut rice, in a medium saucepan, combine the rice, coconut milk, water, and salt. Bring to a boil over high heat and then cover and reduce the heat to low. Cook for 15 minutes, remove from the heat, and let sit covered for 5 minutes. Set aside.

2. For the stir-fry sauce, in a medium bowl, whisk together the soy sauce, ¼ cup of the water, honey, lime juice, oyster sauce, and chili paste. In a small bowl, combine the cornstarch and remaining 1 tablespoon water until dissolved. Whisk into the sauce and set aside.

3. Meanwhile, for the tofu, cut the block into 3 slices and press firmly with paper towels to absorb excess moisture. Cut the slices into cubes and toss with salt, pepper, and cornstarch. Heat the vegetable oil in a large skillet over medium heat. Cook the tofu for 2 minutes without flipping the pieces to allow them to become golden brown. Stir and continue to cook until all the sides are golden, total of about 6 minutes. Transfer the tofu to a plate.

4. For the stir-fry, using the same skillet over medium heat, add the onions, sugar snap peas, red pepper, carrot, garlic, and ginger. Cook, stirring, for 4 minutes, until the vegetables have softened. Add the stir-fry sauce and tofu and continue cooking for 1–2 minutes, stirring until the sauce thickens and the tofu and vegetables are well coated. Remove from the heat and stir in the basil. Serve over the coconut rice.

Make it gluten-free: Use gluten-free tamari or gluten-free soy sauce, and gluten-free oyster sauce

moroccan couscous

WITH CHICKPEAS & HARISSA

ant to Rock the Casbah, or at the very least, the Kitchen? No sweat. Grab a jar of harissa, the versatile North African spice mix that's a fierce combo of chili peppers, red peppers, garlic, salt, and olive oil. Imparting huge flavor, aroma, and spice, harissa's the perfect boost to this simple and speedy (done in 20 minutes) side dish, where mild couscous soaks up all the flavors, and red onions are sautéed to bring out their sweetness, with iron-rich spinach and creamy, protein-packed chickpeas rounding out the dish. Add the cooling freshness of mint, tartness of lemon, and sweet crunch of pomegranate seeds, and get ready to Shake Up the Souk, warm spices and all.

SERVES: 4-6   PREP TIME: 10 MINS   COOK TIME: 10 MINS

2 cups vegetable or chicken broth

1 cup couscous

1 tbsp olive oil

1 small red onion, chopped

1 red bell pepper, chopped

1 garlic clove, minced

1–2 tbsp harissa paste, depending on desired spice level

2 cups packed spinach, chopped

1 cup canned chickpeas, rinsed and drained

¼ tsp kosher salt

¼ tsp freshly ground black pepper

¼ cup fresh mint, chopped

1 tbsp fresh lemon juice

½ tsp lemon zest

1 cup pomegranate seeds, for garnish

1. In a small saucepan, bring the broth to a boil. Stir in the couscous, cover, and remove from the heat. Let stand for 5 minutes and then fluff with a fork.

2. Add the olive oil to a large skillet over medium heat. Add the red onion and cook for 3–4 minutes, until softened. Stir in the red peppers, garlic, and harissa. Cook for 1 minute. Add the cooked couscous, chopped spinach, chickpeas, salt, and pepper. Continue to cook for 1 minute, until the spinach is wilted. Stir in the mint, lemon juice, and lemon zest. Remove from the heat and garnish each serving with pomegranate seeds.

A good spicy challenge strikes a balance between flavor and fear.

—ADAM RICHMAN

tomato sauce with pappardelle

At book signings, you get three types of people: the avid fan, the can-I-just-have-a-cookie person, and the one who will amble by our table and declare, "Thanks, but I don't cook." Well, slow your stroll because now thanks to this no-sweat, no-cook pasta sauce, I can reply, "No problem. We have just the recipe for you." Simple and speedy to pull off, tomatoes, zucchini, garlic, and fresh herbs marinate together in olive oil to develop flavors and 15 minutes later, are tossed with freshly cooked pasta and Parmesan cheese. Easier than microwaving a meal (and a whole lot healthier), this bright, fragrant, and flavorful dish will definitely ignite a passion for not cooking.

SERVES: 4   PREP TIME: 10 MINS (+ marinating)   COOK TIME: 15 MINS

3 tbsp olive oil

2 garlic cloves, finely minced

1½ cups halved cherry tomatoes

1 large zucchini, diced

3 tbsp chopped fresh basil

2 tbsp chopped fresh flat-leaf parsley

½ tsp kosher salt

½ tsp freshly ground black pepper

¼ tsp crushed red pepper flakes

½ lb uncooked pappardelle pasta

¼ cup freshly grated Parmesan cheese

¼ cup shaved Parmesan cheese, for garnish

1. In a large bowl, combine the olive oil, garlic, tomatoes, zucchini, basil, parsley, salt, pepper, and red pepper flakes. Toss and let marinate for 15 minutes.

2. While the tomato mixture marinates, cook the pappardelle pasta in a large pot of boiling salted water until al dente. Drain the pasta.

3. Toss the hot pasta with the tomato mixture and grated Parmesan. Serve immediately and garnish each serving with shaved Parmesan.

Make it gluten-free: Use gluten-free pasta

lessons *from* lisa

Since olive oil is the base of your sauce, make sure to use a high-quality olive oil.

avocado pesto pasta
WITH ITALIAN CHICKEN

I'm a huge fan of the portmanteau, when two words are combined to make one. While considering our moniker (Jusa? JuLisa? Luli?), I came up with one to categorize this incredible dish: ItalCal. Borrowing pesto, the traditional Italian favorite, and merging it with vibrant California avocados, our shero (she/hero) has cooked up delicious weeknight wellness. Lighter and fresher than the classic pesto, avocado lends creaminess and nutrients to the garlicky, velvety pine nut and basil sauce, which coats tender pasta and pairs ridonkulously (ridiculously/donkey) well with simple baked Italian-herbed chicken. Get ready to dish out ginormous (giant/enormous) bowls of this ItalCal cuisine.

SERVES: 4   PREP TIME: 15 MINS   COOK TIME: 30 MINS

Baked Italian Chicken

4 boneless, skinless chicken breasts, pounded to an even 1-inch thickness

2 tbsp olive oil

1 tbsp dried Italian seasoning

½ tsp garlic powder

½ tsp kosher salt

¼ tsp freshly ground black pepper

Avocado Pesto Pasta

¾ lb uncooked linguine

¼ cup pine nuts

1 cup packed fresh basil

1 garlic clove

1 large ripe avocado, pitted

¼ cup olive oil

1 tbsp fresh lemon juice

1 tsp kosher salt

¼ tsp freshly ground black pepper

Pinch red pepper flakes

½ cup freshly grated Parmesan cheese, divided

Fresh basil, for garnish

1. For the chicken, preheat the oven to 425°F. Line a baking sheet with parchment paper.

2. In a large bowl, toss the chicken with the olive oil, Italian seasoning, garlic powder, salt, and pepper. Place the chicken on the baking sheet and bake for 15 minutes. Allow the chicken to rest for 5 minutes before slicing thinly.

3. For the pasta, bring a large pot of salted water to a boil. Cook the linguine until al dente. Reserve ¼ cup of pasta water. Drain the linguine and set aside.

4. While the pasta is cooking, prepare the pesto. In a small skillet over medium heat, toast the pine nuts, stirring frequently, until lightly toasted and golden, 2–3 minutes. Remove from the skillet and cool slightly.

5. Add the pine nuts, basil, and garlic to a food processor. Pulse on and off until well chopped. Add the avocado, olive oil, lemon juice, salt, pepper, and red pepper flakes. Process until the pesto is creamy and smooth.

6. Toss the linguine with the pesto and ¼ cup Parmesan. Add as much pasta water as you like to loosen the texture. Sprinkle the remaining Parmesan over the linguine and top with the sliced chicken. Garnish with fresh basil and serve immediately.

+ **Make it gluten-free: Use gluten-free pasta**

zucchini noodles

You may already know this, but puttanesca loosely translates to "in the style of prostitutes." Kind of appropriate, when you consider that Lisa, aka lady of the kitchen, has created a super-easy sauce that's both full-bodied and supremely satisfying. To put it bluntly, it's a sure thing, a seductive siren that will get you hooked on its robust flavors and intoxicating aroma. Briny olives and capers, spicy chili flakes, and juicy tomatoes all combine in this chunky, tangy, rich, and savory Italian sauce made up of simple ingredients. When you spread this atop raw zucchini noodles, you can rest assured that this healthy, invigorating dish won't weigh you down or empty your wallet.

SERVES: 4   PREP TIME: 15 MINS   COOK TIME: 15 MINS

Puttanesca Sauce

2 tbsp olive oil

1 small yellow onion, chopped

3 garlic cloves, minced

¼–½ tsp crushed red pepper flakes (according to how much spice you like)

¼ tsp kosher salt

¼ tsp freshly ground black pepper

½ cup pitted Kalamata olives, chopped

3 tbsp capers, drained and coarsely chopped

1 tbsp olive brine

1 (28 oz) can whole tomatoes, crushed by hand

¼ cup chopped fresh flat-leaf parsley

2 tbsp chopped fresh basil

4 medium zucchini, ends removed

Freshly grated Parmesan cheese, to serve

1. For the sauce, in a large skillet, heat the olive oil over medium heat. Add the onion and cook for 3 minutes. Add the garlic, red pepper flakes, salt, and pepper, stirring for 1 minute. Add the olives, capers, and olive brine, cooking for another minute. Stir in the tomatoes and bring to a boil. Lower the heat and simmer the sauce for 10 minutes, stirring occasionally. Remove from the heat and stir in the parsley and basil.

2. While the sauce is cooking, use a spiralizer to create the zucchini noodles.

3. Place the noodles in a large serving bowl, toss with the puttanesca sauce, and serve with Parmesan cheese. Serve immediately.

I even got exotic capers. I didn't know what those were, but they're like salty peas.

— BUMPER, PITCH PERFECT 2

autumn pumpkin
& FRESH HERB FUSILLI

Pumpkins have been pigeonholed as something to put on your front porch or in your pie plate. Well, not anymore, because out-of-her-gourd-Gnat has found a way to bring this healthy powerhouse (more fiber than kale, more potassium than bananas, and full of magnesium, iron, and vitamins) to the main event, aka weekday dinner, with this 25-minute meal. While every creamy bite may feel indulgent, it isn't—there's no cream in this velvety, simple sauce, with wholesome pumpkin puree adding a rich sweetness, along with savory sage, earthy rosemary, and fresh Parmesan. Comforting and combined to deliver the warmth, flavors, and aromas of fall, you no longer have to wait for dessert to get your pumpkin fix.

SERVES: 4   PREP TIME: 10 MINS   COOK TIME: 15 MINS

1 tbsp butter

1 tbsp olive oil

1 small yellow onion, chopped

2 garlic cloves, minced

1 tsp minced fresh sage

1 tsp minced fresh rosemary

½ tsp kosher salt

¼ tsp freshly ground black pepper

Pinch cayenne pepper

1½ cups (15 oz can) pumpkin puree

1½ cups chicken broth

½ cup freshly grated Parmesan cheese, divided

¾ lb uncooked fusilli pasta

1 cup baby arugula, for garnish

1. In a large skillet or saucepan over medium heat, melt the butter and olive oil. Add the onion and cook until softened, 3 minutes. Add the garlic, sage, rosemary, salt, pepper, and cayenne. Cook, stirring constantly, for 1 minute. Stir in the pumpkin puree and chicken broth. Allow the mixture to simmer over medium heat, stirring occasionally, for 8 minutes. Remove from the heat and stir in ¼ cup of the Parmesan.

2. While the sauce simmers, bring a large pot of cold salted water to a boil and cook the fusilli until al dente. Reserve ¼ cup of pasta water and drain the pasta.

3. Stir the pasta into the pumpkin sauce and reheat over low heat, adding a splash of the reserved pasta water if necessary to loosen the sauce.

4. To serve, sprinkle each serving with the remaining ¼ cup Parmesan and a small handful of arugula.

+ Make it gluten-free: Use gluten-free pasta

lessons *from* lisa

★ If you can't find fresh sage, fresh marjoram is a good substitute.

turkey ragu

Lisa can't lie (unless she's telling me how good I look in my jeans), so you can rest assured that when she says this lightened-up ragu delivers all the heartiness and flavor of the classic Italian sauce, it's a fact. Wholesome, fast, and filling, it's almost too good to be true. While this sauce seems decadent, it's healthy, with lean turkey and white wine taking the place of red meat and heavy cream, the depth of flavor conjuring up a long-simmering, authentic three-day Bolognese. The honest truth is that it only takes 45 minutes. And, while you might imagine this sauce is labor intensive, it's in fact super easy, with your food processor doing all the work. But don't take my word for it (I've been known to fib)—the proof is in Can't-Lie-Lisa's thick, rich-tasting ragu.

SERVES: 6   PREP TIME: 10 MINS.   COOK TIME: 35 MINS

1 medium red onion, coarsely chopped

2 celery stalks, chopped

2 carrots, peeled and chopped

3 garlic cloves, minced

½ cup chopped fresh flat-leaf parsley

2 tsp chopped fresh rosemary

¼ tsp crushed red pepper flakes

1½ lb ground turkey

1½ tsp kosher salt

¾ tsp freshly ground black pepper

1 cup dry white wine

1 (5.5 oz) can tomato paste

1 (28 oz) can crushed tomatoes

1 lb uncooked spaghetti

Freshly grated Parmesan cheese, to serve

1. Using a food processor or blender, combine the red onion, celery, carrots, garlic, parsley, rosemary, and crushed red pepper flakes. Pulse on and off until the ingredients are finely chopped.

2. Transfer the vegetables to a large pot and add the ground turkey. Place over medium-high heat and cook, breaking up the turkey with a wooden spoon. Continue cooking for 10 minutes until the turkey is cooked through and the vegetables are softened. Add the salt and pepper. Add the white wine and increase the heat to high, letting it cook down for 3 minutes. Stir in the tomato paste and crushed tomatoes and bring to a boil. Reduce the heat to low, partially cover, and cook the sauce for 20 minutes, stirring occasionally.

3. While the sauce cooks, bring a large pot of salted cold water to a boil. Cook the spaghetti until al dente and drain well. Toss with the ragu sauce and serve with the Parmesan cheese.

Make it gluten-free: Use gluten-free pasta

eggplant bolognese

Y ou can learn a lot about people by their most frequently used emojis. Based on the keyboards I've seen, I'd say there are lots of people hungry for eggplant. Not ones to deny wishes, we've set aside the meat and put the popular purple nightshade front and center in this incredibly easy and hearty vegetarian Bolognese sauce. With chunks of eggplant roasted until caramelized and mushrooms sautéed with onions and garlic, this delicious, aromatic, and deeply satisfying Bolognese serves up bites that eggplant addicts everywhere have been clamoring for.

SERVES: 4–6   PREP TIME: 15 MINS   COOK TIME: 35 MINS

2 small eggplants, cut into 1-inch cubes (about 4½ cups)

4 tbsp olive oil, divided

1¼ tsp kosher salt, divided

¼ tsp freshly ground black pepper

1 small yellow onion, chopped

¾ lb mixed mushrooms, such as shiitake and Portobello, stemmed and chopped

3 garlic cloves, minced

1 tsp dried oregano

½ tsp red pepper flakes

¼ cup dry red wine

1 (28 oz) can San Marzano tomatoes

1 lb uncooked rigatoni pasta

¼ cup coarsely chopped fresh basil

Freshly grated Parmesan cheese, for serving

1. Preheat the oven to 450°F. Line a baking sheet with aluminum foil and coat with nonstick cooking spray.

2. Toss the eggplants in a bowl with 2 tablespoons of the olive oil, ¼ teaspoon of the salt, and the pepper. Transfer to the prepared baking sheet and roast for 15–16 minutes, stirring halfway, until tender and golden. Remove from the oven and set aside.

3. In a large skillet over medium heat, add the remaining 2 tablespoons of olive oil. Add the onion, stirring to coat. Stir in the mushrooms and remaining teaspoon of salt. Cook, stirring frequently, until the moisture has evaporated, about 8 minutes. Add the garlic, oregano, and red pepper flakes and cook for 1 minute. Stir in the red wine, stirring continuously for about 1 minute. Using your hands, crush the tomatoes as you add them to the skillet. Lower the heat and simmer the sauce for 10 minutes.

4. Meanwhile, bring a large pot of lightly salted water to a boil. Cook the rigatoni according to package directions until tender but slightly al dente. Drain and place in a serving bowl. Remove the sauce from the heat and stir in the roasted eggplant and fresh basil. Top the pasta with sauce and finish with the fresh Parmesan cheese.

+ **Make it gluten-free: Use gluten-free pasta**

lessons *from* lisa

★ *Serve leftover sauce with eggs for brunch.*

southwestern chicken & rice

I've no idea who let the dogs out and I find it hard to imagine that everybody was kung fu fighting. But what I can tell you with 100 percent certainty is that there's nothing fleeting about the success of this one-pan wonder. Guaranteed to be in heavy rotation, this meal is a hitmaker, a huge win for every weeknight warrior needing to get a wholesome, family-friendly meal on the table. Quick and simple, this all-in-one dish is the real deal—chicken is seasoned with Tex-Mex spices and cooked up in the same skillet with long-grain rice, peppers, onions, tomatoes, corn, and black beans. Unlike "La Macarena," this fuss-free, perfectly spiced, and satisfying dish has some serious staying power.

SERVES: 6   PREP TIME: 10 MINS   COOK TIME: 35 MINS

Spice Rub

¾ tsp kosher salt

½ tsp ground cumin

½ tsp smoked paprika

½ tsp chili powder

¼ tsp freshly ground black pepper

Chicken and Rice

4 boneless, skinless chicken breasts, pounded to even thickness

2 tbsp olive oil

1 small yellow onion, chopped

1 red bell pepper, chopped

1 garlic clove, minced

1 tsp kosher salt

½ tsp ground cumin

½ tsp chili powder

continued on next page

1. For the spice rub, combine salt, cumin, smoked paprika, chili powder, and pepper.

2. For the chicken, season both sides of the chicken breasts with the spice rub.

3. Heat the olive oil in a large skillet over medium-high heat. Add the chicken and cook 5 minutes per side, or until cooked through and no longer pink. Once the chicken is cool enough to handle, chop into bite-sized pieces and set aside.

4. In the same skillet over medium heat, add the onion, red peppers, garlic, salt, cumin, and chili powder. Cook for 4 minutes, stirring frequently, until the onions are softened. Add the rice and stir for 1 minute. Add the drained tomatoes and chicken broth. Bring to a boil, cover, and reduce the heat, simmering for 15 minutes, until the rice is cooked. Stir in the black beans, corn, and chopped chicken. Sprinkle the Monterey Jack cheese evenly over top. Cover and let the cheese melt for 2 minutes. Serve each portion with a spoonful of sour cream, chopped avocado, cilantro, and a lime wedge.

ingredients continued

1½ cups jasmine rice (or any long-grain rice)

1 (14 oz) can diced tomatoes, drained

3½ cups chicken broth

1 cup canned black beans, rinsed and drained

1 cup fresh or thawed frozen corn

¾ cup shredded Monterey Jack cheese

Garnish

¾ cup sour cream

1 large ripe avocado, chopped

Cilantro

Lime wedges

orange chicken

I 've got sticky notes everywhere. While some are cryptic messages I can't decipher ("Fly") and others uplifting clichés ("Collect moments not things"), one Post-It, the one with the digits to my favorite Chinese food restaurant, has been ignored ever since Lisa created a recipe inspired by my go-to takeout dish. This Sticky Orange Chicken has it all, minus the deadly deep-fried batter: chicken is browned in the pan to give it a nice crust, finished in the oven to keep it succulent, and coated in a delectable orange marmalade sauce that's sweet, tangy, and, you guessed it, sticky. Healthy, easy, and irresistible, this orange chicken is destined to become your house special, the answer to all those sticky weeknight dinner situations.

SERVES: 4   PREP TIME: 10 MINS   COOK TIME: 20 MINS

4 boneless, skinless chicken breasts

2 tbsp olive oil, divided

½ tsp garlic powder

½ tsp ground ginger

¼ tsp paprika

¾ tsp kosher salt

¼ tsp freshly ground black pepper

Sticky Orange Sauce

⅓ cup orange marmalade

¼ cup orange juice

2 tbsp rice vinegar

2 tbsp soy sauce

1 tbsp honey

1 garlic clove, minced

¼ tsp ground ginger

1 tbsp cornstarch

2 tbsp water

1 navel orange, thinly sliced, for garnish

Sliced green onions, for garnish

1. Preheat the oven to 425°F. Line a baking sheet with aluminum foil and coat with nonstick cooking spray.

2. Rub the chicken breasts with 1 tablespoon of the olive oil.

3. In a small bowl, combine the garlic powder, ginger, paprika, salt, and pepper. Sprinkle over both sides of chicken breasts.

4. In a large skillet, heat the remaining tablespoon of olive oil over medium-high heat. Add the chicken and sear for 2 minutes per side, until golden on the outside. Transfer the chicken to the prepared baking sheet and bake for 12–14 minutes until cooked through. Remove from the oven and let the chicken rest for 5 minutes before slicing on the diagonal.

5. While the chicken is baking, prepare the orange sauce. In a small saucepan, combine the orange marmalade, orange juice, rice vinegar, soy sauce, honey, garlic, and ginger. Bring to a boil over medium heat and cook for 1 minute.

6. In a small bowl, combine the cornstarch and water, mixing to dissolve the cornstarch. Whisk the cornstarch mixture into the saucepan, whisking continuously until the sauce thickens.

7. To serve, spoon the orange sauce over the sliced chicken and garnish with orange slices and green onions.

+ **Make it gluten-free: Use gluten-free tamari or gluten-free soy sauce**

sesame-baked
chicken strips

WITH SLAW

Sometimes there's an itch you just gotta scratch, and in our case, it's the constant yen for feel-good comfort food. While we've nixed our quest for "healthy" mac 'n' cheese, Lisa's streamlined chicken fingers for the adult diet and palate with these baked-not-fried scrumptious strips dipped in a hoisin-lime mixture, coated with sesame seeds, and baked until crunchy. The perfect balance of flavors and textures proves that yes, my sis is really up to scratch.

Quick Pickled Slaw

1½ cups English cucumber, cut into ½-inch pieces

1½ cups thinly sliced red cabbage

¾ cup peeled and thinly sliced carrots

⅓ cup rice vinegar

2 tbsp sugar

1 tbsp fresh lime juice

½ tsp kosher salt

Dipping Sauce

½ cup light mayonnaise

1 tbsp mirin

1 tbsp soy sauce

½ tsp Sriracha hot sauce

Sesame Chicken Strips

¼ cup flour

½ tsp kosher salt, divided

2 eggs

2 tbsp hoisin sauce

1 tbsp fresh lime juice

1 cup panko (Japanese breadcrumbs)

½ cup breadcrumbs

3 tbsp white sesame seeds

3 tbsp black sesame seeds

4 boneless, skinless chicken breasts, cut in strips

3 tbsp olive oil

1. For the slaw, place the cucumbers, cabbage, and carrots in a small serving bowl.

2. In a saucepan, combine the rice vinegar, sugar, lime juice, and salt. Heat over medium heat for 2 minutes. Let cool for 10 minutes and pour over the vegetables. Cover and refrigerate for 1 hour, or up to 5 days.

3. For the dipping sauce, whisk together the mayonnaise, mirin, soy sauce, and Sriracha. Refrigerate until ready to serve.

4. For the chicken strips, preheat the oven to 400°F. Place a wire cooling rack over a baking sheet and spray the rack with nonstick cooking spray.

5. Place the flour and ¼ teaspoon of the salt in a shallow bowl. In a medium bowl, whisk together the eggs, hoisin sauce, and lime juice. In a third bowl, combine the panko, breadcrumbs, white and black sesame seeds, and the remaining ¼ teaspoon of salt.

6. Coat the chicken strips in flour and then dip in the egg mixture, letting any excess drip off. Dredge in the panko–sesame seed mixture, pressing to make the mixture stick. Place the chicken strips on prepared cooling rack, drizzle with olive oil, and bake for 15 minutes, or until the chicken is cooked through. Serve with dipping sauce and pickled slaw.

Quite frankly, I just don't give a cluck.

—ANONYMOUS

sheet-pan dinner

Ever wonder why there aren't commercials for dishpan hands anymore? Growing up, given the airplay it got, it felt like an epidemic, and Madge the manicurist (remember the "You're soaking in it" slogan?) was the savior. Forty years later, Lisa is still haunted by the drudgery of dishwashing and has come up with the surefire way to forever eradicate unsightly hands: the one-pan dinner. This recipe has it all—juicy baked chicken, lemony herbed potatoes, peppers and zucchini, and the Mediterranean trifecta of tzatziki, feta, and olives—on a single sheet pan. So quick and delicious, with your lady-of-leisure hands intact, the only thing you'll be left to ponder is how Calgon will take you away.

SERVES: 4   PREP TIME: 15 MINS   COOK TIME: 20 MINS

Tzatziki Sauce

1 cup plain Greek yogurt

1 cup grated English cucumber

2 tbsp white wine vinegar

2 tbsp olive oil

1 tbsp chopped fresh dill

1 garlic clove, finely minced

½ tsp kosher salt

Spice Mix

1 tbsp dried oregano

1 tsp dried basil

1 tsp dried thyme

½ tsp lemon zest

½ tsp kosher salt

¼ tsp garlic powder

¼ tsp freshly ground black pepper

Chicken and Vegetables

4 boneless, skinless chicken breasts, cut in half on the diagonal

2 tbsp olive oil, divided

continued above

1 lb new potatoes, cut in half

2 red bell peppers, cut in chunks

1 large zucchini, cut into ½-inch-thick half moons

1 (19 oz) can diced tomatoes, drained

1 lemon, washed and thinly sliced

2 garlic cloves, sliced

¾ cup crumbled feta cheese

18 Kalamata olives, pitted

1. Preheat the oven to 425°F. Line a rimmed baking sheet with aluminum foil and coat with nonstick cooking spray.

2. For the tzatziki sauce, in a medium bowl, combine the yogurt, grated cucumber, white wine vinegar, olive oil, dill, garlic, and salt. Whisk well to combine. Refrigerate until ready to use.

3. For the spice mix, in a small bowl, combine the oregano, basil, thyme, lemon zest, salt, garlic powder, and pepper. Divide the spice mixture in half.

4. In a large bowl, toss the chicken breasts with 1 tablespoon of the olive oil and half the spice mixture. Spread the chicken out over the prepared baking sheet.

5. In another bowl, toss together the potatoes, red peppers, zucchini, diced tomatoes, the remaining tablespoon of olive oil, and the remaining spice mix. Arrange the vegetables around the chicken. Scatter the lemon slices and garlic slices throughout the pan. Bake in the preheated oven for 20 minutes, or until the chicken is cooked through. Top the chicken and vegetables with feta cheese and olives. Serve with tzatziki sauce.

chicken pad SEE EW

I wish we could have a do-over. While we rocked it on *Family Feud* (Lisa encouraged us with, "Good answer, good answer," our bro was lightning fast on the buzzer, and I got to make out with Richard Dawson), I goofed in the Fast Money round. You might have too if you were the second person to answer, "Name something associated with Thai cooking." Once Pad Thai was said, I was done for. Until now. Meet Chicken Pad See Ew, Thailand's other scrumptious, super-popular street food, rice noodles coated in a sweet and savory sauce, with chicken, Chinese broccoli, and eggs scrambled in. Fast and super simple to make, this Chicken Pad See Ew is definitely the answer everyone is looking for when craving winning family food. Survey says, "Delicious dinner."

SERVES: 4–6   PREP TIME: 15 MINS (+ soaking)   COOK TIME: <10 MINS

1 (8 oz) package dried wide rice stick noodles or square rice flakes

½ lb boneless, skinless chicken breasts, thinly sliced

1 tsp dark soy sauce

1 tsp vegetable oil

2 tsp cornstarch

Sweet and Savory Sauce

2 tbsp sweet soy sauce (also known as kecap manis)

1 tbsp rice vinegar

2 tsp dark soy sauce

2 tsp oyster sauce

1 tbsp vegetable oil

2 garlic cloves, minced

¾ lb Chinese broccoli, leaves and stems separated, stems cut into thin sticks

2 eggs, lightly whisked

1. To prepare the rice noodles, place them in a large bowl and completely cover with boiling water. Soak for 15–20 minutes, depending on the thickness of your noodles. Drain, rinse under cold water, and drain well before setting aside.

2. In a medium bowl, combine the chicken with the dark soy sauce, vegetable oil, and cornstarch. Set aside.

3. For the sweet and savory sauce, in a small bowl, whisk together the sweet soy sauce, rice vinegar, dark soy sauce, and oyster sauce until well combined. Set aside.

4. In a wok or large skillet, heat the vegetable oil and garlic over high heat for 1 minute. Add the chicken and Chinese broccoli stems and stir-fry for 3 minutes. Lower the heat to medium and push the chicken and Chinese broccoli to the side of your wok. Add the eggs, allowing them to set slightly before scrambling. After 1 minute, toss the egg with the chicken mixture. Return the heat to high and add the drained rice noodles, sweet and savory sauce, and Chinese broccoli leaves. Stir continuously for 2 minutes until the leaves are wilted and the sauce is incorporated. Serve immediately.

Make it gluten-free: Use gluten-free tamari or gluten-free soy sauce, and gluten-free oyster sauce

grilled chicken

This recipe is for those who claim to read our books cover to cover. First, thanks, thanks so much. Second, this is a test and I'll know you're telling the truth if you hug my sister tight and whisper in her ear, "I read the fine print." Finally, and best of all, your prize for being a superfan is this fast and delicious chicken recipe that's definitely going to get you dinnertime devotees of your own. The ultimate in easy, this recipe uses a sweet and spicy rub to coat the chicken to give it a great crust and lock in the juiciness, which is then amped up with smoky flavors from the grill and finished off with a homemade maple-chipotle barbecue sauce. Read it and eat, friends, read it and eat.

SERVES: 6   **PREP TIME: 10 MINS**   **COOK TIME: 25 MINS**

Maple-Chipotle Barbecue Sauce

½ cup ketchup

4 tbsp pure maple syrup

2 tbsp apple cider vinegar

2 finely chopped canned chipotle peppers in adobo sauce, seeds removed (use 1 for less spice)

2 tsp Dijon mustard

2 tsp Worcestershire sauce

½ tsp garlic powder

½ tsp smoked paprika

½ tsp kosher salt

Spice Rub

1 tsp smoked paprika

1 tsp brown sugar

½ tsp kosher salt

½ tsp ground cumin

½ tsp garlic powder

¼ tsp chipotle powder

¼ tsp freshly ground black pepper

6 boneless, skinless chicken breasts

1 tbsp olive oil

1. For the barbecue sauce, in a saucepan, whisk together the ketchup, maple syrup, apple cider vinegar, chipotle peppers, mustard, Worcestershire sauce, garlic powder, smoked paprika, and salt. Bring the mixture to a boil, reduce the heat to low, and simmer for 10 minutes, stirring occasionally. Set aside ¼ cup of the sauce for basting.

2. For the spice rub, in a small bowl, combine the smoked paprika, brown sugar, salt, cumin, garlic powder, chipotle powder, and pepper.

3. Place the chicken in a large bowl and toss with the olive oil. Sprinkle the spice rub over the chicken, coating well on both sides. Let the chicken marinate while the barbecue preheats.

4. Preheat a lightly oiled grill to medium-high. Grill the chicken for 5–7 minutes per side, depending on thickness, until cooked through. For the final minute of cooking, baste both sides with barbecue sauce and cook for a further 30 seconds per side. Serve with the remaining barbecue sauce.

+ Make it gluten-free: Use gluten-free chipotle peppers, and gluten-free Worcestershire sauce

chicken tacos

I'm not in denial. I fully admit I can't quit these tacos. Lisa, Queen of the Chicken Cartel, has me under her spell with these terrific tacos, guaranteed to ignite appetites, deliver flavor fixes, and satisfy crunchy cravings everywhere. One bite and you too will be done for, hooked on crispy baked chicken tossed in sweet and savory homemade barbecue sauce (which takes five minutes and is totally worth it) and wrapped in a soft tortilla with crunchy fresh coleslaw and creamy avocado dressing. Simple to make and impossible to stop eating, this delicious dinnertime habit is one you're never going to want to kick.

SERVES: 4–6   PREP TIME: 25 MINS   COOK TIME: 20 MINS

Barbecue Sauce

¾ cup ketchup

⅓ cup brown sugar

3 tbsp water

2 tbsp apple cider vinegar

1 tbsp honey

2 tsp Worcestershire sauce

1 tsp mustard powder

½ tsp kosher salt

¼ tsp garlic powder

¼ tsp freshly ground black
   pepper

Breaded Baked Chicken

¼ cup flour

¼ tsp paprika

½ tsp kosher salt, divided

½ tsp freshly ground black
   pepper, divided

2 eggs

¾ cup panko (Japanese
   breadcrumbs)

continued on next page

1. For the barbecue sauce, in a small saucepan, combine the ketchup, brown sugar, water, apple cider vinegar, honey, Worcestershire sauce, mustard powder, salt, garlic powder, and pepper. Bring the mixture to a boil over medium heat. Lower the heat and simmer for 4 minutes, whisking occasionally. Remove from the heat.

2. For the chicken, preheat the oven to 375°F. Line a baking sheet with aluminum foil and coat with nonstick cooking spray.

3. Place the flour, paprika, ¼ teaspoon of the salt, and ¼ teaspoon of the pepper in a large bowl. In a medium bowl, whisk the eggs. In a third bowl, combine the panko, breadcrumbs, the remaining ¼ teaspoon of salt, and the remaining ¼ teaspoon of pepper.

4. Toss the chicken in the flour bowl, shake off any excess, and dip each piece in the eggs, letting the excess drip off. Dredge in the panko mixture, pressing to make the mixture stick. Place on the baking sheet and coat the chicken pieces with olive oil–flavored cooking spray. Bake for 15 minutes, or until the chicken is cooked through. Toss the chicken with the barbecue sauce until well coated.

5. For the coleslaw, in a mixing bowl, whisk together the olive oil, lime juice, honey, and salt. Add the cabbage, carrots, parsley, and green onions. Mix to combine and set aside.

¾ cup breadcrumbs

3 boneless, skinless chicken breasts, cut into 2-inch pieces

Crunchy Coleslaw

2 tbsp olive oil

1 tbsp fresh lime juice

1 tsp honey

Pinch kosher salt

4 cups shredded green and purple cabbage

1½ cups peeled and shredded carrots

½ cup chopped fresh flat-leaf parsley

2 tbsp chopped green onions

Avocado Dressing

1 large ripe avocado

½ cup light sour cream

2 tbsp light mayonnaise

1 tbsp fresh lime juice

1 garlic clove, minced

½ tsp kosher salt

¼ tsp ground cumin

⅛ tsp cayenne pepper

10–12 (8-inch) flour tortillas, warmed

Cotija cheese, crumbled, for garnish

Jalapeños, sliced, for garnish (optional)

6. To prepare the avocado dressing, combine the avocado, sour cream, mayonnaise, lime juice, garlic, salt, cumin, and cayenne pepper in a blender. Blend until smooth.

7. To assemble, place a generous serving of coleslaw on the base of a warmed tortilla. Top with about 3 pieces of chicken, drizzle avocado dressing over top, and garnish with cotija cheese and jalapeño slices. Serve immediately.

ON A TACO
bender.

THE ULTIMATE
veggie burger

Lisa, a clever culinary chemist, has had a veggie burger breakthrough in her one-woman research kitchen. Tired of dry and crumbly meatless messes, after much experimentation, she has successfully created a veggie burger with bite, a creative compound of Mediterranean spices, superb slaw, and zesty spread. Cauliflower and chickpeas are blended with cumin, tahini, and citrus, formed into patties, baked until golden, and topped with crunchy fennel apple slaw and a spicy avocado herb spread. With an abundance of fresh flavor and textures, these veggie burgers pass Lisa's Law of Appetite (wholesome, delicious, and inspiring) with flying colors.

MAKES: 8 VEGGIE BURGERS   PREP TIME: 20 MINS (+ refrigeration)
COOK TIME: 20 MINS

Veggie Burgers

5 cups cauliflower florets (1 large head)

1½ cups canned chickpeas, rinsed and drained

5 tsp olive oil, divided

1 small yellow onion, chopped

2 garlic cloves, minced

1 tsp ground cumin

½ tsp ground turmeric

½ tsp kosher salt

½ tsp freshly ground black pepper

¼ tsp red pepper flakes

½ cup breadcrumbs

2 tbsp tahini

2 tbsp fresh lemon juice

1 tsp lemon zest

Fennel Slaw

2 tbsp plain Greek yogurt

2 tbsp chopped fresh flat-leaf parsley

continued on next page

1. For the burgers, in a large pot of salted boiling water, cook the cauliflower florets over medium heat for 5 minutes. Add the chickpeas and cook for 2 minutes more. Drain well.

2. Using a food processor, in 2 batches, pulse the cauliflower and chickpeas 2–3 times, until coarsely chopped (not pureed paste, as you want texture in your burger). Place in a large mixing bowl and set aside.

3. In a medium skillet, heat 3 teaspoons of the olive oil over medium heat. Add the onion and cook for 3 minutes. Stir in the garlic, cumin, turmeric, salt, pepper, and red pepper flakes, stirring constantly for 1 minute.

4. Remove from the heat and add to the mixing bowl with the cauliflower mixture. Add the breadcrumbs, tahini, lemon juice, and lemon zest to the mixing bowl. Mix well until combined.

5. Form into 8 patties and place on a parchment-lined baking sheet. Refrigerate the burgers for 30 minutes.

6. Preheat the oven to 400°F. Brush the tops of the burgers with the remaining 2 teaspoons of olive oil. Bake in the preheated oven for 10 minutes, flip, and bake for 10 minutes more.

7. While the burgers are baking, prepare the fennel slaw and avocado spread. For the fennel slaw, whisk together the yogurt, parsley, mayonnaise, lemon juice, lemon zest, salt, and pepper. Add the fennel and apple and toss well to coat.

1 tbsp light mayonnaise

1 tbsp fresh lemon juice

½ tsp lemon zest

⅛ tsp kosher salt

⅛ tsp freshly ground black
pepper

1 small fennel bulb, halved,
cored, and thinly sliced

1 Granny Smith apple, cored and
cut into matchsticks

Avocado Spread

1 large ripe avocado

¼ cup plain Greek yogurt

2 tbsp light mayonnaise

2 tbsp fresh lime juice

2 tbsp chopped fresh flat-leaf
parsley

1 tbsp chopped jalapeño pepper,
seeds removed

½ tsp kosher salt

¼ tsp ground cumin

¼ tsp freshly ground black
pepper

Pinch cayenne pepper (optional)

8 soft burger buns

8. For the avocado spread, using a food processor, blend the avocado, yogurt, mayonnaise, lime juice, parsley, jalapeño, salt, cumin, pepper, and cayenne pepper until well combined.

9. To assemble, spread the avocado mixture on both the tops and bottoms of the buns. Place a burger on the bottom bun and top with a scoop of fennel slaw and top of the bun. Serve immediately.

+ **Make it gluten-free:** Use gluten-free breadcrumbs, and gluten-free or lettuce wraps

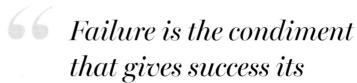

Failure is the condiment that gives success its flavor. —TRUMAN CAPOTE

TAKE A *bite*

teriyaki turkey burgers

WITH GRILLED PINEAPPLE

Goddess Gnat's quite the *wahine* (woman)—with a graceful twist, she's taken the traditionally tasteless turkey burger and danced it into something utterly delicious and tropical. These perfectly seasoned—garlic, ginger, teriyaki sauce—and moist turkey burgers are topped with caramelized pineapple, red onions, and a creamy teriyaki spread and sandwiched between toasted buns. Shake your booty because every bite of these low-fat burgers (yes, paradise found) is an eruption of sweet and savory flavors, a smoothly choreographed and tasty trip to the Aloha State. *Mahalo Lisa, mahalo.*

SERVES: 4   PREP TIME: 20 MINS (+ refrigeration)   COOK TIME: 25 MINS

Teriyaki Sauce

1 tbsp cornstarch

1 tbsp water

¼ cup soy sauce

¼ cup mirin

2 tbsp brown sugar

1 tbsp sake

Turkey Burger

1 lb ground turkey

1 egg

½ cup panko (Japanese breadcrumbs)

2 tbsp finely chopped red onion

2 tbsp chopped fresh flat-leaf parsley

1 garlic clove, minced

1 tsp grated fresh ginger

¼ tsp freshly ground black pepper

continued on next page

1. For the teriyaki sauce, combine the cornstarch and water in a small dish and stir to dissolve. Set aside.

2. In a small saucepan over medium-low heat, combine the soy sauce, mirin, brown sugar, and sake. Bring to a boil and whisk in the cornstarch mixture. Continue to whisk for 3 minutes, until slightly thickened. Remove from the heat and allow to cool.

3. For the turkey burgers, in a large bowl, combine the ground turkey, egg, panko, 3 tablespoons of the teriyaki sauce, red onion, parsley, garlic, ginger, and pepper. Mix just until combined. Form into 4 patties, and using your thumb, make a small indentation in the center of each burger. Place on a plate, cover, and refrigerate for 30 minutes before grilling.

4. For the teriyaki spread, in a small bowl, whisk together the mayonnaise, 3 tablespoons of the teriyaki sauce, lime juice, and Sriracha. Cover and refrigerate until you are ready to assemble the burgers.

5. Preheat a lightly oiled grill to medium-high heat. Place the turkey patties on the grill and cook for 6–8 minutes per side, or until cooked through (reaching an internal temperature of 165°F). During the final minute on the grill, generously brush both sides of the burgers with teriyaki sauce. Remove the burgers from the grill.

Teriyaki Spread

¼ cup light mayonnaise

1 tsp fresh lime juice

1 tsp Sriracha hot sauce

Pineapple and Onions

4 slices fresh pineapple

1 red onion, cut in ½-inch slices

2 tsp vegetable oil

Pinch kosher salt and freshly
  ground black pepper

4 burger buns

4 lettuce leaves (butter, Bibb,
  or Boston)

6. Brush both sides of the pineapple slices and red onions with the vegetable oil and sprinkle with salt and pepper. Place on the grill until charred, about 3 minutes per side. Remove from the grill and quickly toast the burger buns on the grill.

7. To assemble, spread both sides of the toasted buns with the teriyaki spread. Top the buns with lettuce, followed by a turkey burger, pineapple, and red onion. Drizzle with the extra teriyaki sauce. Serve immediately.

+ **Make it gluten-free: Use gluten-free tamari or gluten-free soy sauce, gluten-free panko, and gluten-free buns or lettuce wraps**

lessons *from* lisa

★ *Not looking to grill outdoors? You can make these burgers in a grill pan over medium heat. The timing is the same as on the barbecue.*

top 10 comfort foods

MADE HEALTHIER

spice-rubbed grilled salmon

WITH AVOCADO DRESSING

An unmistakable aroma fills the summer air: it's the intoxicating scent otherwise known as, "I'm having a backyard barbecue, and you're not invited so keep on walking." Well, envy no longer because we're giving you the chance to have your own cookout, complete with smoky smells and salivating neighbors. Rubbed with a homemade blend of savory cumin, oregano, paprika, sweet brown sugar, and zesty lime, this simple, scrumptious, and speedy salmon is perfect for last-minute meals or friend-filled feasts. The grill imparts even more flavor to the spice-crusted fish, leaving it moist inside and crisp outside. Paired with a tangy, refreshing, and creamy avocado yogurt sauce, this healthy salmon, full of protein, vitamin D, and omega-3s, will have everyone drooling at dusk.

SERVES: 4   PREP TIME: 15 MINS   COOK TIME: 10 MINS

Spice Rub

2 tsp brown sugar

1 tsp ground cumin

1 tsp dried oregano

1 tsp kosher salt

½ tsp freshly ground black pepper

½ tsp smoked paprika

½ tsp lime zest

4 salmon fillets (6 oz each)

2 tsp olive oil

Avocado Dressing

1 small ripe avocado, pitted

¼ cup Greek yogurt

2 tbsp chopped fresh flat-leaf parsley

1 tbsp fresh lemon juice

1 small garlic clove, minced

¼ tsp kosher salt

¼ tsp freshly ground black pepper

1. Preheat grill to medium-high. Coat a grill rack with nonstick cooking spray.

2. For the spice rub, in a small bowl, combine the brown sugar, cumin, oregano, salt, pepper, smoked paprika, and lime zest. Mix well.

3. Brush the salmon fillets with the olive oil and divide the spice rub between the pieces to coat them well. Place the salmon, skin side up, on the prepared grill rack. Grill for 4–6 minutes on the first side, flip, and grill 4–5 minutes more, until cooked through.

4. While the salmon is grilling, prepare the avocado dressing. In a blender, combine the avocado, yogurt, parsley, lemon juice, garlic, salt, and pepper. Blend until smooth. Serve alongside the grilled salmon.

lessons *from* lisa

★ *Buy salmon with the skin on it because when grilling, it helps keep the flesh together.*

filet-o-fish

I do deserve a break today, and you know what? So do you, and you're going to get it here thanks to Golden Gnat (over five billion Biters served) and her keen give-the-people-what-they-want palate. Though not a grad of Hamburger U, she's put the healthy in this happy meal with a rejigged riff on the classic fish sandwich. Processed cheese? Gone. Fried filet? Replaced with buttermilk and panko–coated flaky white fish that is baked until crunchy. The tangy tartar sauce has been lightened up and the mushy steamed bun has been swapped out for a sweet toasted brioche. C'mon, sing it with me people . . . duh duh duh da dah, we're lovin' Lisa.

SERVES: 4   PREP TIME: 15 MINS   COOK TIME: 10 MINS

Tartar Sauce

½ cup light mayonnaise

¼ cup plain Greek yogurt

2 tbsp chopped dill pickles

2 tbsp apple cider vinegar

1 tbsp chopped fresh flat-leaf parsley

1 garlic clove, minced

2 tsp capers, drained and chopped

2 tsp finely chopped chives

¼ tsp kosher salt

¼ tsp freshly ground black pepper

Baked Fish

½ cup buttermilk

½ cup panko (Japanese breadcrumbs)

¼ cup flour

¼ tsp mustard powder

¼ tsp paprika

continued above

¼ tsp kosher salt

¼ tsp freshly ground black pepper

4 white fish fillets, such as halibut, cod, grouper, or snapper (6 oz each)

2 tsp olive oil

4 brioche buns, toasted

4 romaine or butter lettuce leaves

1 tomato, sliced into 4 slices

4 dill pickles, sliced

1. For the tartar sauce, whisk together the mayonnaise, yogurt, pickles, apple cider vinegar, parsley, garlic, capers, chives, salt, and pepper until well combined. Cover and refrigerate until ready to assemble.

2. Preheat the oven to 425°F and line a baking sheet with parchment paper.

3. For the baked fish, place the buttermilk in a bowl. In another bowl, combine the panko crumbs, flour, mustard powder, paprika, salt, and pepper. Dip the fish into the buttermilk and then into the panko mixture. Press well to make the coating stick on all sides. Place on the prepared baking sheet, drizzle with olive oil, and bake for 10 minutes, until the fish is cooked through and flakes easily.

4. To assemble, spread a generous amount of tartar sauce on each side of the buns. Place a lettuce leaf on the bottom bun and top with the fish, tomato, pickles, and top bun. Serve immediately.

cod

WITH ALMOND HORSERADISH CRUST

Isn't it kind of ironic that horseradish, which we eat at Passover to remind us of the bitter years of slavery, has a starring role in this toil-free fish dish? A fiery condiment, horseradish, along with shallots, zesty lemon, earthy thyme, and a crunchy almond and fresh breadcrumb topping, does wonders for mild cod. Served up in under 30 minutes (your oven does all the heavy lifting), this fish stays miraculously moist and tender nestled under its golden crust. Tasty and liberating (what are you going to do with that free half hour?), here's your chance to get your horseradish fix without the pain and suffering of gefilte fish.

SERVES: 4   PREP TIME: 10 MINS   COOK TIME: 15 MINS

2 tbsp olive oil, divided

1 cup fresh breadcrumbs
(see lessons from Lisa)

½ cup slivered almonds

1 tbsp chopped shallots

2 tbsp chopped fresh flat-leaf
parsley

1 tbsp jarred horseradish, liquid
squeezed out before measuring

1 tsp lemon zest

1 tsp chopped fresh thyme

¾ tsp kosher salt, divided

½ tsp freshly ground black
pepper, divided

4 cod fillets (6 oz each)

1 tbsp Dijon mustard

Fresh lemon, cut into wedges,
for garnish

1. Preheat the oven to 425°F. Line a baking sheet with parchment paper.

2. In a medium skillet, heat 1 tablespoon of the olive oil over medium heat. Add the breadcrumbs, almonds, and shallots. Stir frequently for 4–5 minutes, until the mixture is lightly toasted. Remove from the heat and stir in the parsley, horseradish, lemon zest, thyme, ½ teaspoon of the salt, and ¼ teaspoon of the pepper.

3. Pat the cod dry with paper towel. Season the fish with the remaining salt and pepper. Place the cod on the prepared baking sheet, skin side down. Brush the top of each piece of fish with the mustard. Press the breadcrumb mixture on top of the fish and drizzle with the remaining tablespoon of olive oil. Bake in the preheated oven for 10–12 minutes, until cooked through. Serve with a wedge of lemon.

+ **Make it gluten-free:** Use gluten-free breadcrumbs

lessons *from* lisa

....

★ *To make 1 cup of fresh breadcrumbs, take 3–4 slices of day-old bread, and pulse a few times in a food processor until you have small crumbs.*

halibut

PICCATA

Contrary to popular belief, it's ridiculously simple to successfully cook fish—all you need to do is dip your toe in the water, and we couldn't think of a more delicious, confidence-boosting way to do it than with this low-on-intimidation, high-on-taste recipe. Mild halibut, the ultimate blank canvas for bright, zesty, and bold flavors, is sautéed until golden, paired with a white wine, lemon, and caper sauce, and complemented with savory sun-dried tomatoes and iron-rich spinach. So impressive (we're talking third-date-dinner or meal with the mother-in-law), this delicious piccata proves that you're the perfect catch.

SERVES: 4   PREP TIME: 10 MINS   COOK TIME: 15 MINS

4 halibut fillets (6 oz each)

½ tsp kosher salt

¼ tsp freshly ground black pepper

¼ cup flour

3 tbsp butter, divided

1 tbsp olive oil

2 garlic cloves, minced

⅓ cup dry white wine

⅓ cup chicken broth

3 tbsp fresh lemon juice

2 tbsp capers, rinsed and drained

2 tbsp coarsely chopped oil-packed sun-dried tomatoes

4 cups packed baby spinach

2 tbsp chopped fresh flat-leaf parsley

Lemon slices, for garnish

1. Pat the halibut dry with paper towel. Season both sides with salt and pepper. Dredge the fish in flour and shake off any excess.

2. In a large nonstick skillet over medium-high heat, add 1 tablespoon of the butter and the olive oil. Add the halibut and sear until the bottom is golden, about 4 minutes. Flip the fish over and continue to cook for 4–5 minutes, until cooked through. Remove the fish to a plate and wipe the skillet clean with paper towel.

3. Add the remaining 2 tablespoons of butter to the skillet and melt over medium heat. Add the garlic and cook for 30 seconds. Stir in the white wine, cooking for 2 minutes until almost evaporated. Add the chicken broth, lemon juice, capers, and sun-dried tomatoes. Bring to a boil, then reduce the heat and simmer the sauce for 2 minutes. Stir in the spinach and parsley, cooking for 1 minute until the spinach is wilted. Return the halibut to the skillet and spoon the sauce over top of the fish to reheat. Serve the halibut with lemon slices.

Bait the hook well: this fish will bite.

—WILLIAM SHAKESPEARE, MUCH ADO ABOUT NOTHING

shrimp
BURRITO BOWLS

OK, so even back in 1785, poet William Cowper knew that "variety's the very spice of life." Fast-forward two centuries and you've got Lisa, our in-house Palate Laureate, well-versed in spice and everything nice, bringing her art to these Shrimp Burrito Bowls. No poetic license necessary, the composition of these bountiful bowls can't be beat— smoky and spicy shrimp, creamy and tangy chipotle dressing, rice studded with lime, black beans, and fresh herbs, and peppers, tomatoes, and avocado, create a healthy, energy-packed combo that only our Bard of the Bite could so lyrically pull together.

Marinade and Shrimp

1 tbsp olive oil

1 tbsp fresh lime juice

1 tbsp chopped canned chipotle pepper in adobo sauce

½ tsp smoked paprika

¼ tsp dried oregano

¼ tsp garlic powder

¼ tsp ground cumin

¼ tsp kosher salt

1 lb (about 20) raw jumbo shrimp, peeled and deveined

1 tbsp olive oil, divided

Creamy Chipotle Dressing

½ cup light mayonnaise

¼ cup buttermilk

2 tbsp chopped fresh flat-leaf parsley

1 tbsp chopped canned chipotle pepper in adobo sauce

1 tsp fresh lime juice

¼ tsp ground cumin

½ tsp kosher salt

Bowls

4 cups cooked white rice

1 cup canned black beans, rinsed and drained

¼ cup chopped fresh flat-leaf parsley

1 tbsp fresh lime juice

½ tsp kosher salt

3 cups chopped romaine lettuce

1 red bell pepper, chopped

1 yellow bell pepper, chopped

1 cup halved cherry tomatoes

1 large ripe avocado, sliced

1. For the marinade, whisk together the olive oil, lime juice, chopped chipotle peppers, smoked paprika, oregano, garlic powder, cumin, and salt. Add the shrimp and marinate at room temperature for 15 minutes.

2. To prepare the chipotle dressing, in a blender, combine the mayonnaise, buttermilk, parsley, chipotle peppers, lime juice, cumin, and salt. Blend until smooth. Refrigerate until ready to use.

3. To cook the shrimp, heat 1½ teaspoons of the olive oil in a large skillet over medium-high heat. Add half the shrimp and sear for about 2 minutes per side, until opaque and cooked through. Repeat with the remaining 1½ teaspoons of olive oil and the remaining shrimp.

4. To assemble the bowls, in a large bowl, toss the cooked rice with the black beans, parsley, lime juice, and salt. Divide between 4 serving bowls. Top each bowl with the cooked shrimp, lettuce, red and yellow peppers, cherry tomatoes, and avocado slices. Drizzle with dressing and serve.

+ **Make it gluten-free: Use gluten-free chipotle peppers**

lessons *from* lisa

In place of white rice, you can also use brown rice, quinoa, or cauliflower rice.

bbq
sloppy
joes
WITH SLAW

o you feel like a hot mess sometimes? We do all the time. So it's no surprise we can't resist this marvelous mess of a sandwich, especially since Lisa's put an unexpected tasty twist on it with the addition of smoked paprika, lending a barbecue flavor and touch of heat, pairing perfectly with lean beef, fresh vegetables, garlic, and spices. Combine this classic comfort food with a refreshing crunchy slaw and tangy sliced pickles, and you've got the ultimate go-to and scrumptiously sloppy weeknight meal. Whether between the buns, on nachos, on baked potatoes, or on your shirt, these BBQ Sloppy Joes are a hot mess, untidy yet undeniably alluring, aromatic, and totally awesome.

SERVES: 6   PREP TIME: 15 MINS   COOK TIME: 30 MINS

BBQ Sloppy Joes

1 tbsp olive oil

1 medium yellow onion, chopped

1 red bell pepper, chopped

1 green bell pepper, chopped

2 garlic cloves, minced

1 tsp kosher salt

½ tsp freshly ground black pepper

1½ lb lean ground beef

1 (14 oz) can diced tomatoes

¼ cup tomato paste

2 tbsp Worcestershire sauce

2 tbsp brown sugar

2 tbsp apple cider vinegar

1 tbsp smoked paprika

1 tbsp Dijon mustard

½ tsp ground cumin

½ tsp dried oregano

2 tbsp chopped fresh flat-leaf parsley

Slaw

4 cups chopped napa cabbage

1 cup chopped red cabbage

½ cup chopped peeled carrots

¼ cup chopped fresh flat-leaf parsley

Slaw Dressing

¼ cup light sour cream

3 tbsp light mayonnaise

1 tbsp apple cider vinegar

1 tsp honey

¼ tsp kosher salt

¼ tsp freshly ground black pepper

6 brioche buns, toasted

24 dill pickle slices

1. For the BBQ sloppy joes, heat the olive oil in a large skillet over medium heat. Add the onion, red pepper, and green pepper, cooking for 4 minutes, until softened. Stir in the garlic, salt, and pepper, cooking for 1 minute more. Turn the heat to medium-high and add the ground beef. Break up the meat until it is cooked through and no longer pink, about 6 minutes. Drain any excess liquid from the pan.

2. Stir in the diced tomatoes, tomato paste, Worcestershire sauce, brown sugar, apple cider vinegar, smoked paprika, mustard, cumin, and oregano. Bring to a boil then lower the heat, simmering partially covered for 20 minutes. Remove from the heat and stir in the parsley.

3. Prepare the slaw while the meat mixture cooks. Toss the napa cabbage, red cabbage, carrots, and parsley together.

4. To make the slaw dressing, in a small bowl, whisk together the sour cream, mayonnaise, apple cider vinegar, honey, salt, and pepper. Mix the coleslaw with the dressing.

5. To assemble, spoon the sloppy joe mixture on the toasted buns. Top with coleslaw and sliced pickles, and serve.

Make it gluten-free: Use gluten-free Worcestershire, and gluten-free buns or lettuce wraps

continued above

ricotta meatballs
IN CHUNKY TOMATO SAUCE

Here's a New York proverb for you: "A nickel will get you on the subway, but garlic will get you a seat." OK, so it isn't a nickel anymore, but the second part still holds true, and, in the case of these tender meatballs loaded with Italian flavors, you'll be firmly in the dinnertime driver's seat. The perfect presence of garlic (not too much, not too little) can be found throughout this dish, from the baked-not-fried ricotta-laden meatballs to the quick and chunky tomato sauce. In the case of these marvelous meatballs, the only seat anyone is going to be fighting for is one at the table.

MAKES: 26–28 MEATBALLS   PREP TIME: 20 MINS   COOK TIME: 35 MINS

Ricotta Meatballs

1½ cups whole-milk ricotta cheese

1 cup freshly grated Parmesan cheese

½ cup breadcrumbs

3 garlic cloves, minced

2 eggs

¼ cup chopped fresh flat-leaf parsley

1½ tsp kosher salt

1 tsp dried oregano

½ tsp dried basil

½ tsp freshly ground black pepper

¼ tsp red pepper flakes

2 lb lean ground beef

Chunky Tomato Sauce

2 tbsp olive oil

1 medium yellow onion, chopped

3 garlic cloves, minced

1 tsp dried oregano

continued above

1 tsp kosher salt

½ tsp freshly ground black pepper

¼ tsp red pepper flakes

2 (28 oz each) cans San Marzano tomatoes

Freshly grated Parmesan cheese, for garnish

1. Preheat the oven to 400°F and line a baking sheet with parchment paper. Set aside.

2. For the meatballs, in a large bowl, combine the ricotta, Parmesan, breadcrumbs, garlic, eggs, parsley, salt, oregano, basil, pepper, and red pepper flakes. Mix well to combine. Add the ground beef and mix thoroughly by hand until combined, being careful not to overmix. Roll 2 heaping tablespoons of meat mixture into a ball and place on the baking sheet. Repeat until all meatballs are rolled. Bake for 10 minutes, flip the meatballs, and bake for 10 minutes more.

3. While the meatballs bake, prepare the sauce. In a large pot, heat the olive oil over medium heat. Add the onion, garlic, oregano, salt, pepper, and red pepper flakes. Cook for 4–5 minutes, until the onion is softened.

4. In a bowl, break up the tomatoes using your hands or a wooden spoon. Add them to the onion mixture and bring to a boil. Reduce the heat to a simmer and add the cooked meatballs. Cook for 30 minutes, occasionally shaking the pot to mix. Garnish with extra Parmesan cheese and serve.

+ **Make it gluten-free: Use gluten-free breadcrumbs**

beef & broccoli

LO MEIN

When it comes to plating, I've never bought into the whole, "It all goes to the same place" mentality. I dream of a world of compartmentalized bone china and walks to help those afflicted with brumotactillophobia, the fear of food touching. I'd be top fundraiser. That said, it should surprise you that this mash-up of two Chinese-style dishes, saucy beef and broccoli with gingery lo mein noodles, is one of my faves. A complete meal that can be cooked in 15 minutes, this delectable duo has hints of spice, savory sauce that coats tender noodles, perfectly cooked beef, and still-crunchy greens, resulting in scrumptious sensory overload.

SERVES: 4   PREP TIME: 15 MINS   COOK TIME: 15 MINS

Stir-Fry Sauce

¾ cup beef broth

5 tbsp dry sherry

3 tbsp soy sauce

2 tbsp oyster sauce

1 tbsp brown sugar

1 tsp Sriracha hot sauce

2 tbsp cornstarch

2 tbsp water

Stir-Fry

1 (8 oz) package lo mein noodles, or any thin noodle

1 tsp sesame oil

3½ cups broccoli florets

1½ cups sugar snap peas, trimmed

1 lb sirloin steak, thinly sliced against the grain

2 tbsp cornstarch

2 tbsp vegetable oil, divided

2 tbsp fresh ginger, minced

2 garlic cloves, minced

2 bunches green onions, sliced into ½-inch pieces on the diagonal

1 (7.7 oz) can sliced water chestnuts, rinsed and drained

1. To prepare the sauce, whisk together the beef broth, sherry, soy sauce, oyster sauce, brown sugar, and Sriracha.

2. In a small bowl, stir the cornstarch and water together to dissolve the cornstarch. Add to the stir-fry sauce and whisk well to combine.

3. In a large pot of boiling water, cook the noodles according to the package directions. Using tongs, remove the noodles, drain, and toss with the sesame oil. Add the broccoli and snap peas to the boiling water and blanch over low heat for 2 minutes. Drain the vegetables and immediately run under cold water to stop cooking. Drain well and set aside.

4. In a medium bowl, toss the sliced beef with the cornstarch.

5. In a wok or large flat-bottomed skillet, heat 1 tablespoon of the vegetable oil over medium-high heat. Add half the sliced beef and cook for 1 minute. Flip and continue cooking for 1–2 minutes, until no longer pink. Remove from the pan and cook the remaining beef. Transfer to a plate and set aside.

6. In the same skillet over medium heat, add the remaining tablespoon of vegetable oil. Add the ginger, garlic, and green onions and cook, stirring constantly, for 1 minute. Add the sliced water chestnuts, stir-fry sauce, noodles, broccoli, sugar snap peas, cooked beef, and lo mein noodles. Stir well to combine and continue to cook until the sauce thickens and coats the mixture, 1–2 minutes.

BANH MI
burgers

While some spin-offs fail miserably (read: *Joanie Loves Chachi*), others become showstoppers (hello, *Frasier*) like this ready-for-prime-time Banh Mi Burger, the offspring of a classic Vietnamese sandwich. Created by Lisa, our critically acclaimed leading lady, she plays on banh mi's savory, crunchy, sweet, and sour elements, sandwiching burgers with an Asian twist between toasted brioche buns and topping them with crisp, cooling quick-pickled vegetables and a scene-stealing spicy sauce. With its high-def textures and fresh flavors, this must-eat dinner is guaranteed to get green lit.

SERVES: 4   PREP TIME: 15 MINS   COOK TIME: 15 MINS (+ pickling)

Quick-Pickled Vegetables

1 large carrot, peeled and thinly sliced

1½ cups thinly sliced English cucumber

1 small daikon radish, thinly sliced

½ cup rice vinegar

½ cup water

¼ cup sugar

Spicy Burger Sauce

½ cup light mayonnaise

1 tbsp fresh lime juice

2 green onions, finely chopped

2 tsp Sriracha hot sauce

¼ tsp kosher salt

Burgers

1½ lb lean ground beef

1 tbsp fish sauce

1 tbsp fresh lime juice

2 tsp Sriracha hot sauce

1 garlic clove, finely minced

1 tsp grated fresh ginger

1 tsp sugar

Pinch kosher salt, to season burger patties

4 brioche burger buns, toasted

Handful fresh cilantro leaves

1. For the pickled vegetables, place the carrots, cucumbers, and daikon radishes in a heatproof bowl. In a small saucepan, bring the rice vinegar, water, and sugar to a boil over high heat. Stir to dissolve the sugar and pour over the vegetables. Cover and chill for a minimum of 20 minutes.

2. For the spicy burger sauce, in a small bowl, whisk together the mayonnaise, lime juice, green onions, Sriracha, and salt. Cover and refrigerate until ready to assemble.

3. For the burgers, preheat the grill to medium-high and lightly oil the grilling surface.

4. In a large bowl, mix the ground beef, fish sauce, lime juice, Sriracha, garlic, ginger, and sugar. Shape into 4 burger patties and sprinkle both sides with a pinch of kosher salt. Place the patties on a preheated grill and cook for 6–7 minutes per side, depending on the desired doneness. Remove from the grill.

5. To assemble, spread the burger sauce on the inside of the toasted brioche buns and add the burgers. Drain the pickled vegetables and top the burgers with a selection of them, finishing with the cilantro leaves.

Make it gluten-free: Use gluten-free buns

lessons *from* lisa

⁎ *If you don't have the use of a grill, heat a cast-iron skillet over medium-high heat and cook, following the same timing as the grill.*

⁎ *Don't be alarmed by fish sauce—it may smell pungent, but it doesn't taste that way—it adds a savory saltiness to these burgers.*

HEALTHY asian-inspired meatloaf

isa's a culinary alchemist. With the power of her palate, she can take something traditionally bland and unhealthy and transform it into pure flavor-packed bliss. She's worked some serious meatloaf magic when divining this dinner: undetectable to the naked eye (and mouth), lean turkey and beef are blended to lighten up the traditionally fat-laden loaf, then combined with ginger, garlic, and hoisin sauce, giving each bite an Asian flair. Homey and mouthwatering, served for dinner, enjoyed cold the next day, or sandwiched between slices of bread, this treasured meatloaf is solid gold.

SERVES: 6   PREP TIME: 10 MINS   COOK TIME: 65 MINS

Hoisin Glaze

3 tbsp ketchup

2 tbsp hoisin sauce

½ tsp Sriracha hot sauce

Meatloaf

1 cup panko (Japanese breadcrumbs)

¼ cup diced green onions

2 garlic cloves, minced

2 tsp grated fresh ginger

1 egg

3 tbsp hoisin sauce

1 tbsp soy sauce

2 tsp sesame oil

2 tsp Sriracha hot sauce

1 lb lean ground turkey

1 lb lean ground beef

1. Preheat the oven to 350°F. Line a rimmed baking sheet with aluminum foil and coat with nonstick cooking spray.

2. For the hoisin glaze, in a small bowl, whisk together the ketchup, hoisin, and Sriracha. Cover and set aside.

3. For the meatloaf, in a large bowl, combine the panko, green onions, garlic, ginger, egg, hoisin sauce, soy sauce, sesame oil, and Sriracha. Mix well and add the ground turkey and ground beef. Combine all ingredients, but do not overmix.

4. On the prepared baking sheet, shape the meat mixture into a long loaf, about 10 inches long and 5 inches wide. Bake for 45 minutes, remove from the oven, and pour the glaze over the meatloaf. Continue baking for 20 minutes more, or until the meatloaf has reached an internal temperature of 160°F–165°F. Remove from the oven and let sit for 10 minutes before slicing.

+ **Make it gluten-free: Use gluten-free hoisin sauce, gluten-free panko, and gluten-free tamari or gluten-free soy sauce**

 A little magic can take you a long way. —ROALD DAHL

THE ULTIMATE chocolate chip cookies

Check the Internet and see how many people claim to have the secret to the best-ever chocolate chip cookie. Tons, I tell you, and they're all wrong, because they don't have the sweet symphony that only our very own virtuoso and cookie conductor can create. While she had me playing the triangle, Maestro Lisa went and dreamed up a cookie composition like no other, better than you could ever imagine—it's studded with melt-in-your-mouth chocolate, the edges are crunchy, the insides are chewy, and the genius addition of cereal lends a crispy bite. Hitting all the right notes, these delectable desserts are Lisa's opus and should be titled *Cookie No. 1*.

MAKES: 18 LARGE COOKIES   **PREP TIME: 10 MINS**   **COOK TIME: 10 MINS**

1 cup butter, room temperature

1 cup brown sugar

¾ cup sugar

2 eggs

1 tsp vanilla extract

2 cups flour

1 tsp baking soda

¾ tsp kosher salt

1½ cups lightly crushed Rice Krispies cereal

1½ cups lightly crushed Corn Flakes cereal

1 cup semisweet chocolate chips

1 cup dark chocolate chips

1. Preheat the oven to 350°F. Line a baking sheet with parchment paper.

2. Using an electric mixer, cream the butter, brown sugar, and sugar on medium speed for 2 minutes. Add the eggs and vanilla, continuing to mix for about 2 minutes until fluffy, scraping down the sides of the bowl as needed. On low speed, add the flour, baking soda, salt, Rice Krispies, Corn Flakes, and both types of chocolate. Mix just until the flour disappears, being careful not to overmix.

3. Drop ¼ cup of batter for each cookie on the prepared baking sheet and pat down slightly. Bake for 9–10 minutes until edges begin to brown. Cool cookies.

Today, me will live in the moment unless it's unpleasant in which case me will eat a cookie.

—COOKIE MONSTER, SESAME STREET

OATMEAL, peanut butter & chocolate blondies

Lisa isn't a writer, but somehow she instinctively knew to follow the Rule of Three (think: Three Little Pigs, Three Musketeers), the theory that three elements form the most memorable, satisfying, and perfect pattern. Here, she's taken a trio of classic cookies—peanut butter, oatmeal, and chocolate chip—and rolled them into one blow-your-mind bar. Soft and chewy, these triple-threat blondies are golden goodness, with creamy peanut butter, chocolate, and oats in every bite, deserving of three cheers for Lisa. Hip hip hooray.

MAKES: 20 BLONDIES   PREP TIME: 10 MINS   COOK TIME: 30 MINS

¾ cup butter, room temperature

½ cup creamy peanut butter

¾ cup sugar

¾ cup brown sugar

2 eggs

2 tsp vanilla extract

2 cups flour

½ tsp baking soda

½ tsp kosher salt

1 cup old-fashioned oats

1½ cups peanut butter chips

1½ cups chopped semisweet chocolate

1. Preheat the oven to 350ºF. Coat a 9-by-13-inch baking pan with nonstick cooking spray. Line the bottom with parchment paper.

2. Using an electric mixer, on medium speed, cream together the butter, peanut butter, sugar, and brown sugar until light and fluffy, about 2 minutes. Beat in the eggs and vanilla for another 2 minutes. Add the flour, baking soda, salt, oats, peanut butter chips, and chocolate. Mix on low speed, just until the flour disappears, being careful not to overmix.

3. Spread the batter evenly in the prepared pan. Bake for 26–28 minutes, until golden around the edges. Allow to cool for 1 hour before removing from the pan.

If two wrongs don't make a right, try three.

—LAURENCE J. PETER

cheesecake bars

W hile I'm a dedicated dessert enabler, I won't use my usual "Trust me, it's only one Weight Watchers point" schtick here. It's not. Nor is it sugar-free, dairy-free, or gluten-free. Nor should it be. In fact, this jaw-dropping dessert is dedicated to our favorite squad, Team Sweet Tooth, and is the definitive and delicious answer to every cheesecake and cookie craving out there. Each divine bar is a marvelous mash-up of two classic desserts, beginning with a golden graham cracker crust, topped with creamy cheesecake and finished with a covering of snickerdoodle dough. Full of sugar and spice (aka cinnamon) and everything nice, these luscious layered bars sell themselves, no sweet-talking required.

MAKES: 25 CHEESECAKE BARS   PREP TIME: 20 MINS
COOK TIME: 45 MINS (+ cooling)

Graham Cracker Crust

2 cups graham cracker crumbs

⅓ cup sugar

½ cup melted butter

Snickerdoodle Dough

½ cup butter, room temperature

½ cup sugar

¼ cup brown sugar

1 egg

1 tsp vanilla extract

1¼ cups flour

½ tsp baking soda

½ tsp cream of tartar

½ tsp ground cinnamon

¼ tsp kosher salt

Cheesecake Layer

2 (8 oz each) packages cream
  cheese, room temperature

½ cup sugar

continued on next page

1. Preheat the oven to 350°F. Coat a 9-by-13-inch baking pan with nonstick cooking spray and line with parchment paper.

2. For the graham cracker crust, combine the graham crumbs and sugar in a bowl. Add the melted butter and mix with a fork until combined.

3. Transfer to the prepared baking pan and press the crumb mixture firmly along the bottom. Bake the crust for 10 minutes. Remove from the oven and let crumb mixture cool slightly. Leave the oven at 350°F.

4. For the snickerdoodle dough, using an electric mixer, cream the butter, sugar, and brown sugar on medium speed until well combined. Add the egg and vanilla, continuing to mix for 2 minutes, until light and fluffy. On low speed, add the flour, baking soda, cream of tartar, cinnamon, and salt. Mix just until the flour disappears. Set the dough aside while preparing the cheesecake layer.

5. For the cheesecake, using an electric mixer, combine the cream cheese and sugar on medium speed until well combined. Add the eggs on low speed, one at a time, beating well after each addition. Add the cream, flour, vanilla, and cinnamon on low speed, mixing until smooth and creamy.

2 eggs

¼ cup heavy cream

2 tsp flour

1 tsp vanilla extract

½ tsp ground cinnamon

4 tbsp sugar + 1 tsp ground
  cinnamon, mixed and divided

6. To assemble, sprinkle 2 tablespoons of the cinnamon sugar over the baked graham crust. Pour the cheesecake batter evenly over top. Crumble the snickerdoodle dough into pieces atop the cheesecake layer (it does not need to be fully covered). Sprinkle the remaining 2 tablespoons of cinnamon sugar over the snickerdoodle layer. Bake for 32 minutes. Remove and let cool before refrigerating. Cover and refrigerate at least 2 hours before cutting.

lessons *from* lisa

★ To quickly soften cream cheese, place it in a resealable bag, seal the bag, and immerse it in warm water for 10 minutes.

★ Cream of tartar, often used to stabilize egg whites, is used in snickerdoodles to give a chewy texture and tangy flavor.

I treat my body like a temple, Laverne. You choose to treat yours like an amusement park.

—SHIRLEY FEENEY, LAVERNE & SHIRLEY

carrot layer cake

We have this friend. Let's just call her Sharolyn Shoffman. She has a big mouth (loves to eat and talk, often simultaneously), so you can imagine the decade-long monologue she's served us with, wanting more nut-free dessert recipes for her peanut-allergic kids. Well, Sharolyn, it's not just that we heard you; it's that we love your kids so much and don't want to deprive them of carrot cake for another minute. Brace yourselves, kids (and adults alike), because this carrot cake is next level. Sweet and moist, this classic (albeit walnut-free) cake is loaded with carrots, cinnamon, ginger, and nutmeg and iced with the ultimate super-simple cream cheese frosting and garnished with a crunchy shortbread crumble. Sharolyn, it's time you got baking and "Let them eat cake."

SERVES: 10–12   PREP TIME: 20 MINS   COOK TIME: 45 MINS

Shortbread Crumble

1 cup flour

½ cup sugar

½ cup butter, room temperature

Carrot Cake

2½ cups flour

2 tsp baking powder

1 tsp baking soda

2 tsp ground cinnamon

1 tsp ground ginger

1 tsp kosher salt

¼ tsp ground nutmeg

¾ cup vegetable oil

4 eggs

1¼ cups brown sugar

½ cup sugar

¾ cup buttermilk

2 tsp vanilla extract

3 cups peeled and grated carrots

continued on next page

1. Preheat the oven to 350°F.

2. For the crumble, combine the flour and sugar in a bowl. Cut in the butter, until mixture is in pea-sized pieces.

3. Spread the crumble over a parchment-lined baking sheet and bake for 12 minutes, stirring once halfway through cooking. When the crumbs are golden, remove from the oven and set aside to cool.

4. For the cake, coat two 8-inch round baking pans with nonstick cooking spray and line the bottoms with parchment paper.

5. In a large bowl, combine the flour, baking powder, baking soda, cinnamon, ginger, salt, and nutmeg. In another bowl, whisk together the vegetable oil, eggs, brown sugar, sugar, buttermilk, and vanilla until fluffy and well combined. Pour the wet ingredients into the dry ingredients, along with the grated carrots. Fold the ingredients together just until combined, being careful not to overmix.

6. Pour the batter evenly into the prepared pans. Bake at 350°F for 34–36 minutes, or until a toothpick inserted in the center comes out clean. Let the cakes cool before frosting.

Cream Cheese Frosting

1 (8 oz) package cream cheese, room temperature

½ cup butter, room temperature

4 cups icing sugar

1 tsp vanilla extract

Pinch kosher salt

7. For the frosting, using an electric mixer, combine the cream cheese and butter on medium speed. On low speed, add the icing sugar, vanilla, and salt. Increase the speed gradually, mixing until the frosting has a smooth spreading consistency.

8. To assemble, place 1 cake layer on a serving dish. Top with 1¼ cups of the frosting and spread evenly over the layer. Top with the remaining layer and spread the remaining frosting over the top and sides. Garnish the top and sides of the cake with the crumble. Refrigerate until ready to serve.

DIG *in*

THIS ONE TAKES THE
cake.

strawberry pie bars

"Even if you're yawning, you can yawn a smile." —STRAWBERRY SHO

This ginger-haired gal, her cat, Custard, and boy toy, Huckleberry Pie, all make me berry happy. I mean, who doesn't want to live in a world (more specifically, in Berry Bitty City) where the goal is to smile *while* yawning? And though she lived in a cake, I think she would have done better in a bar; my Apple Dumplin sister must agree, as she has created these easy berrylicious squares that taste just like fresh strawberry pie. No rolling pin required, creamy lemon vanilla filling and sweet strawberries are piled on a crunchy graham cracker crust and finished with a golden crumble topping, each bite bursting with juicy berry flavor. Just wait until Blueberry Muffin, Orange Blossom, and Plum Pudding try them. The gang is surely going to be smiling while chewing.

MAKES: 16 SQUARE BARS   PREP TIME: 15 MINS   COOK TIME: 45 MINS

Graham Crust

1½ cups graham cracker crumbs

3 tbsp brown sugar

6 tbsp melted butter

Crumble Topping

⅔ cup flour

⅓ cup sugar

¼ cup melted butter

Strawberry Filling

½ cup sour cream

⅓ cup sugar

2 tbsp flour

1 egg

½ tsp vanilla extract

½ tsp lemon zest

Pinch kosher salt

2½ cups hulled and chopped fresh strawberries

1. Preheat the oven to 350°F. Coat a 9-inch square baking pan with nonstick cooking spray and line with parchment paper.

2. For the crust, in a medium bowl, combine the graham crumbs, brown sugar, and melted butter. Mix until well combined and press evenly into the prepared baking pan. Bake the crust for 8 minutes. Remove from the oven and set aside.

3. For the crumble topping, in a small bowl, mix the flour, sugar, and melted butter until crumbly. Set aside.

4. For the strawberry filling, in a large bowl, whisk together the sour cream, sugar, flour, egg, vanilla, lemon zest, and salt. Fold in the chopped strawberries and pour into the prepared crust. Sprinkle with the crumble and bake for 33–35 minutes until the top is golden. Allow to cool before cutting. These are best stored in the refrigerator.

lessons *from* lisa

★ Buy strawberries that are red and blemish free—if the shoulders (the part under the stem) are white, the berries were picked too early.

SO
FORKIN'
GOOD.

banana sheet cake

WITH BANANA FROSTING

I cheated in Mr. Cheung's math class. I mean, c'mon, I knew I'd never need to know pi's 26th digit as an adult (turns out, it's 3, so yes, that was a cheat sheet tucked in my Reebok Pump). And now, I'm forced to confess again—this cake is the ultimate cheat sheet, the perfect slab that'll make you look and feel like an honor roll baker. The formula is as easy as 1-2-3: *moist banana cake + creamy banana icing − effort ÷ 10 = one dreamy dessert.* Flat and rectangular (yeah, yeah, I know, straight sides, right angles), not only is this cake simple to cut (don't have to worry about the radius), but also to frost (dump-'n'-spread method) and bring along to the next picnic, barbecue, or classroom. We've done the mouthwatering math, and the answer's always the same: A+.

SERVES: 10–12   PREP TIME: 10 MINS   COOK TIME: 30 MINS

Banana Cake

2½ cups flour

1 tsp baking powder

1 tsp baking soda

½ tsp kosher salt

½ cup butter, room temperature

¾ cup sugar

½ cup brown sugar

2 eggs

1 tsp vanilla extract

1¾ cups mashed very ripe bananas (about 4)

1 tbsp fresh lemon juice

¾ cup buttermilk

Banana Frosting

¼ cup butter, softened

½ cup mashed bananas

1 tsp fresh lemon juice

3½ cups icing sugar

1. Preheat the oven to 350°F. Coat a 9-by-13-inch baking pan with nonstick cooking spray and line with parchment paper.

2. For the banana cake, in a large bowl, combine the flour, baking powder, baking soda, and salt. Set aside. Using an electric mixer, cream the butter, sugar, and brown sugar on medium speed for 2 minutes. Add the eggs one at a time, beating well after each addition. Mix in the vanilla, mashed bananas, and lemon juice. On low speed, add half the flour mixture, then the buttermilk, and finish with the remaining flour mixture.

3. Spread the batter evenly in the prepared baking pan and bake for 28–30 minutes, until a toothpick inserted in the center comes out clean. Allow to cool completely before frosting.

4. For the frosting, using an electric mixer, combine the butter, bananas, lemon juice, and icing sugar on low speed. Once combined, increase the speed to medium until the frosting develops a smooth spreading consistency. Frost the top of the banana cake and refrigerate until ready to serve.

lessons *from* lisa

The riper your bananas, the better your cake will be. To ripen bananas quickly, place them in a paper bag with apples, tomatoes, or avocados.

This cake freezes really well, but don't frost before freezing.

SPEEDY cherry berry crisp

O K, so most baked goods have gotten their due in the world of idioms: easy as pie, smart cookie, piece of cake. Well, what about the crisp, the easiest, smartest, and most delectable of desserts? Cinch as a crisp? Cozy as a crisp? Whatever the expression, I can easily put into words what's to love about this quick, can't-go-wrong crisp—a great last-minute dessert (35 minutes total), flavor pops from juicy, lemon-zesty cherries and blueberries, and the aroma of cinnamon and nutmeg wafts from the buttery crumble topping. Warm, gooey, sweet fresh fruit covered by a crunchy golden streusel, it'll be gobbled up in no time, but hey, that's the way the crisp crumbles.

SERVES: 6   PREP TIME: 10 MINS   COOK TIME: 25 MINS

Crumble Topping

1 cup old-fashioned oats

1 cup flour

½ cup brown sugar

½ tsp ground cinnamon

¼ tsp ground nutmeg

¼ tsp kosher salt

½ cup butter, cut into cubes

Cherry Blueberry Filling

3 cups fresh cherries, pitted and halved

3 cups fresh blueberries

¼ cup sugar

2 tbsp cornstarch

1 tsp lemon zest

1. Preheat the oven to 375°F. Coat an 8- or 9-inch square baking dish with nonstick cooking spray.

2. For the crumble topping, in a bowl, combine the oats, flour, brown sugar, cinnamon, nutmeg, and salt. Cut in the butter until the mixture resembles coarse crumbs. Set aside.

3. For the filling, in a large bowl, gently toss the cherries, blueberries, sugar, cornstarch, and lemon zest. Place in the prepared baking dish and sprinkle the crumble evenly over the fruit. Bake for 25 minutes, until the topping is golden.

> *I love toppings. Sometimes I go to restaurants and I just order toppings.*
>
> —ORLANDO CASTILLO, TORTILLA SOUP, 2001

CARAMEL

apple
bundt
cake

This Bundt is no bunt. My slugger sis isn't simply tapping the ball with a bat; she's swinging for the fences with this winning dessert. The moist and fluffy cake is loaded with fresh apples, toffee bits, and a hint of cinnamon, and topped off with a 5-minute homemade caramel sauce. Easy yet impressive, this glorious Bundt knocks it out of the dessert ballpark, scoring on the triple play of tender apple chunks, sweet crunchy toffee, and luscious caramel. Get ready to step up to the plate because this melt-in-your-mouth cake is a major league marvel.

MAKES: 12 SERVINGS, 1 CUP CARAMEL SAUCE   PREP TIME: 15 MINS
COOK TIME: 70 MINS

Bundt Cake

3 eggs

2 cups sugar

1 cup vegetable oil

1 cup sour cream

2 tsp vanilla extract

2½ cups flour

1 tsp baking powder

½ tsp baking soda

½ tsp ground cinnamon

1 tsp kosher salt

2 Granny Smith apples, peeled, cored, and chopped

1¼ cups Skor or Heath Toffee Bits

Caramel Sauce

1 cup sugar

⅓ cup butter, softened

½ cup heavy cream, warmed

¼ tsp kosher salt

1. Preheat the oven to 350°F. Coat a 10-inch Bundt pan with nonstick cooking spray and flour the pan, making sure each side is covered. Tap out the excess flour.

2. For the cake, in a large bowl, whisk the eggs, sugar, and vegetable oil until the mixture looks lighter in color and appears fluffy. Whisk in the sour cream and vanilla until well combined. Fold in the flour, baking powder, baking soda, cinnamon, salt, apples, and toffee bits. Mix until all ingredients are combined.

3. Scoop the batter into the prepared pan. Bake for 65 minutes, or until a toothpick inserted in the center comes out clean. Remove from the oven and gently loosen the edges. Allow to cool in the pan for 20 minutes before flipping out. Allow to cool completely and place on a serving platter.

4. For the caramel sauce, in a medium saucepan over medium heat, add the sugar. Stir continuously until the sugar is melted and a deep amber color. Remove from the heat and stir in the butter until melted. Add the cream and salt (the mixture will bubble up when you add the cream). Return to the heat and stir for 1 minute, until the caramel sauce is smooth.

5. Pour the caramel sauce into a glass container and set aside to cool slightly. It will thicken as it cools.

6. To serve, drizzle the caramel sauce over the Bundt cake and serve each portion with extra caramel sauce.

oatmeal cookies

It's rumored it was a date, not an apple, that was the real fruit in the Garden of Eden. This makes perfect sense. You see, Lisa, the all-powerful Cookie Creator, has taken this antioxidant-, mineral-, and fiber-rich fruit and transformed it into a blissfully delicious dessert. We're talking paradise, people. Brilliantly swapping chocolate out for dates adds a great texture, flavor, and a healthy kick. As you bite into these big chewy cookies, loaded with old-fashioned oats and tart cranberries, you'll bear witness to the Almighty baker that's the apple of my eye.

MAKES: 16 LARGE COOKIES   PREP TIME: 10 MINS   COOK TIME: 15 MINS

1 cup butter, room temperature

1 cup brown sugar

½ cup sugar

2 eggs

1 tbsp molasses

1 tsp vanilla extract

3 cups old-fashioned oats

1½ cups flour

1 tbsp cornstarch

1 tsp baking soda

1 tsp ground cinnamon

1 tsp kosher salt

1 cup chopped dried, pitted dates

1 cup dried cranberries

1. Preheat the oven to 350°F. Line a baking sheet with parchment paper.

2. Using an electric mixer, cream butter, brown sugar, and sugar on medium speed for 2 minutes. Add the eggs one at a time, mixing well after each addition, scraping down the sides of the bowl as needed. Add the molasses and vanilla extract, continuing to mix until fluffy, about 2 minutes. On low speed, add the oats, flour, cornstarch, baking soda, cinnamon, salt, dates, and cranberries. Mix just until the flour disappears and the ingredients are mixed in. Do not overmix.

3. Drop ¼ cup batter on the prepared baking sheet. Pat the batter down slightly and bake 10–12 minutes, just until the edges begin to brown. Cool the cookies on a wire rack.

The only way to get rid of temptation is to yield to it . . . I can resist everything except temptation. —OSCAR WILDE

gatherings

While it took us a bit to figure out that the quest for the "perfect party" is futile, and being hostaphobic is wasted energy, we're shortcutting the learning for you. So, forget polishing the silver and pressing linens, people, because what makes a great gathering are awesome eats and a relaxed, welcoming atmosphere. How to get your hosting zen on? All you need are our crowd-pleasing, foolproof recipes, easy options that cover off both the nutrient-rich and the indulgent loosen-the-belt variety. Perfect for everything from the impromptu get-together to the planned holiday feast for family and friends, these special occasion eats are sure to add fuel to the fun and mouthwatering memories to mealtime.

Bottoms up, because these simple and speedy cocktail recipes are going to transform you into a master mixologist.

WHITE CITRUS SANGRIA

2 (750 ml) bottles dry white wine

1 cup orange juice

½ cup brandy

½ cup Triple Sec

½ cup simple syrup

2 lemons, sliced

2 limes, cut into small slices

2 navel or blood oranges, sliced

3 cups sparkling water

Fresh mint, for garnish

SERVES: 10–12

1. In a large pitcher, combine the white wine, orange juice, brandy, Triple Sec, simple syrup, and sliced lemons, limes, and oranges. Stir to combine. Refrigerate for at least 2 hours before serving. Just before serving, add the sparkling water and serve over ice. Garnish with the fresh mint.

ROSEMARY ELDERFLOWER MARTINI

4 oz vodka

3 oz elderflower liqueur

1 oz fresh lemon juice

½ oz simple syrup

4 dashes orange bitters

1 rosemary sprig (with 2 more for garnish)

SERVES: 2

1. Add the vodka, elderflower liqueur, lemon juice, simple syrup, orange bitters, and 1 rosemary sprig to a cocktail shaker filled with ice. Shake and divide into 2 martini glasses. Garnish each with a rosemary sprig.

MIXED BERRY MARGARITA

Berry Simple Syrup

1 cup water

½ cup sugar

¾ cup raspberries

½ cup blueberries

Lime, cut in wedges, to rim glass and garnish

Sea salt, to rim glass

Ice

6 oz tequila

¼ cup fresh lime juice

SERVES: 2

1. For the berry simple syrup, in a medium saucepan over high heat, combine the water, sugar, raspberries, and blueberries. Bring to a boil. Reduce the heat to medium-low and simmer for 4 minutes, stirring occasionally. Remove from the heat, strain the syrup, and discard the solids (the solids can be frozen and saved for smoothies). Refrigerate the syrup and allow to cool completely before preparing the margaritas.

2. Moisten the rims of 2 margarita glasses with the lime wedge and dip each glass into sea salt to coat the rim.

3. In a cocktail shaker filled with ice, add the tequila, ½ cup of the berry simple syrup, and the lime juice. Shake well for about 15 seconds until chilled. Divide between glasses filled with ice and garnish with the lime wedges.

SWEET & SAVORY **tomato jam**

Tomato jam is, simply put, our jam. A snap to make (should be called *Jam for Dummies*), this sweet and spicy spread works amazingly well with strong cheese flavors, not to mention with grilled cheese sandwiches, steak, and chicken. Keep it in the fridge for up to a week, but chances are, it'll be gone in a day.

MAKES: 1¾ CUPS TOMATO JAM   PREP TIME: 15 MINS   COOK TIME: 65 MINS

½ cup brown sugar

3 tbsp apple cider vinegar

3 tbsp water

3 lb (weight before they've been cored) plum tomatoes, cored, seeded, and coarsely chopped

1 cinnamon stick

2 tbsp fresh lemon juice

1 tsp freshly grated ginger

1 tsp kosher salt

½ tsp red pepper flakes

1. In a large saucepan over medium heat, combine the brown sugar, apple cider vinegar, and water. Stir until the sugar dissolves and the mixture comes to a boil, about 5 minutes. Stir in the tomatoes, cinnamon stick, lemon juice, ginger, salt, and red pepper flakes. Cook over low heat, stirring occasionally, for 1 hour or until much of the liquid has evaporated and the mixture has thickened to a jam-like consistency. Remove cinnamon stick after 30 minutes of cooking, unless you like a very strong cinnamon flavor.

2. Place the tomato jam in a glass container, cover, and refrigerate. Serve with an assortment of soft (Brie, goat), firm (Parmesan, Manchego), aged (cheddar, Gouda, Gruyère) and blue (Gorgonzola, Stilta) cheeses, and some fresh and dried fruit, roasted nuts, and honey.

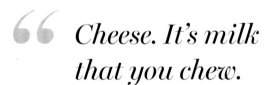

Cheese. It's milk that you chew.

—CHANDLER BING, *FRIENDS*

butternut squash, apple & fennel SOUP

A s the temperature plummets, we all suffer from a little PSL (aka pumpkin spice latte) fatigue, right? OK, so let's put this out there to that well-known Seattle coffee company: the time is ripe for BAFS (aka butternut apple fennel soup), each taste the embodiment of fall festivities. Butternut squash, apples, and fennel are simple ingredients, but, when roasted and combined, are elevated to an obsession-worthy trio. Velvety and vegetarian, this pureed soup is topped with spiced pistachios, adding the perfect salty crunch. Yes, we can feel the excitement mounting for BAFS, the healthiest, most satisfying and scrumptiously steamy venti to hit the renowned roaster.

SERVES: 8–10   PREP TIME: 25 MINS   COOK TIME: 35 MINS

Spiced Pistachios

1 cup shelled pistachios

1 tsp olive oil

½ tsp sugar

¼ tsp dried thyme

¼ tsp paprika

¼ tsp kosher salt

Butternut Squash Soup

4 cups cubed butternut squash

1 fennel bulb, trimmed top and bottom, cut into 8 pieces

2 tbsp olive oil, divided

¾ tsp kosher salt, divided

¼ tsp freshly ground black pepper

1 medium yellow onion, chopped

2 carrots, peeled and chopped

2 celery stalks, chopped

1 Granny Smith apple, peeled, cored, and chopped

continued on next page

1. For the pistachios, preheat the oven to 325°F. Line a baking sheet with aluminum foil and coat with nonstick cooking spray.

2. In a mixing bowl, combine the pistachios, olive oil, sugar, thyme, paprika, and salt. Spread on the prepared baking sheet and bake for 7–8 minutes, until lightly toasted. Remove from the oven and set aside to cool.

3. For the squash soup, preheat the oven to 425°F. Line a rimmed baking sheet with aluminum foil and coat with nonstick cooking spray.

4. In a large bowl, toss together the butternut squash, fennel, 1 tablespoon of the olive oil, ¼ teaspoon of the salt, and the pepper. Spread in a single layer on the prepared baking sheet. Roast for 25 minutes, stirring once halfway through cooking.

5. While the butternut squash and fennel are roasting, heat the remaining tablespoon of the olive oil in a large soup pot over medium heat. Add the onion, carrots, and celery, cooking until softened, about 8 minutes. Add the apple, garlic, thyme, ginger, cumin, the remaining ½ teaspoon of salt, and the red pepper flakes. Cook, stirring, for 1 minute. Add the vegetable broth and squash mixture, bring to a boil, reduce the heat, and simmer the soup uncovered for 15 minutes.

2 garlic cloves, minced

1 tsp chopped fresh thyme

½ tsp ground ginger

½ tsp ground cumin

¼ tsp red pepper flakes

5 cups vegetable broth

6. Remove from the heat and puree the soup in 2 batches using a countertop blender, or in the pot using a handheld immersion blender. Top the servings with roasted pistachios.

lessons *from* lisa

★ *Buy fennel bulbs with the stalks and fronds still attached.*

★ *Roasted fennel tastes like sweet celery, not licorice.*

SOUP TO

nuts.

WINE +
DINNER =
WINNER.

EASY tofu mushroom wonton soup

This warming wonton soup got me thinking about homophones (words that sound the same but mean different things), like deer and dear, or wonton and wanton, the word used to describe a promiscuous seductress. So, with the slip of a finger, this "easy" wanton wonton soup sings a steamy siren song, tempting you with its ambrosial broth and divine dumplings. Infused with fresh garlic, ginger, and green onions, and taken next level with Asian aromatics, the flavor and fragrance of this time-saving broth are breathtaking. Complemented with toothsome tofu mushroom-stuffed wontons, you've got irresistible, inviting bowls that beckon you with their come-hither healthiness—spellbinding spoonfuls so mouthwatering your taste buds will be enthralled.

MAKES: 6 SERVINGS, 35 WONTONS   PREP TIME: 40 MINS   COOK TIME: 30 MINS

Soup

8 cups low-salt chicken broth

3 slices fresh ginger

3 green onions, cut in half

2 garlic cloves, smashed

2 tbsp soy sauce

2 tbsp mirin

½ tsp sesame oil

Tofu Mushroom Wontons

1 tbsp vegetable oil

1 (6 oz) package firm tofu, pressed between paper towels and cubed

½ cup shiitake mushrooms, stemmed, peeled, and chopped

¼ cup water chestnuts, chopped

2 tbsp chopped green onions

2 garlic cloves, minced

2 tsp grated fresh ginger

2 tbsp dry sherry cooking wine

continued on next page

1. For the soup, in a large soup pot, combine the chicken broth, ginger, green onions, garlic, soy sauce, mirin, and sesame oil. Bring to a boil over medium heat. Cover, lower the heat, and simmer for 15 minutes. Remove the ginger, green onions, and garlic from the soup and discard.

2. For the wontons, heat the vegetable oil over medium heat in a skillet. Add the tofu, mushrooms, water chestnuts, and green onions. Cook, stirring, for 3 minutes. Add the garlic and ginger, cooking for 2 minutes more. Stir in the sherry, soy sauce, and sesame oil to combine and remove from the heat.

3. Transfer the mixture to a food processor and pulse on and off until the mixture is pureed.

4. While you are forming the wontons, bring a large pot of water to boil over medium heat.

5. Place a wonton wrapper on a flat surface, keeping the remaining wrappers covered with a damp towel. Scoop a heaping teaspoon of filling in the center. Dip your finger in some water and moisten the edges of the wrapper. Fold the wrapper diagonally in half over the filling and press the edges to seal. Bring the top corners inward, using a little more water, and press to seal. Repeat until all the filling is used. Cover the filled wontons with a damp towel if you're not cooking them right away.

1 tbsp soy sauce

1 tsp sesame oil

35 wonton wrappers

1¼ cups baby bok choy, washed and cut in half

Green onions, chopped, for garnish

6. Add the wontons to the boiling water and cook about 3 minutes, until tender. Remove with a slotted spoon and place directly into serving bowls. At this point, the wontons can be frozen for a great last-minute meal.

7. Just before serving, add the bok choy to the soup pot and cook for 2 minutes over low heat. Ladle the hot soup over the wontons and garnish each bowl with the chopped green onions.

I'm just looking for a reasonable ratio of wontons to soup . . .

—ABBY YATES, GHOSTBUSTERS, 2016

top 10
hosting
HACKS

Entertaining? Don't sweat it. You don't have to break your back (or the bank) to host like a boss—these simple tips will bring life to the party.

01. Cut flower stems diagonally and add a few drops of vodka and a teaspoon of sugar to the water to delay wilting

02. Make a themed playlist to avoid awkward silence

03. Infuse the water pitcher with fruit and fresh herbs (strawberries, lemons, mint)

04. Jazz up paper napkins using an ink stamp

05. DIY Buffet Bars (Bloody Mary, taco, baked potato, waffle, hot chocolate) are awesome

06. Berries frozen in water make pretty ice cubes

07. Line the buffet with kraft paper and write the dish names on it with a marker

08. Think at least half a bottle of wine per person (note: there are four glasses in a bottle)

09. Ice-breaking activities (read: Dance Dance Revolution, beer pong) are fun

10. Don't waste time serving fruit at dessert—it's not a party without cake

kale & brussels sprout CAESAR SALAD

Lisa and I have had the same Barbie game going since childhood. Mine, Barbara Millicent Roberts, boots around in her pink 'Vette, hopping from her Dreamhouse to Ken's, while Skipper (aka Lisa's doll) does the cooking and cleaning. Always looking for inspiration (her big sis doesn't like same old same old), Skipper turned to the cabbage family and discovered Brussels sprouts (a mini cabbage perfect for Barb!), guaranteed to keep her 18-inch waist intact. Sure to become a cult classic, this Caesar salad has a lemony dressing that pairs perfectly with shredded kale and Brussels sprouts, along with crunchy almonds and garlicky breadcrumb gremolata. Just wait until Malibu Barbie, Cat Burglar Barbie, and Astronaut Barbie try it.

SERVES: 6–8 SIDES   **PREP TIME: 20 MINS**   **COOK TIME: 5 MINS**

Caesar Dressing

¼ cup olive oil

1 tbsp apple cider vinegar

1 tbsp fresh lemon juice

1 garlic clove

1 tsp Dijon mustard

½ tsp kosher salt

¼ tsp freshly ground black pepper

½ cup freshly grated Parmesan cheese

Breadcrumb Gremolata

2 cups bread cubes, day-old bread, crusts removed

1 tbsp olive oil

1 garlic clove, minced

¼ cup freshly grated Parmesan cheese

2 tbsp finely chopped fresh flat-leaf parsley

continued on next page

1. For the dressing, in a blender, combine the olive oil, apple cider vinegar, lemon juice, garlic, mustard, salt, and pepper. Once they are well blended, add the Parmesan and pulse 2 times to combine. Set the dressing aside.

2. For the gremolata, place the bread cubes in a food processor and pulse on and off a few times to turn into breadcrumbs.

3. In a skillet over medium-low heat, heat the olive oil. Add the garlic and stir constantly for 30 seconds. Add the breadcrumbs and cook for 5–6 minutes, frequently stirring, until they start to become golden. Remove from the heat and toss the breadcrumbs in a bowl with Parmesan, parsley, lemon zest, salt, and pepper. Set aside.

4. For the salad, place the chopped kale, Brussels sprouts, and roasted almonds in a serving bowl. Toss with the dressing and top each serving with gremolata.

+ Make it gluten-free: Use gluten-free bread

lessons *from* lisa

★ *Choose firm, compact, bright green Brussels sprouts. Avoid sprouts with wilted or loose outer leaves.*

ingredients continued

½ tsp lemon zest

⅛ tsp kosher salt

⅛ tsp freshly ground black pepper

Salad

6 cups (about 2 bunches) finely chopped kale, thick stems discarded

3 cups finely shredded Brussels sprouts

½ cup coarsely chopped roasted almonds

watermelon & beet PANZANELLA SALAD

Tell me more, tell me more, was it love at first bite? Well, of course it was. Superbly refreshing and showcasing the season's bounty, this salad is the epitome of summer lovin'. Worthy of a song and dance, fresh cut watermelon and sweet roasted beets (aka nature's Pink Ladies), crunchy French (too much to call it Frenchie?) bread, fresh herbs, tangy feta, and peppery arugula are all dressed in a vibrant lime vinaigrette. Gather the gang (and grab your skintight leather leggings) because they're going to be hopelessly devoted to this beauty, devouring it at lightning speed. Yes, Panzanella is the word.

SERVES: 4   PREP TIME: 15 MINS   COOK TIME: 55 MINS

2 small golden beets

1 tbsp + 1 tsp olive oil, divided

3½ cups cubed French bread

¼ tsp kosher salt

3 cups arugula

3 cups cubed seedless watermelon

¼ cup chopped fresh basil

2 tbsp chopped fresh mint

½ cup cubed feta cheese

Lime Vinaigrette

¼ cup olive oil

2 tbsp fresh lime juice

2 tsp apple cider vinegar

1 tbsp honey

½ tsp kosher salt

¼ tsp freshly ground black pepper

1. Preheat the oven to 400°F.

2. Scrub the beets clean and cut off the stems. Rub the beets with 1 teaspoon of the olive oil. Wrap the beets together in aluminum foil, closing the foil to make a package. Roast in the preheated oven for 40–45 minutes, until fork tender. When the beets are cool enough to handle, use your fingers or a knife to peel off the skin. Slice the beets and set aside.

3. In a large bowl, toss the bread cubes with the remaining 1 tablespoon of olive oil and the salt.

4. Spread the bread in a single layer on a parchment-lined baking sheet. Bake for 10 minutes, stirring halfway through the cooking time. Remove from the oven and set aside until ready to assemble the salad.

5. For the lime vinaigrette, whisk the olive oil, lime juice, apple cider vinegar, honey, salt, and pepper until well combined.

6. To assemble, in a large serving bowl, combine the arugula, watermelon, basil, mint, feta cheese, sliced beets, and toasted bread cubes. Toss with a few tablespoons of dressing to coat. Serve immediately, drizzling more dressing over each serving if desired.

+ Make it gluten-free: Use gluten-free bread

58 mind-blowing things YOU'VE GOT TO EAT BEFORE YOU DIE

Sporting our elastic-waist pants, we've been super lucky when it comes to eating our way around the globe. Here's a list of our all-time greatest, most epic bites:

01. Chocolate Chip Walnut Cookie, Levain Bakery, New York

02. Ralph's Corned Beef Sandwich, The Polo Bar, New York

03. Cassava Chips with Thinly Sliced Beef, Mani, Sao Paulo

04. Ribeye Steak, Don Julio, Buenos Aires

05. Japanese Fried Chicken Appetizer, Ivan Ramen, New York

06. Shisito Pepper Sushi, Umu, London

07. Chocolate Rugelach, Marzipan Bakery, Jerusalem

08. Mediterranean Lobster, Park Fora, Istanbul

09. The New York Style Burger, Uncle Fletch, Santiago

10. Mashed Potatoes, L'Atelier Etoile de Joel Robuchon, Paris

11. Beef Marmalade and Pickles, Burnt Ends, Singapore

12. Taglierini with Truffles, Buca Mario, Florence

13. Pho Ga, Pho Thin, Hanoi

14. Secret Breakfast Ice Cream, Humphry Slocombe, San Francisco

15. Gruyere, Caramelized Onion & Arugula Pizza, Gjelina, Venice Beach

16. Viener Schnitzel, Meissl & Schadn, Vienna

17. Tonnarelli "in the Parmesan Wheel", Novikov, London

18. Pad See Ew, Khao San Road, Toronto

19. Burrata Pizza, Buca Osteria & Bar, Toronto

20. Cinnamon Buns, Ann Sather, Chicago

21. Brisket Sandwich, Franklin Barbecue, Austin

22. Shakshuka with Braised Eggs, Ottolenghi, London

23. Roasted Strawberry & Toasted White Chocolate Ice Cream, Salt & Straw, Los Angeles

24. Roasted Red Beets, Byblos, Toronto

25. Chocolate Babka French Toast, Russ & Daughters Café, New York

26. Potato Knish, Yonah Schimmel Knishes, New York

27. Sausage Brioche Sibilia, Les Halles de Lyon Paul Bocuse, Lyon

28. **Silver-Service Kosher Hot Dog with a Deviled Egg,** Palm Beach Grill, Palm Beach

29. **Gazoz,** Levinsky 41, Tel Aviv

30. **Sabich Sandwich,** Sabich Tchernihovsky, Tel Aviv

31. **Salted Caramel Scone,** Baker and Scone, Toronto

32. **Fried Dough,** Loosie's Kitchen, Brooklyn

33. **Whoopie Pies,** Two Fat Cats Bakery, Portland

34. **Sesame Bagel,** St-Viateur Bagel Shop, Montreal

35. **Braised Beef, Mushroom & Onions Sandwich,** Stockyard, Philadelphia

36. **Empanadas,** Gustazo Cuban Kitchen and Bar, Boston

37. **Dry Aged Bone-In New York,** SW Steakhouse, Las Vegas

38. **Salmon Oshi Sushi,** Miku, Vancouver

39. **Uncle Rube Sandwich,** Steingold's, Chicago

40. **Fettuccine alla Bolognese,** Scalinatella, New York

41. **The Rebel Within Muffin,** Craftsman and Wolves, San Francisco

42. **Fire-Baked Focaccia,** Etta, Chicago

43. **Loaded Deviled Eggs,** Waypoint Public, San Diego

44. **Roast Chicken,** Pinch Kitchen, Miami

45. **Coconut Cake,** KYU, Miami

46. **Ramen, Motomachi** Shokudo, Vancouver

47. **Lamb Popsicles,** Vij's, Vancouver

48. **Poutine,** Chez Tousignant, Montreal

49. **Milos Special,** Estiatorio Milos, New York

50. **Station Burger,** Richmond Station, Toronto

51. **Tasting Menu,** Alo, Toronto

52. **Crab Cake,** Faidley's, Baltimore

53. **Hummus,** Zahav, Philadelphia

54. **Morning Bun,** Tartine Bakery, San Francisco

55. **Whole Chicken,** Prince's Hot Chicken Shack, Nashville

56. **Seven-Layer Chocolate Cake,** Abe & Louie's, Boston

57. **Mish-Mash Omelet,** Beautys Luncheonette, Montreal

58. **Roasted Marshmallow Ice Cream,** Greg's Ice Cream, Toronto

tabbouleh salad

WITH ISRAELI COUSCOUS

Lisa sent me a note on this salad. It read, "Tabbouleh for JULIE!!! You're welcome for the title suggestion." Extremely helpful, and while I didn't bite on her creative captioning, I'm chowing down on her culinary genius, which is so evident in this fast, fresh, and fantastic salad. In it, she swapped out traditional bulgur for another Middle Eastern staple, Israeli (aka pearl) couscous, giving the salad a chewy texture, each forkful loaded with everything from mint, parsley, and chives to cucumbers, peppers, and tomatoes. Tossed in a zesty lemon cumin dressing, this is one dazzlingly-delicious-tabbouleh-for-Julie-that-is-super-cooly.

SERVES: 6–8   PREP TIME: 15 MINS   COOK TIME: 10 MINS (+chilling)

Lemon Cumin Dressing

¼ cup olive oil

2 tbsp fresh lemon juice

½ tsp lemon zest

½ tsp ground cumin

½ tsp kosher salt

⅛ tsp cayenne pepper

Salad

2 cups Israeli couscous

3 cups chicken broth

1 English cucumber, finely chopped (about 2 cups)

1½ cups cherry tomatoes, halved

1 green bell pepper, seeded and finely chopped

1 cup finely chopped fresh flat-leaf parsley

½ cup finely chopped fresh mint

¼ cup finely chopped chives

1. For the dressing, whisk together the olive oil, lemon juice, lemon zest, cumin, salt, and cayenne pepper. Set aside.

2. For the couscous, in a large saucepan, bring the couscous and broth to a boil. Cover, reduce the heat, and simmer for 10 minutes. Remove from the heat, drain out any remaining liquid, and place in a large serving bowl.

3. Add the cucumber, cherry tomatoes, green pepper, parsley, mint, and chives to the serving bowl. Toss with the dressing and refrigerate for 1 hour to chill and blend the flavors.

+ Make it gluten-free: Replace couscous with quinoa

When the uncreative tell the creative what to do, it stops being art. —TONY BENNETT

grilled vegetable & halloumi SALAD

Lisa's a super-literal gal. I asked her for grilled cheese, expecting toasted buttery bread oozing with gooey cheese. What she served up was radically healthier and dare I say, tastier, a salad of tender grilled vegetables tossed in a tangy dressing and topped with grilled halloumi cheese. Yes, cheese that has been grilled. Hailing from Cyprus, halloumi's a salty cheese that's rich in protein and calcium, and best of all, has a high melting point that makes it ideal for grilling. Golden outside, soft inside, the grilled cheese pairs perfectly with the natural sweetness of the charred vegetables and the salty tang of a caper, lemon, honey, and Dijon dressing. At the end of the day (FYI, I mean this literally and figuratively), this vibrant salad makes me grateful for Lisa's linguistic precision.

SERVES: 4–6   PREP TIME: 15 MINS   COOK TIME: 10 MINS

Zesty Dijon Dressing

3 tbsp olive oil

2 tbsp fresh lemon juice

2 tbsp chopped fresh flat-leaf parsley

1 tbsp capers, rinsed, drained, and chopped

2 tsp honey

1 tsp Dijon mustard

½ tsp lemon zest

½ tsp kosher salt

¼ tsp freshly ground black pepper

Grilled Vegetable Salad

2 zucchini, cut into ½-inch-thick rounds

2 red bell peppers, cut into wide strips

1 bunch asparagus, ends removed, cut into thirds

1 small red onion, cut into thin wedges

2 tbsp olive oil, divided

1 (8 oz) package halloumi cheese, sliced into 8 pieces

2 tbsp chopped fresh flat-leaf parsley

1. For the dressing, in a medium bowl, whisk together the olive oil, lemon juice, parsley, capers, honey, mustard, lemon zest, salt, and pepper until well combined. Set aside.

2. For the salad, preheat the grill to medium heat. In a large mixing bowl, toss the zucchini, peppers, asparagus, and red onion with 1 tablespoon of the olive oil. Put the vegetables in a grilling basket and place on the grill. Stir frequently for 5–6 minutes, until the vegetables are tender and lightly charred. Remove from the grill, put in a serving bowl, and toss with a few spoons of the caper dressing.

3. Brush both sides of the sliced halloumi with the remaining tablespoon of olive oil. Grill for 1–2 minutes per side, until lightly charred. Top the salad with the hot halloumi slices, a few more spoons of dressing, and the chopped parsley. Serve immediately.

sesame-soy green beans

I've been told I'm full of beans. Thanks, I think. So happy to be full of 'em, especially after my favorite bean counter (aka Lisa) has gotten her hands on this nutritionally awesome (high in fiber, protein, vitamins, and minerals) and super-versatile veggie. Green beans (aka string beans or snap beans) are cooked quickly, keeping their vibrant color and signature crunch intact, and they're easily jazzed up with Asian flavors. Packed with a tasty punch, sesame oil, soy sauce, garlic, ginger, chili paste, and a bit of honey bring nutty spiciness and a hint of sweetness to this exciting, healthy, and speedy side.

SERVES: 6–8   PREP TIME: 10 MINS   COOK TIME: 5 MINS

1 lb fresh green beans, ends trimmed

1 tbsp soy sauce

1 tsp honey

¼ tsp chili paste (such as sambal oelek)

2 tsp sesame oil

1 garlic clove, finely minced

½ tsp grated fresh ginger

Toasted black or white sesame seeds, for garnish

1. Bring a large pot of cold, salted water to a boil. Add the green beans, lower the heat, and cook for 2 minutes. Remove the beans from the water and plunge them into a bowl of ice water to retain the green color. Drain well.

2. In a small bowl, whisk together the soy sauce, honey, and chili paste and set aside.

3. In a large skillet, heat the sesame oil over medium-high heat. Add the garlic and ginger and cook for 30–60 seconds, until fragrant. Add the green beans and the soy sauce mixture. Stir well to coat and cook for 1–2 minutes, until heated through. Garnish with the sesame seeds.

✛ Make it gluten-free: Use gluten-free tamari, or gluten-free soy sauce, and gluten-free chili paste

lessons *from* lisa

★ Toast sesame seeds in a dry skillet over medium heat for 3–5 minutes, stirring occasionally until lightly browned.

★ A good alternative to sambal oelek is Sriracha hot sauce.

ROCKIN' THE

BEANSTACH

roasted cauliflower steaks
WITH HARISSA TAHINI SAUCE

You might think getting you to like this creamy white cruciferous veg is a fool's errand. And it might be if we didn't have Lisa, our taste tycoon, ace it by brushing cauliflower with honey and olive oil, sprinkling it with seven spices, and roasting it to caramelized perfection. Topped with a spicy (harissa), nutty (tahini), tangy (yogurt) sauce and finished with crunchy roasted almonds and fresh mint, these golden "meaty" steaks prove there's no such thing as a lost cause when Lisa's in the kitchen.

SERVES: 6   PREP TIME: 15 MINS   COOK TIME: 25 MINS

Harissa Tahini Sauce

2 tbsp plain Greek yogurt

1 tbsp tahini

1 tbsp fresh lemon juice

1 tsp harissa paste

½ tsp honey

¼ tsp kosher salt

1–2 tbsp water, divided

Cauliflower

2 heads cauliflower

2 tbsp olive oil

1 tbsp honey

1½ tsp paprika

½ tsp ground cumin

½ tsp kosher salt

¼ tsp freshly ground black pepper

¼ tsp ground sumac

⅛ tsp ground turmeric

⅛ tsp garlic powder

Roasted slivered almonds, for garnish

Fresh mint, coarsely chopped, for garnish

1. For the harissa tahini sauce, whisk together the yogurt, tahini, lemon juice, harissa, honey, and salt. Add the water a little at a time until a smooth creamy texture is formed. Cover and refrigerate the sauce until ready to use.

2. For the cauliflower, preheat the oven to 425°F. Line a baking sheet with parchment paper.

3. Cut the cauliflower into thick slices, about 1½ inches wide, and place them on the prepared baking sheet. From each head of cauliflower, you should get 3–4 cauliflower steaks.

4. In a small bowl, combine the olive oil and honey. Brush on both sides of cauliflower steaks.

5. In a small bowl, combine the paprika, cumin, salt, pepper, sumac, turmeric, and garlic powder. Sprinkle on both sides of the cauliflower. Bake until golden and tender, 22–24 minutes, flipping once halfway through cooking.

6. To serve, place the cauliflower on a platter, spoon harissa tahini sauce over top, and garnish with roasted almonds and fresh mint.

lessons *from* lisa

★ Harissa, a versatile and fiery North African hot chili spice paste, is found ready-made in jars, tubes, and cans.

LIGHTENED-UP brussels sprout gratin

When Lisa nails a recipe, she gets this very self-satisfied look on her face, much like the cat that got the cream. Well, meow. Turns out she not only got all the heavy cream out of this traditionally fat-laden fare, but also transformed an oft-maligned vegetable into a side dish superstar. Perfect (or shall I say, purr-fect?) for even the pickiest of eaters, Brussels sprouts are sautéed with shallots and garlic, then finished in the oven with a light béchamel sauce and Gruyère, resulting in golden-crusted sprouts that are both tender and creamy. Indulgent without turning us all into fat cats, this glorious gratin is outstanding, really the cat's meow of mealtime.

SERVES: 6–8   PREP TIME: 10 MINS   COOK TIME: 25 MINS

Brussels Sprouts

1 tbsp olive oil

2 lb Brussels sprouts, halved

2 shallots, cut in half and thinly sliced

1 garlic clove, minced

¼ tsp kosher salt

¼ tsp freshly ground black pepper

⅛ tsp cayenne pepper

Béchamel Sauce

2 tbsp butter

¼ cup flour

2 cups milk, warmed (2% or whole milk work well)

¾ cup grated Gruyère cheese, divided

¼ tsp kosher salt

Pinch freshly ground black pepper

1. Preheat the oven to 400°F.

2. For the Brussels sprouts, heat the olive oil in a large ovenproof skillet over medium heat. Add the Brussels sprouts, shallots, garlic, salt, pepper, and cayenne pepper. Cook, stirring, until slightly tender and golden, 6–8 minutes. Remove from the heat.

3. For the béchamel sauce, in a small saucepan, melt the butter over medium heat. Whisk in the flour and stir constantly for 1 minute to cook the flour. Slowly add the warmed milk, whisking constantly for 4–5 minutes until thickened. Remove from the heat and stir in ½ cup of the Gruyère, and the salt and pepper.

4. Pour the sauce over the Brussels sprouts and sprinkle the top with the remaining ¼ cup of Gruyère cheese. Bake for 12–14 minutes, turning the broiler on for the final minute to give a golden finish. Serve immediately.

'Meow' means 'woof' in cat. —GEORGE CARLIN

root vegetables

While Spock, Tonto, and Watson are all regular sidekicks, sometimes, there's a superb sidekick, like Chewbacca, who eclipses the hero. Such is the case with these Maple-Roasted Root Vegetables, a side dish that's considered a supporting character, but is in fact numero uno in the mealtime hierarchy. More than just a chum of chicken or mate to meat, these vegetables are standouts, roasted to bring out their natural sweetness. Lightly glazed with maple syrup, caramelized carrots, parsnips, beets, and sweet potatoes, with their vibrant colors and flavors, are a top-notch, healthy side dish that won't play second fiddle at any feast.

SERVES: 4–6   PREP TIME: 15 MINS   COOK TIME: 35 MINS

1 lb rainbow carrots, peeled and left whole

1 lb parsnips, peeled and sliced lengthwise

2 golden beets, peeled and cut into 8 wedges

1 large sweet potato (about 1 lb), peeled and cut in large cubes

3 tbsp olive oil

¾ tsp kosher salt

¼ tsp freshly ground black pepper

3 tbsp maple syrup

Chopped chives, for garnish

1. Preheat the oven to 400°F. Line 1 large or 2 smaller baking sheets with parchment paper.

2. In a large bowl, toss the carrots, parsnips, beets, and sweet potatoes with the olive oil, salt, and pepper.

3. Place the vegetables on the prepared baking sheets in a single layer, making sure to give them space. If they're too crowded, they won't caramelize. Roast for 20 minutes, remove from the oven, stir, and brush the vegetables with the maple syrup. Return to the oven and continue to roast for 12–15 minutes, until the vegetables are tender and caramelized. Garnish with the chopped chives.

lessons *from* lisa

★ These are the perfect holiday side dish because you can do all the vegetable prep a day ahead.

caramelized fennel

WITH PARMESAN & THYME

Lisa, upon giving me this recipe, claimed that fennel, the black licorice-like vegetable, was the star of her favorite side dish. Well, well, well. I was super psyched to have her eat crow, after years of her razzing me ("Are you 90 years old?" she'd quip) about my deep affection for Licorice Allsorts. However, my victory lap was cut short. It seems that when roasted with a bit of olive oil, earthy thyme, and a sprinkling of Parmesan, the natural flavors of anise-like fennel become sweet, creamy, and slightly nutty, not at all like licorice. As I dig into this simple, comforting, and healthy side, I have to admit that I feel like a kid in a candy store.

SERVES: 4   PREP TIME: 5 MINS   COOK TIME: 35 MINS

2 fennel bulbs, trimmed, cored, cut in half and then into wedges

2 tbsp olive oil

1 tsp chopped fresh thyme

½ tsp kosher salt

¼ tsp freshly ground black pepper

Pinch red pepper flakes

3 tbsp freshly grated Parmesan cheese

1 tbsp chopped fresh flat-leaf parsley, for garnish

1. Preheat the oven to 425°F. Coat a 2½-quart oval baking dish with nonstick cooking spray. Place the fennel wedges in the prepared baking dish.

2. In a small bowl, combine the olive oil, thyme, salt, pepper, and red pepper flakes. Brush the mixture generously over fennel. Cover with aluminum foil and roast for 20 minutes. Remove cover and continue to roast for 10 minutes more. Sprinkle Parmesan cheese over top and return to the oven for 5 minutes. Remove from the oven and garnish with chopped parsley.

We're like licorice. Not everybody likes licorice, but the people who like licorice really like licorice. —JERRY GARCIA

ROASTED GARLIC & parmesan mashed potatoes

It seems so simple, yet there is a fine art to making the most marvelous mash. While some find success with pounds of butter (late Michelin-star chef Joël Robuchon's world-famous pommes pureé), others rely on cream (Tyler Florence), horseradish (Oprah), or cream cheese (Pioneer Woman) to snazz up this classic side. What's Lisa's claim to tuber fame? Roasted garlic. The caramelized clove adds sweetness and depth of flavor not usually found in mashed potatoes, and it pairs perfectly with nutty Parmesan and subtle fresh chives. Despite cutting way back on butter, these well-seasoned spuds have a smooth, creamy consistency that makes them the perfect addition to any meaty main course.

SERVES: 4–6   PREP TIME: 15 MINS   COOK TIME: 60 MINS

Roasted Garlic

1 small head garlic

1 tsp olive oil

Mashed Potatoes

2½ lb (about 4 large) Yukon gold potatoes, peeled and cut in large chunks

¾ cup whole milk

3 tbsp butter

½ cup freshly grated Parmesan cheese

½ tsp kosher salt

¼ tsp freshly ground black pepper

2 tbsp chopped fresh chives, divided

1. For the roasted garlic, preheat the oven to 375°F.

2. Slice the top off the head of garlic and drizzle with the olive oil. Wrap the garlic in aluminum foil, place on a baking sheet, and roast for 40–45 minutes, until tender enough to be mashed. Squeeze the cloves out, mash with a fork, and set aside.

3. While the garlic roasts, cook the potatoes in a large pot of boiling salted water for 15–20 minutes, until fork tender. Drain the potatoes very well.

4. In a large bowl, mash the potatoes using a potato ricer or potato masher.

5. In a small saucepan over low heat, heat the milk and butter until the butter is melted and the milk is warmed. Stir into the mashed potatoes along with the roasted garlic, Parmesan, salt, pepper, and 1 tablespoon of the chopped chives. Stir until blended and creamy. Use the remaining chives to garnish the potatoes. Serve warm.

lessons *from* lisa

★ If you don't want to use the whole roasted garlic clove in the mashed potatoes, you can serve it sautéed with bok choy or spinach, as a spread on a roasted vegetable sandwich, on crostini, or with grilled steak or grilled chicken.

asparagus with toasted walnuts & LEMON VINAIGRETTE

The Broadway musical *Hair* was revolutionary, including naked hippies (Lisa accidentally took her nine-year-old daughter to see it), and most of all, my fave tune, "The Age of Asparagus." I mean, really, who wouldn't want to move this nutrient-rich vegetable from understudy to center stage? Our dinnertime director has choreographed this side dish—fresh, crunchy asparagus paired with toasted walnuts, salty Parmesan, and a tangy lemon dressing—to be a true star. Beautiful to the eye and pleasing to the palate, there will be loud applause for this scene-stealer. Encore! Encore!

SERVES: 6   PREP TIME: 10 MINS   COOK TIME: <5 MINS

30 asparagus stalks

Lemon Vinaigrette

2 tbsp olive oil

1 tbsp fresh lemon juice

1 tsp lemon zest

¼ tsp kosher salt

Pinch freshly ground black pepper

2 tbsp chopped fresh flat-leaf parsley

¼ cup shaved fresh Parmesan cheese

¼ cup coarsely chopped toasted walnuts

1. For the asparagus, snap off and discard the tough bottom ends and peel the lower ends with a vegetable peeler.

2. Bring a large pot of salted water to a boil. Add the asparagus, lower the heat, and cook for 2 minutes. Quickly remove the asparagus and plunge them into a bowl of ice water to stop them from overcooking and losing their bright color. Drain well.

3. For the vinaigrette, in a small bowl, whisk together the olive oil, lemon juice, lemon zest, salt, and pepper.

4. To serve, place the room-temperature asparagus on a serving platter and drizzle with the lemon vinaigrette. Top with chopped parsley, shaved Parmesan, and toasted walnuts.

lessons *from* lisa

★ To toast walnuts, spread them in a single layer on a baking sheet and bake at 350°F for 10 minutes, stirring once halfway through baking.

★ Store asparagus in the refrigerator upright with the stems sitting in a container in an inch of water.

★ Female asparagus stalks are plumper than male ones.

HEALTHIER sweet potato casserole

In my mind I've gone to Carolina, y'all. Lisa finds my put-on twang intolerable, but bless her heart, she's indulged my love for Southern cooking, the kind where you get biscuits with your gravy, and created this lightened-up version of a sweet potato classic. How did shuga do it? She roasted the sweet potatoes, which brings out their natural sweetness, meaning she could cut way back on sugar, and she slashed the fat by swapping out heavy cream for almond milk. With a touch of maple syrup for sweetness, cinnamon, nutmeg, and ginger to spice things up, and a crunchy toasted pecan topping, this made-over casserole will have y'all coming back for more. Now that we've got that figured out, won't you join me on the veranda for a mint julep, darlin'?

SERVES: 8–10   PREP TIME: 15 MINS   COOK TIME: 70 MINS

Sweet Potato Mash

1 tbsp olive oil

5 large (about 5 lb) sweet potatoes, halved lengthwise

2 tbsp butter, softened

⅓ cup vanilla unsweetened almond milk

3 tbsp maple syrup

1 egg, lightly whisked

2 tsp vanilla extract

1 tsp kosher salt

½ tsp ground cinnamon

½ tsp ground ginger

¼ tsp ground nutmeg

Toasted Pecan Topping

1 cup Corn Flakes cereal, lightly crushed

½ cup chopped toasted pecans

2 tbsp brown sugar

¼ tsp ground cinnamon

¼ tsp kosher salt

2 tbsp butter, softened

1. Preheat the oven to 400°F and line a baking sheet with parchment paper.

2. For the sweet potato mash, rub the olive oil on the sweet potato halves. Place the sweet potatoes cut side down on the prepared sheet and bake for 35–40 minutes, until fork tender.

3. Remove from the oven and spoon the cooked flesh from the sweet potatoes into a large mixing bowl. Using a potato masher, mash the potatoes with the butter. Add the almond milk, maple syrup, egg, vanilla, salt, cinnamon, ginger, and nutmeg. Stir well until combined.

4. Lower the oven temperature to 350°F and coat a 9-inch square baking dish with nonstick cooking spray. Transfer the potato mixture to the prepared dish.

5. For the toasted pecan topping, in a mixing bowl, combine the Corn Flakes, pecans, brown sugar, cinnamon, and salt. Rub the butter into the mixture until crumbly. Sprinkle the topping over the sweet potatoes and bake for 30 minutes.

+ Make it gluten-free: Use gluten-free Corn Flakes

lessons *from* lisa

★ You can prep this dish a day in advance. Refrigerate the casserole and add the topping right before baking.

acorn squash

When I see "No Entry," I read it as "Welcome." So, it shouldn't surprise you that when Lisa uses something called forbidden rice (aka black rice), I say, "Bring it on." Once reserved for Chinese royalty, this irresistible rice, full of antioxidants, fiber, iron, and vitamin E, is making a tasty appearance in this commoner's kitchen. Mixed with fresh herbs, salty feta, and crunchy pistachios, the onyx-colored grain is mounded high in sweet roasted squash and topped with fresh pomegranate seeds. Hearty yet healthy, filling yet light, this "forbidden" meal is impossible to resist.

Black Rice Filling

1 cup black rice

2 cups water

2 tbsp olive oil

2 tbsp fresh lemon juice

1 tsp lemon zest

¼ tsp kosher salt

¼ cup chopped fresh mint

¼ cup chopped fresh flat-leaf parsley

½ cup crumbled feta cheese

⅓ cup coarsely chopped roasted, salted pistachio nuts

Pomegranate Topping

1 cup pomegranate seeds

1 tbsp olive oil

1 tbsp chopped fresh flat-leaf parsley

1 tsp fresh lemon juice

Pinch kosher salt and freshly ground black pepper

Acorn Squash

3 acorn squashes, halved and seeds removed

1½ tbsp olive oil

½ tsp kosher salt

¼ tsp freshly ground black pepper

1. For the black rice filling, add the rice and water to a medium saucepan. Bring to a boil, cover, and reduce the heat to low. Cook for 40 minutes. Once the rice is cooked, remove from the heat and let sit covered for 10 minutes.

2. Place the rice in a large mixing bowl and stir in the olive oil, lemon juice, lemon zest, salt, mint, parsley, feta, and pistachios. Set aside.

3. For the pomegranate topping, in a small bowl, combine the pomegranate seeds, olive oil, parsley, lemon juice, and salt and pepper. Cover and refrigerate until ready to serve.

4. While the rice is cooking, roast the acorn squash. Preheat the oven to 400°F and line a baking sheet with parchment paper. Brush the squash halves with olive oil and sprinkle with the salt and pepper. Place the squash halves cut side down on the prepared baking sheet. Roast for 25 minutes, until tender and golden.

5. To assemble, divide the black rice filling between the roasted squash halves. Spoon the pomegranate topping over top and serve.

lessons *from* lisa

★ *Choose acorn squashes that feel heavy for their size.*

butternut squash & spinach LASAGNA

To this day, I can't get close enough to my sister. Despite her protests, since childhood (I forced her to push our beds together so we could hold hands) she's been my security blanket. Call me Linus, but Lisa continues to comfort me. Take her luscious lasagna: it's the epitome of feel-good food, an earthy, hearty, vegetarian twist on an Italian classic. Not only am I assuaged by its ambrosial aroma, but also the taste of these layers of love, a warming pan of creamy-yet-creamless roasted butternut squash and ricotta, tender noodles, savory spinach, and cheesy goodness. Easy to assemble and guaranteed to solve any dinnertime dilemma, even with Lisa's need for personal space, this is one delicious dependency I'll never give up.

SERVES: 8–10   PREP TIME: 25 MINS   COOK TIME: 85 MINS

Butternut Squash

2 tsp olive oil

1 butternut squash, cut in half lengthwise, seeds removed

¾ cup ricotta cheese

½ cup milk

¾ tsp kosher salt

¼ tsp freshly ground black pepper

Ricotta Spinach Filling

2 (10 oz) packages frozen chopped spinach, thawed and squeezed dry

2 cups ricotta cheese

1 egg, lightly whisked

½ cup freshly grated Parmesan cheese

½ tsp kosher salt

¼ tsp freshly ground black pepper

Pinch ground nutmeg

continued on next page

1. Preheat the oven to 400°F. Line a baking sheet with parchment paper.

2. For the squash, brush the olive oil over the cut side of the squash. Place the squash cut side down on the baking sheet. Bake for 30–35 minutes, until fork tender.

3. Once cool enough to handle, scoop out the flesh of the squash and transfer to a blender or food processor. Add the ricotta, milk, salt, and pepper. Pulse until smooth and creamy. Transfer to a bowl and set aside.

4. Reduce the oven temperature to 375°F. Coat a 9-by-13-inch baking dish with nonstick cooking spray.

5. For the ricotta spinach filling, in a medium bowl, combine the spinach, ricotta, egg, Parmesan, salt, pepper, and nutmeg. Set aside.

6. In a large pot of salted boiling water, cook the noodles for 6–8 minutes, until al dente. Drain and rinse the noodles under cold water.

12 uncooked lasagna noodles

1 cup shredded mozzarella cheese, divided

1 cup shredded Gruyère cheese, divided

7. To assemble, in the prepared baking dish, spread about ½ cup of the squash mixture on the base. Top with 3 noodles and spread half the ricotta spinach filling over the noodles. Sprinkle with ½ cup of the mozzarella cheese. Top with 3 more noodles. Spread about 1 cup of the squash mixture over the noodles. Sprinkle with ½ cup of the shredded Gruyère and top with 3 more noodles. Spread the remaining ricotta spinach filling on top and sprinkle with the remaining ½ cup of mozzarella. Top with the remaining 3 noodles, spread with the remaining butternut squash mixture, and sprinkle with the remaining ½ cup of Gruyère.

8. Cover with aluminum foil and bake for 35–40 minutes, until bubbling around the edges. Remove the cover, turn the broiler to high, and broil for 4 minutes, until the topping is golden. Remove from the oven and let sit 10 minutes before cutting.

If I can punch you in the throat without moving my feet, you're in my personal space. —ANONYMOUS

mushroom & ricotta
WHITE PIZZA

In my world, there's nothing but Lisa Hut. This girl, she thinks way outside the box and delivers pizza without equal. Lisa's crust is killer. I mean, sure you can buy a prepared one, but rolling your own is easier than you think, and using "00" extra-fine Italian flour yields a perfect 10 crust, one that's light and airy with a crisp exterior. When it comes to toppings, Lisa's mastered balancing taste and texture, allowing ingredients to shine in every bite with a combination of freshly grated mozzarella, dollops of creamy ricotta, and shallot, herb, and garlic-sautéed mushrooms. Trust me, save the airfare and enjoy the ultimate, dreamiest NeapoLisa pie right in the comfort of your home.

MAKES: TWO 12-INCH PIZZAS   PREP TIME: 20 MINS (+ rising)
COOK TIME: 25 MINS

Pizza Dough

1¼ cups warm water

1 tbsp sugar

1 (¼ oz) package active dried yeast

3½ cups "00" flour

3 tbsp olive oil

2 tsp kosher salt

Mushroom Topping

2 tbsp olive oil

1 lb sliced mixed mushrooms (cremini, shiitake, white button)

1 large shallot, thinly sliced

2 garlic cloves, minced

½ tsp dried oregano

½ tsp dried thyme

½ tsp kosher salt

continued on next page

1. For the pizza dough, in the bowl of an electric mixer, combine the warm water, sugar, and yeast. Let sit for 5 minutes. Add the flour, olive oil, and salt, mixing on low speed using the dough hook, until the flour is incorporated. Increase the speed to medium and mix until the dough is smooth, 8 minutes. Place the dough in a lightly oiled bowl, cover, and let rise for 1 hour in a warm place.

2. Preheat the oven to 450°F. Place your pizza stone in the oven 30 minutes before cooking the pizza.

3. While the dough rises, prepare the mushroom topping. In a large skillet, heat the olive oil over medium-high heat. Add the mushrooms and shallot and cook for 10 minutes, stirring occasionally. Add the garlic, oregano, thyme, and salt. Continue cooking for 1 minute. Remove from the heat and set aside.

4. For the pizzas, punch the dough down and divide it in half (each half will be 14 oz). Knead each piece on a lightly floured surface for 1 minute. Cover both dough balls with a clean cloth and allow to rest for 10 minutes.

5. On a lightly floured surface, roll each dough ball into a 12-inch circle. Brush the edges of both pizzas with olive oil, sprinkle with a pinch of salt around the edges, and top with the mozzarella, dollops of ricotta, and the mushroom mixture.

1 tbsp olive oil

Pinch kosher salt

2 cups shredded mozzarella
cheese

1½ cups ricotta cheese

Shaved Parmesan cheese,
for garnish

6. Transfer one pizza at a time to the preheated stone and bake until the crust is golden, 10–12 minutes. Remove from the oven, top with shaved Parmesan cheese. Slice and serve.

lessons *from* lisa

★ An equal amount of all-purpose flour can replace the "00" flour.

★ If you don't have a pizza stone, use a pizza pan and bake as directed.

" *Every pizza is a personal pizza if you try hard and believe in yourself.*

—DEMETRI MARTIN

SLICE, SLICE *baby* →

saffron risotto

WITH CORN & ROASTED RED PEPPERS

Goldcorp, allow me to give you a nugget of advice because you're doing it all wrong. Forget tunneling, dredging, and drilling, and start working the crocus fields, where the spice more valuable (and in some cases, more expensive) than gold is waiting to be harvested. Yes, I'm telling you that saffron (aka red gold) is the most highly prized spice on the rack and, much like Lisa, has the Midas touch when turning recipes into riches. In this easy yet elegant dish, our Golden Girl has taken this precious floral-scented spice and combined it with creamy rice, fresh corn, roasted red peppers, and a dazzling pop of basil, parsley, and lemon. One delicious bite from this pot of gold and you'll know, without a doubt, you've hit the mother lode.

SERVES: 4–6   PREP TIME: 15 MINS   COOK TIME: 25 MINS

4 cups chicken broth

1 large pinch saffron threads

1 tbsp olive oil

1 tbsp butter

1 small yellow onion, finely chopped

2 shallots, finely chopped

½ tsp kosher salt

1½ cups Arborio rice

½ cup dry white wine

1 cup fresh corn (from 3 small ears)

1 red bell pepper, roasted and chopped (about ½ cup)

⅓ cup freshly grated Parmesan cheese

1 tbsp chopped fresh basil

1 tbsp chopped fresh flat-leaf parsley

1 tsp lemon zest

Freshly grated Parmesan cheese, for serving

1. In a medium saucepan, bring the broth to a boil. Turn the heat to low and add the saffron threads to infuse the broth. Continue to simmer the broth.

2. In a large pot over medium heat, heat the olive oil and butter. Add the onion, shallots, and salt, cooking until softened, about 3 minutes. Stir in the rice and cook, stirring, for 1 minute. Add the wine, stirring continuously until it has evaporated.

3. Reduce the heat to medium-low and add ½ cup of the broth, stirring frequently until the liquid is absorbed. Add another ½ cup and repeat, making sure each addition of liquid is absorbed before adding the next.

4. With the last ½ cup of broth, stir in the fresh corn and continue stirring until broth has been absorbed. Remove from the heat and stir in the roasted red pepper, Parmesan, basil, parsley, and lemon zest. Serve immediately, garnished with extra Parmesan if desired.

lessons *from* lisa

★ The total cook time for the risotto is 18–20 minutes, until it's creamy and slightly al dente.

★ Saffron is expensive because it's an extremely labor-intensive crop; each crocus flower has 3 tiny stigmas in the center that are harvested individually.

smoked gouda
MAC & CHEESE

espite going Dutch on this marvelous mac, Lisa isn't a cheapo—she's hugely generous with Gouda, our favorite Dutch export since wooden clogs (note: we look awesome in our klompen). Gouda, one of the world's most popular cheeses, is combined with smoked Gouda and sharp white cheddar, resulting in the perfect balance of flavor, texture, and gooeyness. Finished with a buttery, crispy crumb topping, this twist on a classic crowd-pleaser is one Dutch treat you're not going to want to split.

SERVES: 8–10   PREP TIME: 15 MINS   COOK TIME: 35 MINS

Crumb Topping

3 tbsp butter

1 cup panko (Japanese breadcrumbs)

¼ cup freshly grated Parmesan cheese

¼ tsp dried thyme

¼ tsp paprika

¼ tsp kosher salt

Macaroni

1 lb uncooked short noodle pasta (macaroni, mini farfalle, mini shells)

¼ cup butter

5 tbsp flour

1 tsp mustard powder

¾ tsp kosher salt

Pinch cayenne pepper

3½ cups whole milk, warmed

1½ cups shredded smoked Gouda cheese

1½ cups shredded aged Gouda cheese

3 cups grated sharp white cheddar cheese

1. Preheat the oven to 350°F. Coat a 9-by-13-inch baking dish with nonstick cooking spray.

2. For the crumb topping, melt the butter in a skillet over medium heat. Add the panko and cook, stirring constantly, until golden, 2–3 minutes.

3. Transfer to a bowl and stir in the Parmesan, thyme, paprika, and salt. Set aside.

4. In a large pot of salted boiling water, cook the pasta until al dente, about 5 minutes. Drain, rinse, and set aside.

5. While the pasta is cooking, in a large saucepan, melt the butter over medium heat. Sprinkle in the flour and cook, whisking continuously, for 1 minute. Stir in the mustard powder, salt, and cayenne pepper. Very slowly add the warmed milk, continuously whisking to prevent lumps. Bring the sauce to a boil, then reduce the heat and simmer, whisking frequently, for about 5 minutes, until the sauce has thickened and doesn't feel grainy. Over low heat, stir in the smoked Gouda, aged Gouda, and white cheddar. Cook until the cheese melts and the sauce is smooth, 1–2 minutes. Remove from the heat and stir in the pasta.

6. Transfer to the prepared baking dish and bake for 10 minutes. Remove from the oven, sprinkle the crumb topping evenly over top, and continue to bake for 10 minutes until bubbling and heated through.

lessons *from* lisa

★ *Only cook pasta al dente, as it bakes again in the oven and will have a mushy end texture if overcooked.*

★ *Grating your own cheese takes a few minutes and is worth the small effort—it melts and tastes much better.*

ONE-PAN **roasted chicken dinner**

Many put the no-fail dinner in the same category as Chupacabra and Bigfoot: mythical. Well, the hunt is over, blurry photos and all. It doesn't get easier than this one-pan meal, a tender and juicy spice-rubbed chicken along with perfectly cooked vegetables. Stuffed with fresh herbs, lemon, and garlic, the chicken is coated in an aromatic mix of spices and roasted nestled atop potatoes and carrots. The result is a flavorful meal that will leave everyone breathless. As for you, the ease of this foolproof feast frees you up to continue your quest for the Loch Ness Monster and the Bogeyman.

SERVES: 4   PREP TIME: 15 MINS (+ brining)   COOK TIME: 65 MINS (+ resting)

1 (4–4½ lb) whole roasting chicken

Kosher salt, for rubbing

1 lemon half

4 sprigs fresh thyme

2 sprigs fresh rosemary

2 garlic cloves

Spice Rub

2 tsp ground cumin

2 tsp ground coriander

2 tsp garlic powder

1 tsp paprika

1 tsp sumac

1 tsp kosher salt

½ tsp freshly ground black pepper

4 tbsp + 1 tsp olive oil, divided

continued on next page

1. To prepare the chicken, pat dry with paper towels. Generously season inside and out with salt. Let sit at room temperature for 30 minutes. If you have longer, refrigerate up to 24 hours, making sure to bring the chicken back to room temperature before cooking to ensure even cooking.

2. Preheat the oven to 425°F, placing a 12-inch cast-iron skillet in the oven while preheating. Pat the chicken dry again with paper towels, fill the cavity with the lemon, thyme, rosemary, and garlic, and tie the legs together with kitchen string.

3. For the spice rub, in a small bowl, combine the cumin, coriander, garlic powder, paprika, sumac, salt, and pepper. Remove 1 teaspoon of the spice rub and set aside.

4. Rub 2 tablespoons of the olive oil all over the outside of the chicken and sprinkle with the spice rub. Remove the skillet from the oven and drizzle 1 tablespoon of olive oil in the bottom of the skillet. Carefully place chicken in the skillet.

5. In a medium mixing bowl, toss the red potatoes and fingerlings with 2 teaspoons of olive oil and the remaining teaspoon of spice rub. Scatter the potatoes around the chicken. Roast the chicken for 30 minutes.

Vegetables

¾ lb small red potatoes, washed and dried

¾ lb fingerling potatoes, washed and dried

¾ lb baby heirloom carrots, trimmed

Pinch kosher salt and freshly ground pepper

6. Toss the carrots with the remaining 2 teaspoons of olive oil and a pinch of salt and pepper. Scatter over the potatoes and roast for another 30–35 minutes, or until a thermometer inserted in a thick part of the leg registers 165°F. Remove from the oven and tent with foil for 15 minutes. Remove the kitchen string and serve the chicken and vegetables.

lessons *from* lisa

★ If you don't have a cast-iron skillet, this can easily be made in a roasting pan—no need to preheat the roasting pan as you do the skillet.

DINNER IS
served.

za'atar-crusted chicken

WITH CUCUMBER SALAD

"Winner Winner, Chicken Dinner" is an interesting phrase. While most of us don't think of chicken as a jackpot ("Winner Winner, Lobster Dinner" sounds more like a prize), I'll gladly and eagerly take this mind-blowing chicken as my windfall. Dipped in nutty tahini (which is super high in calcium, amino acids, and healthy fats), chicken is then coated in za'atar (pronounced "za-ah-tar"), a fragrant Middle Eastern spice blend. Baked until golden and crispy, this flavor-packed dish is paired with a refreshing mint and dill cucumber salad, making this 30-minute dinner a trip directly to the winner's circle, with time to spare for your victory lap.

SERVES: 4   PREP TIME: 15 MINS   COOK TIME: 15 MINS

Za'atar Chicken

4 boneless, skinless chicken breasts

½ tsp kosher salt

¼ cup tahini

1 egg

3 tbsp water

1 cup panko (Japanese breadcrumbs)

½ cup slivered almonds

2 tbsp za'atar

1 tbsp toasted sesame seeds

½ tsp ground cumin

½ tsp kosher salt

½ tsp freshly ground black pepper

Pinch cayenne pepper

1 tbsp olive oil

continued on next page

1. For the chicken, preheat the oven to 425°F. Line a rimmed baking sheet with parchment paper and set aside. Season chicken breasts with ½ teaspoon kosher salt.

2. In a shallow dish, whisk together the tahini, egg, and water until smooth. In another shallow dish, combine the panko, almonds, za'atar, sesame seeds, cumin, salt, black pepper, and cayenne pepper. Dip each chicken breast into the tahini mixture and then coat in the panko mixture, pressing well to make the panko stick. Place on the prepared baking sheet, drizzle olive oil over each chicken breast, and bake for 14–15 minutes, until cooked through.

3. While the chicken bakes, prepare the cucumber salad. Cut the cucumber into thin slices.

4. In a small bowl, whisk the yogurt, sour cream, lemon juice, olive oil, lemon zest, sugar, salt, pepper, garlic powder, dill, and mint until well combined. Fold in the cucumbers and serve immediately with the chicken.

Cucumber Salad

1 large English cucumber, unpeeled

¼ cup plain Greek yogurt

¼ cup light sour cream

1 tbsp fresh lemon juice

1 tbsp olive oil

½ tsp lemon zest

½ tsp sugar

½ tsp kosher salt

¼ tsp freshly ground black pepper

¼ tsp garlic powder

2 tbsp chopped fresh dill

2 tbsp chopped fresh mint

+ Make it gluten-free: Use gluten-free panko, and gluten-free za'atar or make your own (see Lessons from Lisa)

lessons *from* lisa

★ If you're not serving this right away, leave the dressing separate from the cucumbers—mixing them too far ahead will create a watery salad.

★ Use a mandoline to cut the cucumbers for speed and consistent slices.

★ To make your own za'atar, stir together 3 tablespoons of sumac, 2 tablespoons of toasted sesame seeds, 2 tablespoons of dried thyme, 1 tablespoon of dried oregano, and 1 teaspoon of kosher salt. Store in an airtight container for up to 3 months.

> *Winning isn't everything. It's the only thing.* —VINCE LOMBARDI

EAT & *enjoy*

#DRINK
BEFORE DINNER

grilled lemon chicken
WITH ROMESCO SAUCE

I told Lisa I'm going to Spain to run with the bulls. She called me on that one (she's seen me run, lapped by babies and seniors alike), but as I panted, jogging in place, I admitted I just wanted to go somewhere I can have romesco sauce at every meal. After she said, "Yeah, I figured," our very own mealtime matador took the bull by the horns and created this superbly fantastic recipe, a lemon, garlic, and herb–marinated chicken that's grilled to juicy perfection and paired with this classic Spanish sauce. Hailing from Tarragona, a coastal city in Spain, romesco is a flavor explosion of roasted peppers, caramelized tomatoes, garlic, almonds, and spices, ideal for those of us looking to thrill our taste buds without breaking a sweat.

SERVES: 6   PREP TIME: 20 MINS (+ marinating)   COOK TIME: 40 MINS

3 tbsp olive oil

1 tbsp lemon zest

3 garlic cloves, crushed

1 tsp dried thyme

1 tsp dried oregano

½ tsp dried basil

½ tsp kosher salt

½ tsp freshly ground black pepper

Pinch red pepper flakes

6 boneless, skinless chicken breasts

Romesco Sauce

4 plum tomatoes, cored and halved (seeds can be left in)

⅓ cup + 2 tsp olive oil, divided

Pinch kosher salt

Pinch freshly ground black pepper

continued on next page

1. For the chicken, in a large bowl, whisk together the olive oil, lemon zest, garlic, thyme, oregano, basil, salt, pepper, and red pepper flakes. Add the chicken to marinade, cover, and refrigerate at least 1 hour and up to 24 hours.

2. Preheat a grill to medium-high and oil the grill grate. Discard the marinade and grill the chicken for 5–6 minutes per side, until cooked through.

3. For the romesco sauce, preheat the oven to 400°F. Place the tomato halves cut side up on a parchment-lined baking sheet. Drizzle with 2 teaspoons of the olive oil and sprinkle with a pinch of kosher salt and pepper. Place in the oven for 25 minutes, until the tomatoes are starting to caramelize around the edges.

4. Remove from the oven, let cool slightly, and place in a blender.

5. To roast the red peppers, place the peppers directly on the burner of a gas stove and turn to high heat. If you don't have a gas burner, you can roast the peppers under a broiler. When one side is charred, rotate the pepper until all sides are charred.

2 red bell peppers

2 slices crusty bread, toasted and cubed (about ¾ cups cubed)

2 garlic cloves, minced

⅓ cup sliced almonds

1 tsp sherry vinegar

½ tsp smoked paprika

½ tsp kosher salt

¼ tsp freshly ground black pepper

6. Place the peppers in a bowl, cover, and let them steam. After 5–10 minutes, slip off the charred skin and remove the core and seeds of the peppers. Add the peppers to the blender along with the toasted bread cubes.

7. In a small skillet, heat the remaining ⅓ cup of olive oil over medium heat. Stir in the garlic and almonds. Cook for 2 minutes, watching carefully. Transfer to the blender and add the sherry vinegar, smoked paprika, salt, and pepper. Blend until smooth and serve alongside the chicken.

+ **Make it gluten-free: Use gluten-free bread**

> *Nobody ever lives their life all the way up except bull-fighters.*
>
> —ERNEST HEMINGWAY, *THE SUN ALSO RISES*

top 10 easy yet elegant recipes even

YOUR MOTHER-IN LAW WILL LOVE

While she may offer up "helpful" advice on everything from properly loading a dishwasher to perfect parenting, your mother-in-law will be left speechless by these surefire winners.

chicken scaloppine
WITH MUSHROOMS & WHITE WINE

Did you know that at any one time, 0.7 percent of the world's population is drunk? I like knowing this. It means I'm not alone as I sip—this recipe only uses a quarter of that bottle of vino—while cooking up a storm. Not only is this thinly pounded chicken paired with white wine and garlic-sautéed mushrooms, but it's also enhanced with zesty lemon and a little butter (note: our lightened-up version omits quarts of cream), making the end result fantastically fast and flavorful. Easy to make (even when not sober as a judge), you'll be eating, drinking, and merrymaking in no time with this 35-minute-start-to-finish feast. Cheers!

SERVES: 4   PREP TIME: 10 MINS   COOK TIME: 25 MINS

¼ cup flour

½ tsp kosher salt

½ tsp freshly ground black pepper

2 tbsp olive oil, divided

4 boneless, skinless chicken breasts, butterflied (sliced horizontally) and pounded thin

Mushroom and White Wine Sauce

4 cups brown or white sliced mushrooms

2 garlic cloves, chopped

¼ tsp kosher salt

¼ tsp freshly ground black pepper

1 cup dry white wine

1 cup chicken broth

¼ cup fresh lemon juice

2 tbsp capers, rinsed and drained

3 tbsp butter

¼ cup chopped fresh flat-leaf parsley

1 tsp lemon zest

1. Place the flour in a shallow dish and season with salt and pepper.

2. Heat 1 tablespoon of the olive oil in a large skillet over medium-high heat. Dredge the chicken in the flour mixture, shaking off any excess. Place in the hot skillet in 2 batches so you don't overcrowd the pan. Cook 2–3 minutes per side, depending on thickness, until golden brown and cooked completely through. Remove from the skillet and cook the rest of the chicken using the remaining olive oil. Set the chicken aside on a plate.

3. For the mushroom and white wine sauce, using the same skillet, add the mushrooms and sauté for 3 minutes, until tender. Add the garlic, salt, and pepper, continuously stirring for 30 seconds. Add the white wine over medium-high heat and cook for 3 minutes. Stir in the chicken broth, lemon juice, and capers. Once the sauce comes to a boil, reduce the heat and simmer for 5 minutes. Stir in the butter, parsley, and lemon zest. Return the cooked chicken to the skillet and simmer until heated through, 1–2 minutes.

 I cook with wine, sometimes I even add it to the food. —W.C. FIELDS

pecan-crusted chicken WITH ORANGE HONEY GLAZE

I think that most chicken dishes would make front-page news for the wrong reasons: "Rubber Chicken Epidemic Sweeps the Nation!" or "Greasy Schnitzel Loses Its Breading!" While these headlines are attention-grabbers, we've got a hot-off-the-press suppertime scoop you're going to want to sink your teeth into: pecan-crusted chicken, moist and full of toasty, nutty flavor, is baked until golden brown and drizzled with a sweet and savory orange honey glaze. Get ready to eat between the lines because this quick, easy, baked, crunchy, crowd-pleasing chicken is going to be in wide circulation. You can quote me on that.

SERVES: 4   PREP TIME: 15 MINS   COOK TIME: 35 MINS

Pecan Chicken

¼ cup flour

1¼ tsp kosher salt, divided

½ tsp freshly ground black pepper

½ tsp paprika

½ tsp dried thyme

1 egg

2 tbsp honey mustard

1 cup coarsely chopped pecans

1 cup panko (Japanese breadcrumbs)

2 tbsp sesame seeds

½ tsp orange zest

4 boneless, skinless chicken breasts, pounded slightly for even thickness

2 tbsp olive oil

Orange Honey Glaze

½ cup orange juice

¼ cup honey

1. Preheat the oven to 350°F. Line a baking sheet with aluminum foil and coat with nonstick cooking spray.

2. For the pecan chicken, in a shallow bowl, combine the flour, 1 teaspoon of the salt, pepper, paprika, and thyme. In a second bowl, whisk together the egg and honey mustard. In a third, larger bowl, combine the pecans, panko, sesame seeds, orange zest, and the remaining ¼ teaspoon of salt. Coat each chicken breast in the flour mixture, shaking off the excess. Dip in the egg mixture and finally coat in the pecan mixture, pressing well to make the mixture stick.

3. Place the chicken breasts on the prepared baking sheet and drizzle with the olive oil. Bake for 30 minutes and let the chicken rest for 5 minutes before serving.

4. For the glaze, in a small saucepan, heat the orange juice and honey over medium heat. Let the mixture boil for 4 minutes, until slightly thickened. Drizzle over the cooked chicken just before serving.

66 *Some newspapers are fit only to line the bottom of bird cages.*

—SPIRO AGNEW

citrus herb turkey

WITH GRAVY, STUFFING & CRANBERRY SAUCE

Sorry, liquids, but you're outta luck—Lisa has won the Battle of the Bird and we're not going to need you to wash down the traditionally dry-as-dust, bland bird. Our fearless Queen of the Coop has transformed the turkey from drive-you-to-drink choking hazard to first-rate, flavorsome centerpiece, going the extra mile and infusing flavor EVERYWHERE. The bottom of the roasting pan creates a full-flavored gravy, the cavity is stuffed with aromatics to bring flavor from the inside out, a citrus blend is nestled under the turkey skin, allowing flavors to melt into the meat, and the exterior is rubbed with a little butter to make a crisp outer layer while the inside meat stays moist. Get ready to drink up the compliments because a delicious stuffing of leeks, apples, and dried fruit along with a simple-to-make cinnamon orange cranberry sauce rounds out this guaranteed-to-be-gobbled-up spread.

SERVES: 15–20   PREP TIME: 30 MINS   COOK TIME: 4½ HOURS (+ resting)

Roasted Citrus Herb Turkey with Gravy

1 yellow onion, quartered

2 large carrots, peeled and cut into large chunks

2 celery stalks, cut into large chunks

2 dried bay leaves

2 cups turkey or chicken broth

1 (16–18 lb) fresh turkey, cavity empty (remove and discard the neck and giblets)

1 tsp kosher salt

1 tsp freshly ground black pepper

1 small yellow onion, quartered

½ orange, cut into wedges

2 large garlic cloves, crushed

4 sprigs fresh rosemary

4 sprigs fresh thyme

Handful of fresh flat-leaf parsley

continued on next page

1. Scatter the onion, carrots, celery, bay leaves, and broth on the bottom of a roasting pan. Set aside. Preheat the oven to 350°F and place a rack in the lowest position of the oven.

2. For the turkey, pat the skin dry and place breast side up on a roasting rack in the roasting pan. Rub the salt and pepper inside the turkey cavity, then stuff the cavity with the onion, orange, garlic, rosemary, thyme, and parsley.

3. For the citrus herb rub, using a food processor, combine the parsley, olive oil, orange zest, rosemary, oregano, salt, and pepper until chopped.

4. Using your hand, create a large pocket by gently separating the turkey skin from the meat. Spread the rub front and back underneath the skin. Tie the turkey legs together with kitchen twine and tuck the wing tips under the turkey. Rub the outside of the turkey with the softened butter and generously season with salt and pepper.

5. Loosely tent the turkey with aluminum foil and place in the preheated oven. Remove the aluminum foil after the first hour and continue to roast until a meat thermometer inserted into the thickest part of the thigh reads 165°F–170°F, and 160°F for the thickest part of the turkey breast. Total cook time will be 4–4½ hours. Once the turkey is cooked, remove from the oven and transfer to a serving platter. Let rest at least 30 minutes before carving.

Citrus Herb Rub

½ cup chopped fresh flat-leaf parsley

2 tbsp olive oil

1 tbsp orange zest

1 tbsp chopped fresh rosemary

2 tsp dried oregano

1 tsp kosher salt

1 tsp freshly ground black pepper

3 tbsp softened butter

Kosher salt and freshly ground black pepper

Gravy

2 cups chicken broth, approximately

2 tbsp butter

⅓ cup flour

6. While the turkey is resting, prepare the gravy. Take the drippings from the bottom of the roasting pan and strain through a fine-mesh sieve, pushing to extract as much liquid and flavor from the solids as possible. Spoon off any visible fat from the top of the drippings. Add the chicken broth to the drippings to make a total of 4 cups of liquid.

7. In a large saucepan, melt the butter over medium heat. Stir in the flour, stirring constantly for 1 minute. Slowly but continuously whisk in the drippings and broth mixture. Continue to cook until the gravy is the desired thickness. Serve with the turkey.

BUT WAIT. THERE'S MORE...

SERVES: 8–10   PREP TIME: 15 MINS   COOK TIME: 60 MINS

Leek, Apple & Dried Fruit Stuffing

12 cups bread cubes

¼ cup butter

2 cups sliced leeks, white part only

3 celery stalks, chopped

1 Granny Smith apple, peeled, cored, and chopped

1 tbsp chopped fresh sage

2 tsp chopped fresh thyme

1 tsp dried oregano

½ tsp kosher salt

3 eggs, lightly whisked

¾ cup chopped dried apricots

¾ cup dried cherries

3 cups chicken broth

1. Preheat the oven to 350°F. Coat a 9-by-13-inch baking dish with nonstick cooking spray.

2. Place the bread cubes on a rimmed baking sheet and bake for 10 minutes. Stir and continue baking for 5 minutes more. Remove from the oven and allow to cool. Place in a large mixing bowl and set aside.

3. Melt the butter in a large skillet over medium-low heat. Add the leeks and celery, cover, and cook for 8 minutes, stirring occasionally. Stir in the apples, sage, thyme, oregano, and salt. Cook for 2 minutes. Remove from the heat and combine with the bread cubes in the mixing bowl. Stir in the eggs, apricots, and cherries.

4. Transfer to the prepared baking dish and pour the broth evenly over top. Cover with aluminum foil and bake for 20 minutes. Uncover and continue to bake for 10–15 minutes more, until the top is golden.

Cinnamon Orange Cranberry Sauce

3 cups fresh or frozen cranberries

1 cup fresh orange juice

½ cup sugar

1 cinnamon stick

½ tsp orange zest

Pinch kosher salt

1. Rinse the cranberries well and place in a medium saucepan with the orange juice, sugar, and cinnamon stick. Bring to a boil over high heat, reduce the heat to medium, and simmer for 10–15 minutes, until most of the cranberries have popped open. Remove from the heat, discard the cinnamon stick, and stir in the orange zest and salt. Transfer to a serving bowl and refrigerate covered until ready to serve.

EAT, DRINK & BE

merry.

roasted red snapper

WITH ASPARAGUS & ORANGE FENNEL SALAD

I don't like to spill Lisa's secrets, but she was a rabid *Young and the Restless* fan by age seven; she was sure she'd marry Snapper (aka The Hoff) and live happily ever after in Genoa City. While that didn't pan out, I'm pretty sure our lil' whippersnapper still carries the torch, as evidenced by this delicious snapper-centric sheet-pan dinner that turns a simple piece of fish into a superb spread. Lean, firm, and mild red snapper is cooked as one large fillet (no scaling or eyes to contend with, phew) surrounded by asparagus and onions and topped with juicy oranges. Paired with a refreshing citrus, fennel, and mint salad, this healthy and quick supper on a sheet is a breeze to pull together, making Lisa's unrequited crush a lot easier (and tastier) to swallow.

SERVES: 4   PREP TIME: 15 MINS   COOK TIME: 15 MINS

Red Snapper

1½ lb red snapper fillet

2 tbsp olive oil, divided

½ tsp kosher salt, divided

½ tsp freshly ground black pepper, divided

1 bunch asparagus (about 20 stalks)

1 medium red onion, thinly sliced

1 large navel or blood orange, thinly sliced

Orange Fennel Salad

3 navel or blood oranges, peeled and cut into segments

1 fennel bulb, trimmed and thinly sliced

1 tbsp olive oil

2 tsp mirin

1 tbsp chopped fresh mint

1 tbsp chopped fresh flat-leaf parsley

½ tsp kosher salt

¼ tsp freshly ground black pepper

1. Preheat the oven to 425°F. Line a rimmed baking sheet with parchment paper.

2. Pat the red snapper dry with paper towel. Coat both sides of the fish with 1 tablespoon of the olive oil and ¼ teaspoon each of the salt and pepper. Place the red snapper in the center of the prepared baking sheet.

3. Snap off and discard the tough bottom ends of the asparagus and peel the lower ends with a vegetable peeler. In a large bowl, toss the asparagus and red onion with the remaining 1 tablespoon of olive oil, and ¼ teaspoon each of salt and pepper. Place the asparagus and onions on the baking sheet around the sides of the fish. Lay a few orange slices over the snapper and around the baking sheet. Roast for 12–14 minutes, depending on thickness, until cooked through.

4. While the fish is roasting, prepare the orange fennel salad. In a medium bowl, combine the orange segments, sliced fennel, olive oil, mirin, mint, parsley, salt, and pepper. Toss to combine.

5. Cut the red snapper into 4 pieces and serve with the roasted asparagus and orange fennel salad.

sumac-spiced salmon
WITH ALMOND GREMOLATA

What do Lisa and science fiction writer Frank Herbert have in common? They both think that the person who controls the spice controls the universe. I guess that makes Lisa captain of the cosmos, because with this quick, healthy, and super-tasty salmon, she's put us all in control of our dinner destiny. A spice mix of citrusy sumac, aromatic cumin, sweet fennel, and nutty coriander pairs perfectly with salmon, and is enhanced with the addition of a crunchy toasted almond gremolata. The lesson is simple: raid your spice cabinet, and you too can become the master of mealtime in this flavor-packed universe.

SERVES: 4   PREP TIME: 15 MINS   COOK TIME: 10 MINS

Sumac-Spiced Salmon

4 salmon fillets (6–8 oz each), skin on

4 tsp olive oil, divided

2 tsp ground sumac

½ tsp ground cumin

½ tsp ground fennel seed

½ tsp kosher salt

½ tsp lime zest

¼ tsp ground coriander seed

¼ tsp freshly ground black pepper

Almond Gremolata

½ cup chopped fresh flat-leaf parsley

¼ cup chopped toasted almonds

1 tbsp olive oil

1 tsp lime zest

1 small garlic clove, finely minced

Pinch kosher salt

Pinch red pepper flakes, optional

1. Preheat the oven to 425°F. Line a baking sheet with parchment paper. Place the salmon on the baking sheet and brush with 2 teaspoons of the olive oil.

2. In a small bowl, combine the sumac, cumin, fennel, salt, lime zest, coriander, and pepper. Sprinkle over top of each piece of salmon. Drizzle the salmon with the remaining 2 teaspoons of olive oil. Bake for 10 minutes, until cooked through.

3. While the salmon is cooking, prepare the gremolata. In a small bowl, toss the parsley, almonds, olive oil, lime zest, garlic, salt, and red pepper flakes. Serve each piece of salmon topped with approximately 1 tablespoon of almond gremolata.

lessons *from* lisa

★ Toast almonds by spreading them in a single layer on a baking sheet and baking at 350°F for 5–10 minutes, until fragrant and lightly browned, shaking the pan occasionally.

★ Sumac, often found in Middle Eastern cooking, is a dry red powder that adds a lemony kick and brightens up dishes—sprinkle it on hummus, salad, grilled chicken, or bread.

salmon

Do you feel like you're swimming upstream trying to get a healthy and tasty dinner on the table? You can stop fighting the current because the tides have turned—not only will this foolproof salmon become a weeknight staple with your family, but it's also a super-impressive and delicious addition when feeding a crowd. First placed in a sweet and salty marinade (you'll be blown away by the extra flavor 20 minutes can add), the whole fish is then baked, glazed with an easy homemade teriyaki sauce, and finished with green onions and sesame seeds. It's so fast and simple—prepare to get hooked on this go-with-the-flow fish dish.

SERVES: 4–6   PREP TIME: 10 MINS (+ marinating)   COOK TIME: 25 MINS

2 lb salmon fillet, left whole

Marinade

2 tbsp soy sauce

1 tbsp olive oil

1 tbsp brown sugar

1 tbsp rice vinegar

Teriyaki Glaze

¾ cup + 1 tbsp water, divided

¼ cup brown sugar

3 tbsp soy sauce

1 tbsp rice vinegar

1 tbsp honey

1 small garlic clove, finely minced

1 tbsp cornstarch

Chopped green onions,
  for garnish

Sesame seeds, for garnish

1. Preheat the oven to 425°F. Line a baking sheet with parchment paper. Place the salmon in a large resealable plastic bag.

2. For the marinade, in a small bowl, whisk together the soy sauce, olive oil, brown sugar, and rice vinegar. Pour the marinade over the salmon, seal the bag, and let sit for 20 minutes at room temperature.

3. To bake the salmon, remove from the bag, place skin side down on the prepared baking sheet, and discard the marinade. Bake until cooked through, about 15 minutes.

4. While the salmon is cooking, prepare the teriyaki glaze. In a small saucepan over medium heat, combine ¾ cup of the water, brown sugar, soy sauce, rice vinegar, honey, and garlic and bring to a boil. In a small bowl, dissolve the cornstarch in the remaining 1 tablespoon of the water. Add the cornstarch mixture to the saucepan while continuously whisking and cook for 3–4 minutes, until the glaze reaches the desired thickness.

5. When the salmon is cooked, remove from the oven, brush with the teriyaki glaze, and sprinkle with the green onions and sesame seeds. Serve with the remaining teriyaki glaze.

✛ **Make it gluten-free:** Use gluten-free tamari or gluten-free soy sauce

miso-glazed halibut

WITH SOBA NOODLES

I can count on one hand the number of times my sis and I have successfully high-fived. Either we miss completely or one of us comes in Hulk-like while the other half-asses it. Awkward. And that's why I'm so grateful Lisa hasn't left us hanging with this healthy Asian-inspired dish where she covers the ultimate five taste sensations like a boss: sweet, sour, salty, bitter, and the magical flavor bomb known as umami. This recipe has it all—miso delivers savory and salty hits, halibut serves up mild sweetness, nutty soba noodles are coated in a soy, ginger, and sesame sauce, and all is brought together with fresh peppery watercress. Now, thanks to this super-quick and easy recipe, we can once again confidently say, "Gimme five."

SERVES: 4   PREP TIME: 10 MINS   COOK TIME: 20 MINS

Soba Noodles

1 (6 oz) package soba noodles

2 tsp soy sauce

2 tsp rice vinegar

1 tsp sesame oil

1 tsp honey

1 tsp toasted sesame seeds

½ tsp grated fresh ginger

2 cups packed trimmed watercress

Miso Glaze

2 tbsp white miso paste

1 tbsp honey

1 tbsp mirin

1 tbsp soy sauce

1 garlic clove, minced

1 tsp grated fresh ginger

Halibut

4 skinless halibut fillets
(6–8 oz each)

Chopped fresh scallions, for garnish

Toasted sesame seeds, for garnish

1. For the soba noodles, add the noodles to a large pot of boiling water. Cook for 6–8 minutes, until just tender. Drain noodles and dump into a bowl of cold water to prevent the noodles from sticking together. Drain well.

2. In a small bowl, whisk together the soy sauce, rice vinegar, sesame oil, honey, sesame seeds, and ginger. Toss with the soba noodles and watercress. Set aside.

3. Preheat the oven to 425°F and line a baking sheet with parchment paper.

4. For the miso glaze, whisk together the miso paste, honey, mirin, soy sauce, garlic, and ginger. Remove 3 tablespoons and set the remaining glaze aside.

5. Pat the fish dry, place on the prepared baking sheet, and brush with the 3 tablespoons of miso glaze. Bake for 10 minutes, remove from the oven, and turn the oven to broil. Brush the fish with the remaining miso glaze and place under the broiler for 1–2 minutes, until golden and caramelized, watching carefully as it can burn quickly.

6. Place the soba noodles on a serving plate, top with the fish, and garnish with the scallions and sesame seeds.

lessons *from* lisa

★ White (shiro) miso is the sweetest, smoothest, and most delicate miso, making it great in soups and dressings.

mediterranean cod
IN PARCHMENT

The Founding Fathers may have used parchment to scribble a few notes (like the US Constitution), but they had nothing on liberty-loving Lisa, who has taken this precious paper and used it to secure our inalienable dinner rights: Easy, Tasty, and the Pursuit of Healthy. I do declare, she's gone and done it—this impressive yet humble fish dish is all that and more. Mild cod rests atop a foundation of fresh asparagus; then it's assembled with sun-dried tomatoes, olives, and red onions, wrapped up tight, baked, and finished with zesty kale pesto. These fuss-free, flavor-packed parcels may sound good on paper, but trust us, they're even more fantastic on your fork.

SERVES: 4   PREP TIME: 15 MINS   COOK TIME: 15 MINS

1 bunch asparagus, ends trimmed

1 tbsp + 2 tsp olive oil, divided

½ tsp kosher salt, divided

½ tsp freshly ground black pepper, divided

4 skinless cod fillets (6 oz each)

⅓ cup oil-packed sun-dried tomatoes, drained

⅓ cup Kalamata olives, pitted and halved

1 small red onion, cut into thinly sliced rings

3 tbsp white wine

Kale Pesto

1 cup coarsely chopped kale

¼ cup chopped fresh flat-leaf parsley

¼ cup olive oil

¼ cup raw almonds

2 tsp fresh lemon juice

1 small garlic clove

½ tsp kosher salt

1 tsp lemon zest

1. Preheat the oven to 425°F. Cut 4 large sheets of parchment paper (enough to tightly enclose fish).

2. Divide the asparagus and place in the center of each sheet. Drizzle with 2 teaspoons of the olive oil and season asparagus with ¼ teaspoon each of the salt and pepper. Place each cod fillet over the asparagus and season the fish with the remaining ¼ teaspoon each of salt and pepper. Top the fish with the sun-dried tomatoes, olives, and red onion. Drizzle the white wine and the remaining 1 tablespoon of olive oil over each fish packet. To seal the packet, bring the sides of the parchment paper up and crimp tightly to create an enclosed pouch. Place the packets on a baking sheet and bake for 12–14 minutes.

3. While the fish bakes, prepare the pesto. Using a food processor, combine the kale, parsley, olive oil, almonds, lemon juice, garlic, and salt. Pulse on and off until the pesto reaches the desired consistency. Cover and set aside.

4. Remove the fish from the oven and let the packets rest for 5 minutes before opening. Cut open the packets and top with the pesto and lemon zest.

lessons *from* lisa

★ *If you don't have parchment, use aluminum foil lightly coated with nonstick cooking spray.*

★ *You can substitute halibut or tilapia for cod.*

southwestern flank steak
WITH AVOCADO SALSA

If I'm going to keep pace with my superb synchro-swimming, ribbon-dancing partner Dahra (no, the H isn't a typo), I need to fuel up or she's going to leave me in her jazz hand dust. I turn to Lady Gaga for inspiration, recalling her red carpet flank steak dress, hoping I too can dazzle with this protein-rich, versatile, and lean cut. Crusted in spicy, sweet, and smoky Southwestern flavors, the steak is quickly grilled to tender perfection, thinly sliced, and served alongside an applause-worthy avocado salsa. Sure to bring pizzazz to the plate, this satisfying, scrumptious, and dazzling dinner will have me treading tirelessly and high kickin' it with my lively sister-from-another-mister in no time at all.

SERVES: 6–8   PREP TIME: 15 MINS (+ marinating)   COOK TIME: 15 MINS (+ resting)

Spice Rub

1 tbsp brown sugar

2 tsp kosher salt

2 tsp ground cumin

2 tsp smoked paprika

1 tsp chili powder

1 tsp garlic powder

1 tsp ground coriander seed

1 tsp freshly ground black pepper

2½ lb flank steak

Avocado Salsa

½ cup diced red onions, soaked in ice water 5 minutes and drained well

2 firm ripe avocados, peeled, pitted, and chopped

1¼ cups halved cherry tomatoes

1 jalapeño pepper, seeded and finely chopped

¼ cup chopped fresh cilantro

continued on next page

1. For the spice rub, in a small bowl, combine the brown sugar, salt, cumin, smoked paprika, chili powder, garlic powder, ground coriander seed, and pepper.

2. Coat both sides of the steak with the spice rub. Any leftover rub can be used to season the flank steak before grilling. Wrap the seasoned steak tightly with plastic wrap. Refrigerate for at least 2 hours or overnight. Let the steak come to room temperature before cooking.

3. Preheat the grill to medium-high heat and lightly oil the grill grates. Season the steak with any remaining rub and place on the grill. Grill for 6 minutes, flip, and grill for 6 minutes more, until internal temperature reaches 135°F, for medium-rare doneness. Transfer the steak to a cutting board and let rest 10–15 minutes to seal in juices. Slice the steak thinly against the grain to serve.

4. While the steak is resting, prepare the avocado salsa. In a mixing bowl, combine the red onions, avocados, cherry tomatoes, jalapeño, cilantro, lime juice, olive oil, salt, and pepper. Toss gently to coat and serve with the sliced flank steak.

lessons *from* lisa

★ Soak raw red onions in ice-cold water to remove the harsh bite.

ingredients continued

2 tbsp fresh lime juice

1 tbsp olive oil

½ tsp kosher salt

¼ tsp freshly ground black
  pepper

moroccan meatballs

WITH CITRUS COUSCOUS

Lisa can be stubborn. While I had no trouble convincing her to capitalize on meatball madness, I'm having a harder time getting her to agree to starting up a meatball truck (side panel to read "We Got Balls") and rollin' these awesome orbs coast to coast. I'm totally revved up about this Meat-Me-in-Morocco meal of tender, spice-filled, and healthy baked meatballs served with a super-spiced (but not spicy) tomato sauce and an orange, date, and chickpea couscous. Add the freshness of mint, the earthy fragrance of cumin, and the hints of zesty citrus, and you've got your next amazingly easy, impressive, and delicious dinner around the corner. What are we waiting for? Let's get our chuck wagon on the road, Lisa.

SERVES: 6   PREP TIME: 30 MINS   COOK TIME: 40 MINS

Moroccan Meatballs

2 lb lean ground beef

½ cup breadcrumbs

1 egg

1 garlic clove, finely minced

½ tsp freshly grated ginger

½ tsp ground cumin

½ tsp dried oregano

½ tsp kosher salt

Spiced Tomato Sauce

1 tbsp olive oil

1 small red onion, diced

2 garlic cloves, minced

½ tsp freshly grated ginger

2 tsp ground cumin

2 tsp dried oregano

1 tsp fennel seeds

1 tsp kosher salt

¼ tsp cayenne pepper

2 (28 oz) cans whole tomatoes, coarsely chopped

continued on next page

1. For the meatballs, preheat the oven to 400°F. Line a rimmed baking sheet with aluminum foil and coat with nonstick cooking spray. In a large bowl, combine the beef, breadcrumbs, egg, garlic, ginger, cumin, oregano, and salt. Mix well to combine. Roll the meat mixture into 32 meatballs and place on the prepared baking sheet. Bake for 15 minutes, flipping the meatballs halfway through cooking.

2. While the meatballs are baking, prepare the spiced tomato sauce. In a large pot, heat the olive oil over medium heat. Add the onion and cook, stirring frequently, for 4–5 minutes, until softened. Add the garlic, ginger, cumin, oregano, fennel seeds, salt, and cayenne, continuing to cook for 3 minutes. Add the tomatoes, tomato paste, and sugar. Simmer the sauce uncovered for 15 minutes, then add the cooked meatballs and continue to simmer covered for 15 minutes more. Remove from the heat and stir in the orange zest.

3. Meanwhile, prepare the couscous, in a medium saucepan over high heat, combine the water, olive oil, honey, and salt. Bring to a boil. Stir in the couscous, remove from the heat, cover, and let stand for 5 minutes. Stir in the chickpeas, dates, mint, and orange zest.

4. Serve the meatballs and sauce over the couscous and garnish with the fresh mint.

ingredients continued

2 tbsp tomato paste

2 tsp sugar

½ tsp orange zest

Citrus Couscous

3 cups water

2 tbsp olive oil

1 tbsp honey

½ tsp kosher salt

1½ cups couscous

1 cup canned chickpeas, rinsed and drained

½ cup Medjool dates, pitted and chopped

2 tbsp chopped fresh mint

1 tsp orange zest

Fresh mint leaves, for garnish

> *Thank you, horseradish, for being neither a radish nor a horse. What you are is a liar food.* —JIMMY FALLON

roast beef
WITH HORSERADISH SAUCE

Photos of your ex, that "cute" college-era top, those yellowing credit card statements? Bad leftovers, people. Get rid of them and discover the best kind of leftovers—we're talking don't-invite-anyone-over-because-you'll-want-leftovers (in mile-high sandwiches, no less) of this dish for days and days. Yes, we're suggesting you leave everyone out in the cold because you're not going to want to share this roast beef, the ultimate in comfort food. It's been rubbed with spices, left overnight to absorb flavors, and then cooked to juicy perfection and served with a zesty fresh herb and horseradish sauce. Turn out the lights and lock the door (nobody's home, folks) because this super-easy and satisfying classic roast beef is the ideal Sunday night dinner (for one).

SERVES: 6–8   PREP TIME: 15 MINS (+ refrigerating)   COOK TIME: 90 MINS (+ resting)

Spice Rub

4 tsp kosher salt

2 tsp paprika

2 tsp garlic powder

1 tsp dried oregano

1 tsp freshly ground black pepper

Pinch cayenne pepper

1 (4 lb) top sirloin roast (or top round roast)

Fresh Herb Horseradish Sauce

½ cup light sour cream

½ cup light mayonnaise

2 tbsp fresh chopped basil

2 tbsp fresh chopped flat-leaf parsley

2 tbsp jarred horseradish

2 tbsp fresh lemon juice

1 garlic clove, minced

½ tsp kosher salt

¼ tsp freshly ground black pepper

Pinch cayenne pepper

1. For the rub, in a small bowl, combine the salt, paprika, garlic powder, oregano, black pepper, and cayenne pepper.

2. Pat the roast dry with paper towel. Season with the rub mixture, rubbing on all sides of the roast. Wrap tightly in plastic wrap and refrigerate overnight.

3. Remove the roast from the refrigerator 1 hour before cooking to ensure even cooking. Preheat the oven to 450°F and line a rimmed baking sheet with aluminum foil. Place a roasting rack on top of the baking sheet and coat the rack with nonstick cooking spray.

4. Place the roast fat side up on the rack. Insert a meat thermometer into the thickest part of the roast. Place in the preheated oven for 15 minutes. Lower the temperature to 325°F and continue to roast for 1 hour and 20 minutes, or until your thermometer reads between 135°F and 140°F for medium-rare.

5. Remove the roast from the oven and cover loosely with aluminum foil. Allow to rest for 30 minutes before slicing.

6. For the sauce, in a small bowl, whisk together the sour cream, mayonnaise, basil, parsley, horseradish, lemon juice, garlic, salt, pepper, and cayenne pepper. Refrigerate until ready to serve with the sliced roast beef.

beef tenderloin

Monopoly was invented in the 1930s and remains perfect to this day. Beef Wellington, another innovation of that time, hasn't fared so well, missing from menus and holiday tables for decades. Well, it's time to hop on the B & O Railroad because our culinary conductor is giving this Park Place–worthy meal a makeover, pulling out all the passé parts (fatty pâté, soggy puff pastry, to name a few) and keeping the very best elements that make this a richly satisfying winner. At the top of her game, Lisa's wrapped lean yet luscious beef tenderloin in a hugely flavorful mushroom crust, clearly cornering the market on the makings of a delicious, easy, and impressive feast. Tipping my Top Hat and giving you Free Parking on this one, dear sister.

SERVES: 8   PREP TIME: 10 MINS   COOK TIME: 50 MINS (+ resting)

1 (3 lb) beef tenderloin

¾ tsp kosher salt, divided

¾ tsp freshly ground black pepper, divided

½ lb sliced white button mushrooms

1 (0.7 oz) package dried mushrooms (shiitake, portobello, or porcini)

1 small shallot, peeled and coarsely chopped

½ tsp dried thyme

1 tbsp olive oil

2 tbsp Dijon mustard

1. Preheat the oven to 400ºF. Line a rimmed baking sheet with aluminum foil and coat with nonstick cooking spray.

2. Place the tenderloin on the baking sheet and sprinkle with ½ teaspoon each of the salt and pepper.

3. Using a food processor, combine the button mushrooms, dried mushrooms, shallot, thyme, and the remaining ¼ teaspoon each of salt and pepper. Pulse on and off until the mixture is finely minced.

4. In a small skillet, heat the olive oil over medium-low heat. Add the mushroom mixture and cook until the moisture is reduced, 5–6 minutes. Remove from the heat and allow to cool slightly.

5. Spread the mustard over the top and sides of the tenderloin. Pat the mushroom mixture evenly over the beef. Bake in the preheated oven for 45 minutes, or until a meat thermometer reads 145ºF for medium-rare. Remove from the oven and let rest for 15–20 minutes before slicing.

lessons *from* lisa

★ *Ask your butcher to tie the middle and both ends with kitchen twine to keep the shape of the beef tenderloin. If there are too many ties to cut when serving, the mushroom topping will get messy.*

*BEST SERVED

ON A PLATE

biscotti

For 24 years, Lisa has held this recipe close to her ample bosom. That's approximately 8,760 days that anyone who has ever tasted her legendary biscotti has spent pacing their kitchens, waiting for the big reveal. The time is now, so hold onto your *mutandines* (translation: knickers) Nonna, because Lisa's take on this iconic Italian cookie is sure to blow your skirt up. No longer the traditional texture that's harder than Mount Vesuvius, this cookie-like version is studded with almonds and milk chocolate chunks. It's crunchy on the outside but soft enough to keep everyone's teeth intact. The best things really do come to those who wait.

MAKES: 25 BISCOTTI   PREP TIME: 20 MINS   COOK TIME: 30 MINS

1¾ cups flour

1½ cups almond flour

1 cup sugar

¾ cup brown sugar

¾ cup coarsely chopped slivered almonds

4 tbsp cornstarch

2 tsp ground cinnamon

1½ tsp baking powder

½ tsp kosher salt

2 cups chopped milk chocolate

¾ cup butter, room temperature

2 eggs, lightly whisked

2 tsp vanilla extract

Cinnamon Sprinkle

¼ cup sugar

1½ tsp ground cinnamon

1. Preheat the oven to 350°F. Line a baking sheet with parchment paper.

2. In a large mixing bowl, stir the flour, almond flour, sugar, brown sugar, slivered almonds, cornstarch, cinnamon, baking powder, salt, and chocolate until well combined. Using your fingers, cut the butter into the flour until you have a crumb-like mixture. Stir in the eggs and vanilla extract until the dough comes together.

3. Divide the dough into 3 pieces. Shape them into rectangles (about 3 by 9 inches), and smooth the top and sides, patting them into shape. Bake the dough for 25 minutes. Remove from the oven and let cool for 10 minutes. Leave the oven on.

4. Using a large spatula, move each rectangle to a cutting board. Cut into slices ¾–1 inch wide using a serrated knife.

5. For the cinnamon mixture, on a plate, mix the sugar and cinnamon. Take each biscotti slice, dip both sides in the cinnamon mixture and place back on the parchment-lined baking sheet. Once all the biscotti are done, place back in the oven for 6 minutes more. Remove from the oven and carefully transfer to a cooling rack.

sugar cookies

These Confetti Sugar Cookies are ticker-tape-parade-worthy, deserving to be feted among astronauts, athletes, and royalty. Well, OK, maybe more like a float on Main Street that reads, "Eat Me," but whatever the case, we can all easily follow in the steps of Grand Marshal Gnat. With a whir of her whisk, she has us saluting these soft-baked beauties, reveling in the rainbow celebration of color and crunch and admiring the triumphant combo of creamy white chocolate and subtle vanilla flavor. One bite and the confetti will be flying off the plate, and the crowds will be clamoring for more.

MAKES: 18 COOKIES   PREP TIME: 10 MINS   COOK TIME: 10 MINS

1½ cups flour

2 tsp cornstarch

½ tsp baking soda

¼ tsp kosher salt

½ cup butter, room temperature

1 cup sugar

1 egg

2 tsp vanilla extract

1½ cups chopped white chocolate

¼ cup cylinder-shaped sprinkles

1. Preheat the oven to 350°F. Line a baking sheet with parchment paper.

2. In a mixing bowl, combine the flour, cornstarch, baking soda, and salt. Set aside.

3. Using an electric mixer, cream the butter and sugar on medium speed for 2 minutes. Add the egg and vanilla extract and continue mixing until fluffy, about 2 minutes more. On low speed, add the flour mixture, white chocolate, and sprinkles. Mix just until the flour disappears and the ingredients are combined. Do not overmix.

4. For each cookie, drop 2 tablespoons of batter on the prepared baking sheet. Pat the batter down slightly and bake for 8–10 minutes, until the edges are golden. Cool the cookies on a wire rack.

Every cookie is a sugar cookie. A cookie without sugar is a cracker.

—GARY GULMAN

pecan pie bars

Lisa's business card should read "Table Troubleshooter." This gal can solve all our kitchen conundrums and is masterful at managing mealtime stress, especially during the holidays. These gooey Easy Pecan Pie Bars are the perfect case in point. Full of decadence, they're like handheld tasty treaties, smoothing the way with their thick layer of caramelized pecan pie filling sitting atop a buttery shortbread crust. The laid-back cousin to the traditional pie, these bars are super easy to make, to portion out, to freeze, and to take on the road. Really, there just can't be strife in the presence of these sweet, salty, crunchy, and nutty crowd-pleasers. So, bring it on—hot-button topics, drunken relatives, crying babies—because nothing can dampen the mood when there's a plate of these peacekeeping pecan squares present.

MAKES: 25–30 PECAN PIE BARS   PREP TIME: 20 MINS   COOK TIME: 65 MINS

Pecan Pie Filling

1 cup brown sugar

5 tbsp flour

3 tbsp cornstarch

1 tsp kosher salt

6 eggs

2 cups corn syrup

6 tbsp melted butter

1 tbsp vanilla extract

3 cups coarsely chopped pecan halves

Shortbread Crust

2 cups flour

½ cup icing sugar

1 tsp vanilla extract

½ tsp kosher salt

1 cup melted butter

1. Preheat the oven to 350°F. Coat a 9-by-13-inch baking pan with nonstick cooking spray and line with parchment paper, extending the paper over the edges for easier removal.

2. For the pecan filling, in a large bowl, whisk together the brown sugar, flour, cornstarch, and salt until there are no lumps.

3. In a separate bowl, whisk together the eggs, corn syrup, melted butter, and vanilla. Add the liquid mixture to the dry mixture and whisk until combined. Let the mixture stand while preparing the crust.

4. For the crust, in a large bowl, stir together the flour, icing sugar, vanilla, and salt. Add the melted butter and stir until combined. Press the dough onto the bottom of the prepared pan. Poke the crust with a fork 5 or 6 times in different locations to prevent air bubbles. Bake the crust in preheated oven for 20 minutes, until golden.

5. Stir the pecans into the pecan filling and pour the filling evenly over the crust. Bake at 350°F for 45 minutes until the filling is just set; the center should be a little wobbly but not runny. Cool completely, refrigerate, and chill at least 2 hours before cutting.

lessons *from* lisa

★ *Light or dark corn syrup can be used; the dark syrup gives more color and a deeper flavor.*

white chocolate
shortbread WITH PINK PEPPERCORNS

Y ou know how you get a tune stuck in your head and can't get it out? Mine is "Rhythm of the Night" by DeBarge, and has been since 1985. Though tone-deaf, Lisa can often be found humming "Sgt. Pepper's Lonely Hearts Club Band," which is apt because she's both militaristic in the kitchen and a fan of peppering us with surprising bites. Her talent knows no bounds with these buttery shortbread cookies, each morsel studded with floral, sharp pink peppercorns, zesty citrus, and creamy white chocolate. A perfect melody of sweet and savory, these groundbreaking biscuits are sure to make you "More popular than Jesus" at the cookie jar.

MAKES: 20 SHORTBREAD COOKIES   **PREP TIME: 10 MINS**   **COOK TIME: 25 MINS**

1 cup butter, room temperature

1 cup sugar

1 tsp vanilla extract

1 tsp lemon zest

1 tsp pink peppercorns, lightly crushed, divided

1 tsp kosher salt

2 cups flour

1¼ cups chopped white chocolate

1. Preheat the oven to 350°F. Coat a 9-by-13-inch baking pan with nonstick cooking spray and line with parchment paper.

2. Using an electric mixer, cream the butter and sugar on medium speed until fluffy, about 3 minutes, scraping down the sides of the bowl once or twice. Add the vanilla, lemon zest, ½ teaspoon of the pink peppercorns, and the salt, mixing to combine. Using a spatula or wooden spoon, fold in the flour and white chocolate just until combined.

3. Firmly press the dough into the prepared baking pan, spreading it evenly. Sprinkle the remaining ½ teaspoon of pink peppercorns over top. Bake 22–24 minutes, until just firm and lightly golden around the edges.

4. Remove from the pan after 10 minutes and cut into squares, and then cut each square diagonally into triangles. Allow to cool completely.

lessons *from* lisa

★ *If you don't have a mortar and pestle to crush the peppercorns, you can easily crush them between 2 spoons.*

★ *Slice the shortbread while it's still warm for the cleanest cut.*

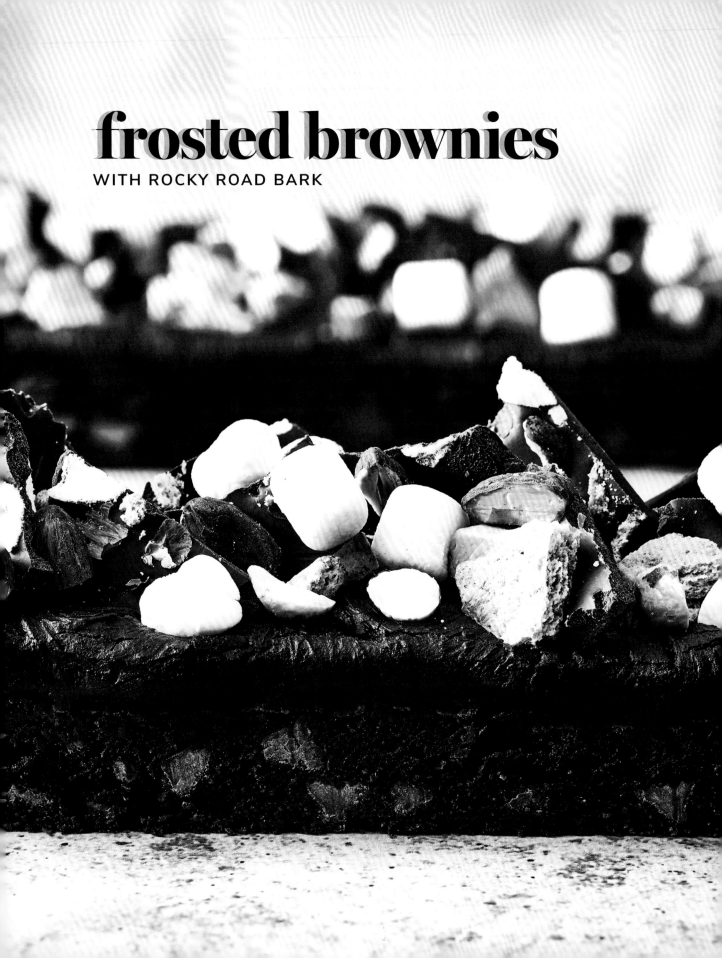

frosted brownies

WITH ROCKY ROAD BARK

N ot that anyone asked me, but I would've added a little more pizazz to L. Frank Baum's classic tale. Can you just imagine Dorothy's delight at discovering Glisa, the *really* good witch who was a whiz at making chocolate dreams come true? Yup, on her quest to Cocoa City, Dottie (like the nickname?) and her buddies would encounter Glisa at the corner of Brownie Boulevard and Rocky Road, serving up these decadent bites topped with thick 'n' fudgy frosting and a magical garnish of chocolate and marshmallows and almonds (oh my!). Ding, dong, one bite of this delicious brownie dessert and the kiddo from Kansas would be knocked right outta her ruby slippers. The End.

MAKES: 20 BROWNIE BARS   PREP TIME: 30 MINS   COOK TIME: 30 MINS

Rocky Road Bark

1½ cups semisweet chocolate chips

½ cup mini marshmallows

¼ cup chopped roasted almonds

2 whole graham crackers, broken into small pieces

Pinch kosher salt

Brownies

¾ cup butter

4 oz unsweetened chocolate

2½ cups sugar

¼ cup vegetable oil

4 eggs

2 tsp vanilla extract

1 cup flour

½ cup cocoa powder, sifted

1 tsp kosher salt

1 cup semisweet chocolate chips

Chocolate Frosting

½ cup butter

¾ cup cocoa powder, sifted

⅓ cup semisweet chocolate chips

2½ cups icing sugar

⅓ cup whole milk

1. For the rocky road bark, melt the chocolate in a microwave-safe dish for 30 seconds and stir. Continue to microwave in 20-second intervals until the chocolate is smooth.

2. Pour the chocolate on a parchment-lined baking sheet and spread evenly with a spatula. Scatter the marshmallows, almonds, and graham crackers over top. Sprinkle with a pinch of salt. Refrigerate and allow to set for 1 hour. When hardened, break into small pieces.

3. For the brownies, preheat the oven to 350°F. Coat a 9-by-13-inch baking pan with nonstick cooking spray and line with parchment paper.

4. In a microwave-safe bowl, melt the butter and unsweetened chocolate until smooth, stirring occasionally. In a large bowl, whisk together the sugar, oil, eggs, and vanilla. Add the melted chocolate mixture, flour, cocoa powder, salt, and chocolate chips, stirring until the mixture is well combined and the flour has disappeared. Spread in the prepared pan and bake for 25–30 minutes. Let cool completely before frosting.

5. For the frosting, combine the butter, cocoa powder, and chocolate in a saucepan over low heat. Continue to whisk until smooth. Remove from the heat and whisk in the icing sugar and milk until a smooth spreading consistency is formed. This frosting needs to be used right away, as it will harden if you wait too long. Frost the cooled brownies and garnish with pieces of the rocky road bark.

lessons *from* lisa

★ These brownies freeze well without frosting or bark.

classic apple pie
WITH STREUSEL TOPPING

Don't let Lisa's innocent look fool you—she's a card shark, especially when it comes to the matching game Concentration. She can't be beat. Trust me, I've tried. What the Queen of Hearts doesn't realize is that with this cinnamon-studded apple pie, she's given me, the Joker with the sieve-like brain, an edge as cinnamon is reported to boost memory. Before I forget to tell you, this sweet and fragrant, warm and uplifting dessert is absolutely unforgettable—cinnamon-spiced tender apples are piled atop a flaky crust and crowned with a crunchy, buttery streusel topping. One bite and already my memory is jogged . . . I just remembered I'd like a scoop of ice cream with it.

SERVES: 6–8   PREP TIME: 30 MINS (+ dough refrigeration)   COOK TIME: 60 MINS

Crust

1¼ cups flour

1 tbsp sugar

½ tsp kosher salt

½ cup cold butter, cubed

3 tbsp cold water

1 tbsp apple cider vinegar

Streusel Topping

1 cup flour

½ cup brown sugar

½ tsp ground cinnamon

¼ tsp kosher salt

½ cup cold butter, cubed

Apple Filling

8 Granny Smith apples, peeled, cored, and cut in chunks

⅓ cup brown sugar

continued on next page

1. For the crust, in a large bowl, mix the flour, sugar, and salt together. Cut in the butter until it forms pea-sized crumbs.

2. Combine the cold water and apple cider vinegar, and add them to the flour mixture. Knead until the dough comes together. Shape into a disk, wrap in plastic, and refrigerate at least 1 hour or overnight.

3. For the streusel topping, in a small bowl, combine the flour, brown sugar, cinnamon, and salt. Cut in the butter with your fingers until the streusel is crumbly. Set aside.

4. Preheat the oven to 425°F. On a lightly floured surface, roll out the chilled dough into a 12-inch circle. Carefully transfer the dough into a 9-inch pie plate. Turn the excess dough hanging over the edge underneath to create a rolled edge. You can flute the edges around the pie for a decorative finish.

3 tbsp flour

1 tbsp fresh lemon juice

1 tsp ground cinnamon

1 tsp vanilla extract

5. For the apple filling, in a large bowl, toss the apples with the brown sugar, flour, lemon juice, cinnamon, and vanilla. Spoon the filling into the crust and sprinkle with the streusel topping. Place the pie on a baking sheet (to catch any drippings) and bake in the preheated oven for 15 minutes. Without opening the oven, reduce the heat to 375°F and bake for 45 minutes more, until the apples are tender. Allow to cool slightly before cutting.

lessons *from* lisa

★ Loosely cover in the last 15 minutes of baking if the topping is starting to brown too quickly.

★ If you want to freeze the pie, bake and cool it completely before wrapping it tightly with plastic wrap. When you want to eat it, thaw overnight in the refrigerator and warm in the oven or serve at room temperature.

I don't think I've ever seen pie advertised. That's how you know it's good. They advertise ice cream and other desserts. They advertise the bejeezus out of yogurt, but I haven't seen one pie commercial. —ADAM CAROLLA

HOW DO YOU LIKE THEM APPLES?

honey galette

In *The Odyssey*, Homer called the pear "A gift from the Gods." Can't disagree when it comes to this golden, juicy fruit, especially when tossed with warm spices, loosely layered on a buttery crust, and drizzled with honey. Yes, this French galette is the epitome of laid-back simplicity, a free-form tart designed for those of us who are put off by conventional pie making and long for a more balanced crust-to-fruit ratio. This perfectly imperfect dessert features dough haphazardly folded around a lightly spiced pear filling and baked up until the fruit is caramel-coated and the crust is light and flaky. The gifts of this pear galette—rustic elegance, simple preparation, flawless flavors—are the gifts that keep on giving.

SERVES: 6–8   PREP TIME: 15 MINS (+ dough refrigeration)   COOK TIME: 40 MINS

Crust

1¼ cups flour

1 tsp sugar

¼ tsp kosher salt

½ cup cold butter, cut into pieces

¼ cup ice water

Pear Filling

4 medium Bosc pears, cored and
  sliced into ¼-inch-thick slices

¼ cup sugar

2 tbsp flour

1 tsp ground cinnamon

¼ tsp ground ginger

¼ tsp ground nutmeg

1 tbsp melted butter

1 tbsp honey + more for garnish

1 egg, lightly whisked

2 tsp coarse sugar

1. For the crust, place the flour, sugar, and salt in a food processor. Pulse to combine. Add the butter and continue to pulse until the mixture resembles coarse meal. Add the ice water and process just until dough starts to come together.

2. Turn the dough out onto a work surface and form into a flat disk. Wrap the dough in plastic wrap and refrigerate for at least 1 hour before rolling.

3. Preheat the oven to 400°F and line a baking sheet with parchment paper.

4. For the filling, in a medium bowl, toss the pears with the sugar, flour, cinnamon, ginger, and nutmeg until well combined. Set aside.

5. On a lightly floured surface, roll out the dough into a 14-inch circle. Transfer the dough to the prepared baking sheet and brush the melted butter and honey over the surface, leaving a 2-inch border. Arrange the pears on top of the butter and honey mixture. Fold up the edges of the crust over the pears. Brush the crust edges with the whisked egg and sprinkle with the coarse sugar.

6. Bake until the pears are bubbling and crust is golden brown, 36–38 minutes. Remove from the oven and drizzle with honey to garnish. Serve warm with ice cream if desired.

chocolate fudge cake

WITH COOKIES 'N' CREAM FROSTING

Lisa's afraid of riding elevators (a "cootie cage on a pulley") and yet has no problem embracing the ultimate mood elevator: chocolate. Friends, this chocolate cake goes straight to the top floor, the penthouse of pleasure, where super-moist fudgy layers are iced with addictive sweet cookie frosting. One bite and you'll immediately experience the release of Cocoatonin (trademark pending, but we have our legal team on it), a natural high flowing through you. Don't delay . . . push the preheat button and hop on this express lift to dizzyingly delicious heights of happiness.

SERVES: 10   PREP TIME: 20 MINS   COOK TIME: 30 MINS

Chocolate Fudge Cake

1¾ cups flour

1 cup sugar

1 cup brown sugar

1 cup cocoa powder, sifted

1½ tsp baking powder

1 tsp baking soda

1 tsp kosher salt

2 eggs

1 tsp vanilla extract

1 cup buttermilk

½ cup vegetable oil

1 cup boiling water

2 tsp instant espresso powder (if you don't have any, use your fave instant coffee)

Cookies 'n' Cream Frosting

1 (8 oz) package cream cheese, room temperature

½ cup butter, room temperature

2 cups icing sugar

2 tsp vanilla extract

15 Oreo cookies, chopped

1. Preheat the oven to 350°F. Coat two 9-inch round baking pans with nonstick cooking spray and line with parchment paper.

2. For the cake, using the whisk attachment of an electric mixer, combine the flour, sugar, brown sugar, cocoa powder, baking powder, baking soda, and salt on low speed. Add the eggs, vanilla, buttermilk, and vegetable oil. Beat at medium speed for 2 minutes, occasionally scraping down the sides of the bowl. In a small measuring cup, combine the boiling water with espresso powder and mix in on low speed. Mix until the batter is smooth.

3. Divide the batter evenly between the prepared pans and bake for 26–28 minutes. Remove from the oven and allow to cool slightly before removing from the pans. Let layers cool completely before frosting.

4. For the frosting, using an electric mixer, combine the cream cheese, butter, icing sugar, and vanilla extract on low speed. Increase the speed to medium and beat until the frosting is smooth. Add the chopped Oreo cookies on low speed, mixing just until combined.

5. To assemble, place one layer on a serving plate and top with 1½ cups of the frosting, spreading evenly. Top with the second layer and frost the top with the remaining frosting. Refrigerate until ready to serve.

molten
chocolate
lava CAKES

isa's saved me from yet another out-for-dinner dilemma, the one where I'm with a bunch of folks and out comes the dessert menu. "Too full," everyone says. Except me, who's drooling for the molten lava cake. The wait staff informs me it'll take an extra 45 minutes. Dirty looks and yawns ensue. What to do? Say, "Check, please" and head home where, thanks to this easy and awesome recipe, I can bake up my own chocolate eruption in just 25 minutes. This rich, decadent dessert is foolproof—intentionally underbaked, the exterior cake is moist and the center irresistibly warm and gooey, each chocolaty bite a reminder that I can have my cake and eat it too.

SERVES: 4   PREP TIME: 10 MINS   COOK TIME: 15 MINS

6 oz chopped semisweet or dark chocolate (just under 1 cup)

½ cup butter

¼ cup sugar

2 tbsp brown sugar

2 eggs

2 egg yolks

3 tbsp flour

¼ tsp kosher salt

Icing sugar, for garnish

1. Preheat the oven to 425°F. Butter four 3-inch ramekins or ovenproof bowls and coat with flour, tapping out any excess. Place ramekins on a baking sheet and set aside.

2. In a medium bowl, melt the chocolate and butter together in a microwave until smooth.

3. In a large bowl, whisk the sugar, brown sugar, eggs, and egg yolks until well combined. Slowly add the melted chocolate mixture to the egg mixture while constantly whisking. Add the flour and salt and stir just until the flour disappears. Divide the batter evenly between the prepared ramekins with about ⅓ cup of batter in each.

4. Bake in the preheated oven for 15–16 minutes, until the sides are firm and the center is still soft. Remove from the oven and let sit for 2–3 minutes. Loosen the cakes from the edges and invert onto a serving plate. Sprinkle with icing sugar if desired.

lessons *from* lisa

★ To make these in advance, leave the filled ramekins refrigerated and let them come to room temperature before baking off.

★ The easiest way to invert these is to place a small serving dish on top of the ramekin, flip it over, and lift the ramekin off.

mocha cupcakes

WITH COFFEE FROSTING

Our ancestors must have been bakers and baristas, because my sister's blood type is Mocha Positive. Lisa can't face the morning grind without her coffee and won't go to bed before chowing down on chocolate. While she's denied me a transfusion, she has compromised and created these bean-and-bar cupcakes, a decadent dessert that pumps joy through my veins. Chocolate and coffee, a classic duo, are combined in these airy, moist, and luscious cupcakes, which are slathered in a smooth espresso frosting. Vital to your existence, these aromatic, toothsome treats give new meaning to "Wake up and smell the coffee."

MAKES: 12 CUPCAKES   **PREP TIME: 15 MINS**   **COOK TIME: 15 MINS**

Mocha Cupcakes

1 cup flour

½ cup cocoa powder, sifted

1 tsp baking powder

½ tsp baking soda

½ tsp kosher salt

1 tbsp instant espresso powder

¼ cup boiling water

½ cup vegetable oil

2 eggs

1 tsp vanilla extract

¾ cup sugar

¼ cup brown sugar

½ cup buttermilk

Coffee Frosting

2 tsp espresso powder

1 tbsp boiling water

1 cup butter, room temperature

3 cups icing sugar

½ tsp vanilla extract

Chocolate espresso beans,
 chopped, for garnish

1. Preheat the oven to 350°F. Line 12 muffin cups with paper liners and spray with nonstick cooking spray.

2. For the cupcakes, in a large bowl, combine the flour, cocoa powder, baking powder, baking soda, and salt, mixing well.

3. In a small bowl, dissolve the espresso powder in boiling water. Let cool slightly.

4. In a medium bowl, whisk together the vegetable oil, eggs, vanilla, sugar, brown sugar, buttermilk, and espresso mixture. Add to the dry ingredients and stir just until combined. Divide the batter into the prepared cupcake pan and bake for 15 minutes, until a toothpick inserted in the center comes out clean. Allow the cupcakes to cool before frosting.

5. For the frosting, in a small dish, dissolve the espresso powder in boiling water.

6. Using an electric mixer, combine the butter and icing sugar on low speed. Once combined, add the vanilla and espresso mixture. Increase the speed to medium until the frosting has a smooth and spreadable consistency. Frost the cooled cupcakes, garnish with espresso beans, and serve.

> **" I am one of the few
> people who looks hot
> eating a cupcake.**
>
> —KELLY KAPOOR, THE OFFICE

WHITE CHOCOLATE
raspberry cake

There are pickup lines, such as, "I can die happy now, cause I've just seen a piece of heaven," that have a zero percent success rate. So listen up, fellas, because we've got a surefire way you won't get shut down: serve up a sweet slice of heaven. Yes, this White Chocolate Raspberry Cake is the ultimate icebreaker, the perfect marriage of tart raspberries and creamy white chocolate. Layers of light and fluffy white cake are spread with raspberry jam, followed by smooth white chocolate frosting, and finished with fresh raspberries. Blissful bite after bite, this cake serves up all the charisma and conversation you'll ever need, so park the whole, "Are you a library book, 'cause I'd like to check you out," nonsense and get baking.

SERVES: 10–12   PREP TIME: 30 MINS (including cake assembly)
COOK TIME: 25 MINS

White Cake

3½ cups cake flour

4 tsp baking powder

1 tsp kosher salt

¾ cup butter, room temperature

½ cup vegetable oil

2 cups sugar

6 egg whites

2 tsp vanilla extract

1½ cups whole milk, room temperature

White Chocolate Frosting

1¼ cups butter, room temperature

4½ cups icing sugar

8 oz white chocolate, melted

¼ cup whole milk

1 tsp vanilla extract

¼ tsp kosher salt

6 tbsp raspberry jam, divided

2 cups fresh raspberries, divided

1. For the cake, preheat the oven to 350°F. Coat three 8-inch baking pans with nonstick cooking spray.

2. In a medium bowl, sift the flour, baking powder, and salt. Set aside.

3. Using an electric mixer, combine the butter, vegetable oil, and sugar on medium speed. Continue mixing for 2 minutes. Add the egg whites and vanilla extract and mix for 4 minutes, until the mixture is light and fluffy. Alternate adding the flour mixture and the milk, beginning and ending with the flour mixture. Do not overmix.

4. Divide the cake batter between the prepared pans. Bake for 25 minutes, or until a toothpick inserted into the center of the cake comes out clean. Allow the cake layers to cool completely before frosting.

5. For the frosting, with an electric mixer, beat the butter and icing sugar on low speed until combined. Once incorporated, add the melted white chocolate, milk, vanilla extract, and salt. Turn the mixer to medium speed until the frosting is smooth.

6. To assemble, place 1 layer on a serving plate and spread 3 tablespoons of raspberry jam over top. Spread ¾ cup of frosting over the jam, followed by ¾ cup of fresh raspberries. Top with the second layer and repeat with 3 tablespoons of raspberry jam, ¾ cup of frosting, and ¾ cup of fresh raspberries. Top with the final cake layer and spread the remaining frosting over the top and sides of the cake. Garnish with the remaining fresh raspberries. Refrigerate until ready to serve.

cinnamon rolls

WITH CREAM CHEESE ICING

I like to be precise with my words. Figuratively, I'm not going to sugarcoat this, but literally, I am. This is one decadent recipe. There's nothing understated, bite-sized, low-cal, or dairy-free about these frosted cinnamon rolls. Guaranteed to break your resolve (and the Internet), gooey, fluffy, and perfectly soft rolls ooze with buttery cinnamon brown sugar and are topped with cream cheese frosting that melts straight into the swirled cracks and crevices. Nothing will get them eating out of your hands (literally and figuratively) like a batch of these messy, marvelous, go-big-or-go-home buns.

MAKES: 12 CINNAMON BUNS   **PREP TIME: 20 MINS (+ rising)**   **COOK TIME: 25 MINS**

Dough

1 cup whole milk, warmed (not hot)

3 tbsp sugar

1 (¼ oz) package instant yeast

1 egg

3 cups flour

1 tsp kosher salt

¼ cup butter, softened

Cinnamon Brown Sugar Filling

⅓ cup butter, softened

1 cup light brown sugar

1½ tbsp flour

1½ tbsp ground cinnamon

1 tbsp whole milk

¼ tsp kosher salt

Cream Cheese Frosting

4 oz cream cheese

¼ cup butter, softened

1½ cups icing sugar

1 tbsp whole milk

¼ tsp vanilla extract

Pinch kosher salt

1. For the dough, in the bowl of an electric mixer, using the dough hook, combine the milk, sugar, yeast, and egg on low speed. Add the flour, salt, and butter and mix on low speed until the flour is incorporated. Increase the speed to medium, and mix for 8 minutes.

2. Remove the dough from the mixer and roll into a large ball on a lightly floured surface. Place in a large bowl that has been coated with nonstick cooking spray. Cover and let rise in a warm place for 1 hour.

3. For the filling, in a food processor, combine the butter, brown sugar, flour, cinnamon, milk, and salt. Pulse to combine until smooth and spreadable. Set aside.

4. Coat a 9-by-13-inch baking pan with nonstick cooking spray and line with parchment paper.

5. After an hour, punch the dough down and on a lightly floured surface, roll the dough into a 12-by-18-inch rectangle. Spread the filling evenly over the dough, leaving a ½-inch border all around. Roll the dough into a tight cylinder and pinch the ends together to seal. Cut into 12 equal pieces and place them in the prepared baking dish. Cover with a damp cloth and let rise for 30 minutes.

6. Preheat the oven to 350°F and bake for 25 minutes until golden on top.

7. For the frosting, in the bowl of an electric mixer, add the cream cheese, butter, icing sugar, milk, vanilla, and salt and beat on low speed. Increase the speed and continue to beat until smooth. Once the cinnamon buns come out of the oven, frost while warm.

thanks

*I feel a very unusual sensation—if it's not
indigestion, I think it must be gratitude.*

—BENJAMIN DISRAELI

· · · · · · · ·

WE THANK

Robert McCullough, our friend and fearless leader, along with our champion, the eagle-eyed, linguistic-lassie Lindsay "LPats" Paterson. As well, a shout-out to Kristin Cochrane, our girl boss crush, along with Susan Burns and the supreme publicity/sales team at Penguin Random House.

Raquel Waldman Buchbinder, you're the ultimate graphic designer and a woman whose brilliance, creativity, kindness, and flare bring every single page of this book to life. You're it, woman.

Maya Visnyei, a photographer with boundless, jaw-dropping skill, artistry, patience, and vision—you capture the beauty of life. An additional thanks to Jasmine DeBoer and huge love to the expert slicers and dicers that are Nicole "WWND" Young, Matt "Yes Guy" Kimura, Kelly Jabbaz, and Cheryl Louvelle. It's only with a dream team like this that you get 160 photos in 10 days. A final thanks to Julia Connelly of Julia Beauty and Alex Walderman of Flawless for making us look alive (and then some).

Heather Reisman, your constant support and vision make book-lovers out of all of us. We also attribute much of our success to Meryl Witkin, the wind beneath our Bite Me wings, as well as the team at Bite Me Creative, gluten-free goddess RonniLyn Pustil, superfans Bonnie Levy and Brenda Goldstein, housewares-haven Hill Home, and Rick Broadhead, our meticulous and enthusiastic agent.

Finally, we send all our love to our inspiring and supportive parents, Larry and Judy Tanenbaum, brother Ken, sis-in-law Jennifer, and nifty nieces and nephews.

JULIE ALSO THANKS
Kenny, Jamie, Perry, Benjy & Billie Jean

DG, CarCar, CW, Double E, Mudz, Andelah, Suselah, Jojo, LDK, DP, MerBear,
LeeMac, D.Dubs & Clunestein

LISA ALSO THANKS
Jordan, Emmy, Lauren, Alex & Sophie

index